TRICKSTER

TRICKSTER

An ANTHROPOLOGICAL —— MEMOIR ——

EILEEN KANE

University of Toronto Press

www.utphighereducation.com

Library and Archives Canada Cataloguing in Publication

Kane, Eileen
    Trickster: an anthropological memoir / Eileen Kane.

Includes bibliographical references.
ISBN 978-1-4426-0177-2 (bound).—ISBN 978-1-4426-0178-9 (pbk.)

1. Kane, Eileen. 2. Anthropologists—United States—Biography. 3. Anthropologists—Ireland—Biography.   I. Title.

2. GN21.K35A3 2010   301.092   C2010-903452-X

We welcome comments and suggestions regarding any aspect of our publications—please feel free to contact us at news@utphighereducation.com or visit our Internet site at www.utphighereducation.com.

North America
5201 Dufferin Street
North York, Ontario, Canada, M3H 5T8

2250 Military Road
Tonawanda, New York, USA, 14150

ORDERS PHONE: 1-800-565-9523
ORDERS FAX: 1-800-221-9985
ORDERS E-MAIL: utpbooks@utpress.utoronto.ca

UK, Ireland, and continental Europe
NBN International
Estover Road, Plymouth, PL6 7PY, UK
ORDERS PHONE: 44 (0) 1752 202301
ORDERS FAX: 44 (0) 1752 202333
ORDERS E-MAIL: enquiries@nbninternational.com

The University of Toronto Press acknowledges the financial support for its publishing activities of the Government of Canada through the Book Publishing Industry Development Program (BPIDP).

Printed in Canada
Book design by George Kirkpatrick

RECYCLED
Paper made from
recycled material
FSC® C103567

For Patrice

Trickster makes this world... (Hyde, 1998)

Coyote: an American Indian Trickster

Trickster ... a
broad-stroked guileless schemer,
inept strategist,
divine comic and creative destroyer,
clever fool and serious joker,
an amoral innocent;
a sly dupe,
a sacred cheat,
and a gaping need;
a boundary-crossing,
shape-changing,
base obsessive.
Man Himself?
Hound of Heaven?

Contents

Foreword

THE ONLY "REAL" people in this book are historical figures such as Jack Wilson (Wovoka) and his nephew; Corbett Mack; my professors; some of my family, and me. Everything written here happened, but what about the other characters? People in Yerington were happy to help me with information about their culture, but I doubt any of them expected to appear many years later as individual personalities in a book. And they haven't; I've used them closely as models but have altered enough details, I hope, to honor the implicit understanding that we shared. For ethnographers who may be interested in local naming, I have followed the local patterns but have used no local names except those mentioned above.

The Northern Paiute people of Nevada, along with many other American Indians, were named by someone else, sometimes by pre-Contact neighbors or later by European settlers. The Paiutes' traditional name, which is used today, is Numu—or "People." At the time I lived with the group, they (when speaking in English), the local white population, and most anthropologists called them "Paiute."

In more recent years, the Paiutes have developed a standardized way of writing their language (see Poldevaart, 1987), but for this story I've used only my original 1964 field notes and journal, and so have used the phonetic spellings of Paiute words that I recorded in them.

BLESSING CEREMONY FOR WATER AND PINE NUTS

From left: Marlin Thompson (Oo'duh wunu'duh), Marge Torres, Christine
Nuesbaum and Lillus Richardson. Marlin Thompson, Christine Nuesbaum and
Lillus Richardson are three of the last four local native speakers. Photo is a gift from
Marlin Thompson, Paiute tribal historian, to the author, 2009.

Acknowledgments

MY GRATITUDE TO Professors Warren d'Azevedo and the late Wayne Suttles and Sven Liljeblad, directors of the 1964 National Science Foundation (NSF) Training Program, and to Don and Kay Fowler for sharing with their trainees their scholarship and lifelong friendships with the people in local American Indian communities. Also, thanks to Lelia Doolan, Brooke Foster, Ward Goodenough, Don Handelman, Joan D. May, Leonard Plotnicov, Patrice Price, and the anonymous readers for their comments. Anne Brackenbury of the University of Toronto Press has provided the kind of support and advice that writers dream of, and freelance editor, Betsy Struthers, the kind of editing that leaves authors thinking they write a lot better than they thought they could. Beate Schwirtlich, production coordinator, and George Kirkpatrick, designer and typesetter, have given the text one last good scouring and sent it out with this elegant face. Alice Kehoe read an early draft, and people who know her generosity will not be surprised that she immediately wrote the Introduction. And, as always, I'm more than grateful to my delightful husband, Paud Murphy, who has read so many drafts that he knows the text by heart and can act out all the parts beautifully.

Finally, I must acknowledge a great debt to the Paiutes of today: Tribal Chairman Elwood Emm and the members of the Tribal Council; Marlin Thompson, tribal historian; Karl Fredericks and the elders and members of the Paiute Tribe for their great kindness to me, then and now.

In addition to the usual ethnographic accounts, you can learn more about the Paiute people from the References and Further Reading section at the end of the book. This contains other important perspectives, which I saved to read when I was finished and which I highly recommend. In particular, for more information about the Paiutes, I recommend the works of Michael Hittman, the 1965 National Science Foundation trainee in Yerington, Nevada, and a long-term friend to the Paiutes; and Alice Beck Kehoe's *The Ghost Dance: Ethnohistory and Revitalization,* as well as her other books on American Indian issues. Two studies by local area people, Edward C.

Johnson, Melvin D. Thom, and Stannard Frank, were published ten years after my story takes place. Very useful ethnographic material can also be found in Paiute newspapers of the 1980s, *Numu Ya Dua'*, copies of which can be ordered from admin@ypt-nsn.gov. For Youngstown, I recommend Sherry Lee Linkon's and John Russo's *Steeltown USA: Work and Memory in Youngstown*, Robert Bruno's *Steelworker Alley: How Class Works in Youngstown*, and Mel Watkins's *Dancing With Strangers: A Memoir*, which recounts the early life of a young black youth, who grew up three streets away from me in Youngstown.

And for tricksters, I urge you to read Lewis Hyde's *Trickster Makes This World: Mischief, Myth, and Art*.

Introduction

Alice Beck Kehoe

I VISITED YERINGTON, NEVADA, in 1995, wanting to see where Wovoka had lived. Wovoka—Jack Wilson to the whites—was the famous Paiute prophet linked to the shocking massacre of Indian people at Wounded Knee, South Dakota, in December 1890. His people have a small reservation outside the town of Yerington.

For supper that night, I chose to go to Yerington's "family restaurant." It was nearly empty, and the young waitress was friendly. I told her I had come because Yerington was where Wovoka had lived. "Who?" she asked. "Wovoka. Jack Wilson. The Paiute Prophet." "Never heard of him." "Are you from Yerington?" "Yes, lived here all my life." "They didn't tell you about Jack Wilson in high school here?" "No, never heard of him."

I didn't ask her whether she had heard of Tecumseh or Sitting Bull, Geronimo or Sacajawea, or even Pocahontas (this visit occurred before the release of the Disney movie). American history is customarily taught as the Manifest Destiny of our great English-speaking nation overcoming the wilderness. First Nations' crucial roles in the economy, even after the Indian Wars ended in the 1880s, are left out—they are not even counted in the gross national product. But Indians are not the only segment of our country's population not given their due in most history textbooks. A son of Norwegian immigrants to the Midwest remarked about Professor Frederick Jackson Turner's claim that American democracy was forged by the pioneers on the wild frontier, "While the Americanization was rapid in the cities because of the more constant intercourse between people, the European immigrants who made up three-fourths of the frontier population in the Middle West remained like foreign colonists in speech and manners for at least one generation" (Holand 1957: 103). Immigrants have made up the bulk of the labor force in the United States and have been the butt of racist policies. Eileen Kane's Irish steelworker people in Youngstown, Ohio, were as little known to the mills' owners and managers as Wovoka's Paiute to the young white woman in Yerington. And a few blocks from Kane's family home, a black youth who, like her, became an academic, lived in another segregated society (Watkins 1998). The book you have here tells it like it was for the excluded Indians and fighting Irish in an America about to crack its class structure with Congress's *Civil Rights Act*.

Eileen Kane drove into Yerington in 1964, not a seasoned anthropologist as I was in 1995, but a young graduate student thrust into anthropology's grand rite of passage, the first fieldwork. Her book vividly recreates the challenge for a young person of making sense out of a strange locale. Here was the opposite of her family back in Youngstown: not people emigrating for the opportunity to make a living, but people dispossessed, shunted into marginal land to look on as invaders prospered from their resources. Yet the Irish (and black) steelworkers in Ohio and the Paiute in Nevada had in common their subordination to white Anglo-Saxon Protestant—WASP— power. The managerial class of whites who oversaw their work and lives disdained Indians, Irish, and blacks as inferior races; despised their religions; and considered their manners of speaking to be crude. Eileen Kane opens readers' eyes to an American class structure that grouped non-WASP laborers together. Ignored by the middle classes, migrant harvesters' seasonal camps, which included Yerington Paiutes, brought together Indians, Hispanics, Asians, and immigrants from Europe in America's lowest social class and facilitated marriages between them (Petrillo 2007).

Back in 1964, Kane's introduction to fieldwork challenged her in another way that she would not realize until years later. She describes how she prepared by reading Harold Driver's compendium of "facts" about all the "Indians" of North America. Everything known about these "primitive peoples"—their kinship systems, economies, beliefs, etc.—was thoroughly organized within this one volume. Mid-twentieth-century graduate students in anthropology were drilled to recognize and annotate these "facts" in the field situations where they were sent to get material for their dissertations. Ethnographic field schools, where professors lived alongside students in order to give them guidance and support, have been around since E.A. Hoebel studied the Kiowa in the 1930s, and Ruth Benedict the Blackfoot in 1939; in the 1960s and 1970s, Harvard's Evon Vogt spent years with a generation of students in the Mexican Maya community of Zinacantan. Many graduate students, like Eileen Kane and I, muddled through fieldwork alone, preferring to immerse ourselves in the new society, sink or swim. Fieldwork was regularized by means of traditional western cultural categories (religion, politics, etc.) and was characterized by stereotypes of "primitive" non-westerners. Students could be flunked if they failed to see what was decreed to be expected; for example, when another young woman reported to her professor that the Yoruba villagers she lived amongst had no "pantheon of gods," he admonished her, "Dig deeper! You're failing to get the data" (personal communication, Justine Cordwell). More seriously, students sent out to record the practices of Pacific Islanders coming under U.S. Trust Territories rule after the Japanese surrender in 1945 were pressured to record "clans" and "clan territories" where none existed in order to impose local government based on these stereotypes (Schneider 1984).

Our generation, Kane's and mine, came of age in the 1960s as imperial powers decided that managing colonies was too expensive compared to simply extracting their resources on a business basis. Anthropology joined other social sciences in observing from a "post-colonial" standpoint, rejecting the racist concept of "primitive societies" and cautiously exploring the positions of our "subjects"—now our collaborators—in national and global scenes. Some analysts, for example, anthropologist John H. Moore, used a Marxist approach to calculate the labor value of exploited people in colonies: he demonstrated that nineteenth-century Cheyenne Indians received \$0.01 (one-tenth of one cent) per hour for their work producing tanned bison hides for the Eastern U.S. and European markets. No wonder, he notes, that John Jacob Astor and other CEOs of the major fur trading companies became multi-millionaires (Moore 1996: 130). During the twentieth century, Cheyenne Indians relegated to an Oklahoma reservation worked as seasonal laborers, as did the Paiutes, on white "family farms," enterprises that could not have survived on the labor of white family members alone. Indians were paid less than white laborers and less than minimum wage; farmers did not report the wages (or contribute required taxes), but Indians accepted this arrangement because they could still receive food stamps and Aid to Families with Dependent Children supplements (Moore 1996: 135). Such situations around American Indian reservations indicate that they constitute "Fourth World" internal colonies, invaded and conquered (generally after two or three centuries of armed resistance) by the U.S. or Canada. Indians were forced onto marginal lands, allowed only minimal education in government and church-run schools, forbidden to homestead, and unable to obtain loan capital for agriculture or businesses because their land was held in trust to the federal government or had been sold off.

Capital: this is what both Paiutes and Youngstown steelworkers lacked. Americans don't like to talk about social class, and they don't like to talk about capitalism. It's a hard fact that the two great Anglo nations of North America, the U.S. and Canada, operate capitalist cultures, and under such cultures people who can't get capital suffer. Private property, primarily in land, is the foundation of capitalism; great fortunes were and are made in North America by speculating in land (most of the Founding Fathers in the U.S. did so). In the nineteenth century, investing capital in industry and transportation and, in the later twentieth century, investing in information technology and funds management created more fortunes for a few. What constitutes a very successful American Indian business? Famous Dave's Barbeque restaurants.

David Anderson is enrolled in Lac Courte Oreilles Lake Superior Band of Ojibwa in northern Wisconsin, grew up in Chicago (like many Indians whose parents moved to cities during World War II, when jobs were available to minorities), and learned to love the barbequed meat his factory-worker father bought from Southern black street-vendors. Anderson didn't need much capital to start a barbeque restaurant, and because he grew up in multi-ethnic Chicago, he could find work and begin his enterprise. Although he is now well-to-do, franchising his restaurants across the country, he can hardly be compared to Jeff Bezos, CEO of Amazon.com, whose mother's family owned a 25,000-acre ranch in Texas; whose grandfather and stepfather were engineers; and who attended Princeton University, went to work on Wall Street, readily met venture capitalists, and is now a billionaire. Anderson and Bezos are both highly intelligent, hard-working businessmen; the differences between them highlight "white privilege," the advantage of being born into a middle-class white professional family, versus the disadvantage of being born into an uneducated non-Anglo working-class family. Eileen Kane, Irish-American working class, had much in common with the Paiutes around Yerington. In this book, readers come to grasp this perhaps startling perspective.

Kane lets us feel how insecure and excited anthropologists are in their first fieldwork. Quickly, the characters she encounter bound upon her stage. The Paiutes are kind to the young woman, yet frustratingly difficult to get to know. Gradually, she becomes aware of commonalities between herself and them. Half a lifetime later, with years of international work under her belt, Kane sees them more clearly. There is depth to this book. And it's a good read.

TRICKSTER

CHAPTER ONE

VOWS

MY FATHER IS doing that peculiar one-step that brides are supposed to do. My legs are a lot longer than his, so I'm almost running in place beside him. We're like two pistons, bobbing and misfiring down the center aisle of Holy Succour Church.

Glancing up toward the front of the church, I spot something no skittish 1960s' bride should see before her marriage. A banana boat. On the altar. I'd guess the scale of the model is about 1:15, maybe 1:20. On the right, the Epistle side, there's my beaming groom, Francis, his jaw suddenly set a little too possessively for my liking. On the left, the Gospel side, there's the boat. It floats seductively, advancing and receding in the May heat. I can hear its happy crew and bohemian passengers. I can smell its tropical cargo.

This is not a vision; the Catholic Church frowns on its members having unofficial visions. Anyhow, I'm not a vision person. Miss Science, that's me. About to become Mrs. Murphy, not that I'm changing my name. No one else seems to notice the boat: not my teary father, not the groom, and apparently not the scrubbed Irish-Americans in the pews. Not even Mrs. Anzivino's son Jimmy, the Youngstown Mafia's community outreach person. My father and I finally arrive at the altar, and the boat sails off into the vestry. Without me. Francis grasps my elbow firmly.

At the reception afterwards in my parents' partly-converted basement, bowed and wiry men who work in the mill with my father tell me he never stops talking about how smart I am, doing that PhD at the University of Pittsburgh. Anthropology. Scholarships galore. My professors can't do without me. Someday I'm going to be a college professor. "He's real proud of you," they all say. "Never talks about nothing else."

The groom's florid uncle, triple whiskey in hand, joins us. "Yeah," he says, "but can you iron a shirt?" How much Francis's jaw looks like his! I've never noticed this before. He doesn't wait for an answer from me; he's hailing Father Jim, or Father Bob, or one of the many Fathers at the altar that day, all of them Friday-night card-pals of the Murphys'. "I was just saying to the blushing bride here..."

Father Jim-Bob raises his bloodless hand magisterially and calls the group to attention. "The Murphys will be off, soon," he says. "But before they go, let us offer up a little prayer for their safe trip."

Instantly, heads bow over highballs. It takes a few seconds before I realize that Francis and I are now the Murphys. Or, rather, Francis is the Murphy, and I am the extra "s".

Prayer over. Awkward little silence. The uncle downs his drink. "Ahhh," he breathes, looking heavenward toward the cold and hot air ducts in the basement ceiling, "Bushmills. 'Tis like an archangel pissing on your tongue."

The groom's father hastily proposes a toast: "To Francis and Eileen. To a happy honeymoon, and then Francis will be off for reserve officer training at Fort Monmouth, and Eileen will be waiting for him in..." He trails off. "To Francis and Eileen!"

Where I'll be "waiting" is mentioned in the last line of my wedding announcement, the next day's lead story on the *Vindicator*'s society page. Although we are more than a pickle fork away from "society," my uncle works for the newspaper and has brought a pile of advance copies to put beside the bar. The female guests pounce, read the announcement, and quickly move away, drinks in hands, loudly loving each other's hats.

ANCIENT RING FEATURED AT KANE WEDDING

A double ring ceremony featuring the traditional Irish wedding ring, two hands clasping a crowned heart, was performed Saturday morning in Holy Succour Church, Youngstown, uniting in marriage Miss Eileen Máire Kane, daughter of Mr. and Mrs. Arthur L. Kane, and Francis Thomas Murphy, son of Mr. and Mrs. Kevin Murphy.

The bride, an Andrew Mellon Fellow at the University of Pittsburgh, and a graduate of Youngstown University, is presently working on a doctorate in anthropology. The bridegroom, also a Youngstown University graduate, is a chemical engineer with the Ford Company.

Carrying a colonial bouquet of white and pink roses and forget-me-nots, the bride wore a full-length lace and taffeta tiered gown and an illusion veil held by white roses and forget-me-nots. The maid of honor, Miss Anne Kane, sister of the bride, and bridesmaid Mary Agnes Kane, a cousin, wore sea mist taffeta gowns with turquoise trains and matching picture hats, and carried baskets of pink and white carnations and violets. Patrice Kane and Alice Murphy, sisters of the bride and bridegroom, were flower girls in tiered sea mist gowns with empire waists, and carried small wicker bird cages. James Leone was best man.

Following a reception held at the home of the bride's parents, the couple will leave for a trip to Rehoboth Beach. Mr. Murphy will enter the Army as a second lieutenant, and the bride will continue her studies in Pittsburgh after three months of anthropological research on an Indian reservation in Nevada.

Does it sound like I entered the church in bad faith that day, given the vision of the boat, my refusal to change my name, my heading for the Indian reservation so soon after the wedding? In fact, I am among the group—myself and the groom's little sisters, mainly—who think the whole idea of the wedding is rather nice.

"Why are you getting married?" my own little sister, 15 years younger than me, asked the night before.

How do you explain these things to a child? "Last year, I dreamed I was getting married to someone, I don't know who, and when I looked back I saw Francis in the back of the church, looking very sad. And I felt sad, too."

Because I believe in scientific evidence, it would be foolish for me to ignore this message from the subconscious. Of course, as a scientist I also recognize that earlier that day I could have heard Eddie Fisher on the radio singing "I'm Walking Behind You," his ballad about a heartbroken lover watching his lost love go up the aisle.

"I'd feel sad, too, if I was marrying someone I didn't know," my sister said. "But if you have to marry a stranger, I want you to pick a tall dark one. Francis is medium and pink."

We older girls know from movies and books that tall dark strangers can end up beer-bellied and undershirted in seedy faded towns—faded towns even worse than Youngstown—swatting at dirty, diapered swarms of kids. I am sensible: Francis is the Boy Next Door. Not literally—his family lives a few blocks away—but in every other way he qualifies for that role. He's quiet. Skinny. Reliable. Safe. Familiar. Freckled.

Medium. Pink.

Enough of reason. Who knows why people marry? The fact is I *have* to get married. I'm not pregnant, but this is Youngstown, 1964, and I'm 23. Our families are vigilantly anti-cohabitation. Contemplating sex? Either marry or send your mother to an early grave. It's our cultural custom.

And Francis and I *have* to leave because Youngstown, Ohio, population 160,000 and falling, has no place for us—the outdated mills, the dark department-store counter, and the typing pool are there for people who can't get to college, and only a tiny range of professions exists for the few who can. After his Army service, Francis, with his Master's in chemical engineering, will have to leave town to find work. And so will I, if I'm to work as an academic, an anthropologist. But to get that work, I have to finish my PhD, and to do that I have to learn how to do fieldwork. Leaving on my own for summer training on an Indian reservation four days after the wedding is not customary, but it's necessary. We're the first in our families ever to go beyond high school; we financed our educations through scholarships and tough family sacrifices. Francis can't stop now, and I won't. The University of Nevada in Reno is running the training program I need, and I'm going.

"I saw the most amazing thing this morning, going up the aisle," I tell Francis as we drive away for our few days' honeymoon in Rehoboth Beach, New Jersey. It's nice to be able to share ridiculous experiences with someone comfortable, someone who has known you and your family for eons, which is another reason a tall dark stranger can't work out as husband material.

"I know, Father Tony wore the wrong color chasuble—you see that? His was for Laetare Sunday. You only wear that on the middle Sunday of Lent."

So he didn't see the banana boat. I say nothing. Maybe there are some things you can't share with a new husband.

We take the country route to Enon Valley and beyond. White wooden gas stations, corn-on-the-cob stands, hex signs on Amish barns, the ice machine in East Palestine that people say is run by the Mafia. We watch for our favorite signs: "Backhoe Work by the Grace of God," hand-painted on a broken board, and "Fin 'n' Fur Kennels and Bible School."

"You know," he says as we pass through New Galilee, "I've been thinking—it's really time we settle down."

"I EXPECTED MORE." I'm stretched out beside Francis on the hotel bed.

He sits up, surprised. "What?"

"I mean New Jersey. I expected a lot of casinos, violence, cocktail lounges. I thought it would be more colorful."

"Than what? Youngstown?" Francis asks. According to the cover of last September's *Saturday Evening Post*, Youngstown is "Crime Town, U.S.A." and "Bomb City, the Murder Capital of the U.S."

We put on our few specially bought honeymoon clothes and set out for the boardwalk, a leaden sea churning on one side and on the other rows of chairs filled with gamblers' wide backsides and racks of unidentifiable orange and turquoise postcards.

"You know," Francis says suddenly, "if you kill someone, I'll be the one who'll be executed for it." Almost moment by moment this man I've married, usually mild and easygoing, is sounding more like a bullfrog, loud and rumbly. Marital responsibilities seem to be overwhelming him.

"That's ridiculous. It means the only person I can be punished for killing is you."

"And I found out the day before the wedding that you won't be able to open a charge account without me signing for it, or take out a loan. And they'll make you use my last name to vote or renew your driver's license." He's reproachful, as if I'm a little faulty.

"Who told you this?"

"My father. The other day, when he gave me The Talk." His father is a marriage counselor.

"Aren't you too old for that?"

"He asked me if I knew everything, and I said yes, so he filled me in on the legal side. Good thing, too. For example, you can't sue me if I injure you by driving carelessly."

"Well, doesn't that lift your heart a little?"

"And if you pick a fight in the streets, it'll be me who has to take over and handle the situation."

"Your father said that?"

"No, my mother." Until the final "I do's," Francis's mother had been hoping he'd become a priest.

"How likely is it I'll pick a fight in the streets on my honeymoon?" At 100 pounds and just under five feet five, trussed up in my new lacy clothes (including, still, my wedding garter), it seems a stretch.

"I don't mean that you'd pick a fight." He pauses, reflecting. "As such." Clearly, his mother's comments have got to him. "I mean if you get into trouble when I'm around, I'll have to handle it."

We've been going out together for seven years and I've never noticed this deeply chivalrous streak before. I lower my eyes demurely when we encounter other shy honeymooners on the boardwalk. I wonder if they, too, although looking so carefree and happy, are also suddenly plunged into this Paleolithic gender divide.

It's not just Francis who's having second thoughts. For my part, I begin to see him as a sperm landmine. He's the eldest of 11 children; now that we're married, he can probably impregnate me simply by sharing a soda straw. The fact that our previous sexual experiences had non-eventful outcomes doesn't matter. The marriage license makes me feel far more permeable. I don't want children yet, nor does he, so I insist that he use three condoms together.

"I can't feel anything," he complains, gamely, as he approaches me, swathed in rubber. We both end up laughing.

After that it seems a good idea to stay apart at night: I pass the time reading in our room, and he goes out gambling. This way, I can't get into a fracas, and he can't knock me up. We both agree this is the safest approach. The honeymoon passes quietly.

We barely mention what we'll be doing during the months ahead when we'll be apart, but we know the time will test each of us: Francis, pacific, non-athletic, and nervous, serving his time in the Army. And me, shy and socially inept, living on an Indian reservation.

"Your mother is worried about you," he says.

Translation: Francis is worried about me.

"She thinks you're unconscious most of the time."

This conflicts sharply with my own notion that very little gets past me.

"Well, maybe not unconscious, exactly. More like oblivious. Hapless." Francis minored in English. "And you don't mingle well."

"What has mingling got to do with fieldwork?" I snap.

He rolls his eyes.

On our last morning, we drive to La Guardia Airport for my flight to Reno. At my gate, we hug, promise to write each other daily, and kiss good-bye, just in time for Francis to drive the 40 miles to Fort Monmouth and report for duty. He plans to fly out and join me in Nevada in September, when we'll drive back together across the country. I have a one-way ticket.

CHAPTER TWO

At Home on the Range

I RIDE INTO YERINGTON, Nevada at noon, down the deserted main street, past the dusty bar, the courthouse, the faded stage-set wooden storefronts. A couple of tough-looking men in Stetsons and boots squint at me, giving nothing away. One spits at a loping yellow dog.

This is the life I imagined: the big sky and me, alone out on the range, maybe sleeping under the stars at night, up with the dawn and out into the crystalline desert air. Free—my only possessions my hat and boots, and maybe my horse, although I'm not all that keen on horses. No steel mills, no mud-colored snow, the only gunshots those of honest cowboys with no known links to the Mafia.

With me in the university van are a professor of anthropology, an archeologist, a Paiute-speaking Swedish linguist, two teaching fellows, and four other wide-eyed trainees en route to their own placements. In my bag, along with a packet of letters from Francis, are a new compass, an engineer's scale, a camera, a tape recorder, some soil conservation maps, blueprint materials, a water canteen, and a snake-bite kit, not one of which I can use with any confidence and for all of which I paid $95.80. I also have four cans of meatballs, three months' worth of tampons, hair curlers, a solid girdle with suspenders, some squashed Hostess Snoballs (these last two items smuggled in by my mother), and, most important, carefully wrapped in waxed paper, my beautiful prized copy of Harold E. Driver's *Indians of North America*, which cost me nearly as much as my wedding dress.

It's a hot day in mid-June. I'm fresh from almost three weeks' fieldwork training at the university in Reno, and itching from Rocky Mountain Spotted Fever inoculations. The drive is spectacular: a high desert river valley stretches to the Desert and Singtase Mountains, the landscape a mix of gray-brown scrub and, surprising to me, rich green fields of grass, alfalfa, onions, and garlic. Yerington, 80 miles away from Reno, is a place designed for northern Ohioans: flat. The bonus is that, although it's flat in the right places—the roads and lawns—it's piped like a piecrust at the horizons with spectacular copper and lavender mountains.

The town, 1,800 people, has a moonscape copper mine, 47 small businesses serving the vast hinterland, and two Paiute reservations. One, the two-acre "Colony" of 130 people, is built on a traditional camping place near Yerington's main street. The other, "the Ranch," 10 miles out of town, has 1,000-plus acres of arable and grazing land, home to eight families of about 40 people. Another 100 or so Paiutes live in the area.

"It's deserted, like a ghost town," I marvel to the professor, as the van rumbles down the wide main street past a cozy-looking diner, the Lyon County Courthouse, the Crescent Garage, an imposing post office, and a few bars.

"Lunchtime. Rotarians have their monthly lunch today."

Both reservations are tribal property, restricted to legally recognized American Indians. I can't live on either, so the professor has found me accommodation in an eccentrically converted garage in the white part of town. Entrance by overhead door only. No sleeping out under the stars for me.

We all pile out of the van to inspect the interior: a rough bunkhouse bed partnered with a dainty white-and-gold reproduction French bedside table, one drawer missing; an old Kelvinator icebox, red Formica table, and two-burner camp stove; and in the office corner, a battered tool bench, legs cut down to make a desk, and a tufted blue armchair. Most of my clothes will hang behind an old curtain stretched across a corner of the room, and some can go on the tailor's dummy beside the tiny green bathroom. No lamps, just a bare overhead bulb.

But how will I meet Paiutes in the middle of a white town? Indians aren't allowed in bars. Actually, I'm not either; in the 1960s, "No Ladies Without Escorts" signs are still posted in many places around the country. If I go in, I could get Francis arrested.

Admittance to the two reservations is only with permission of the Paiutes, and my three letters to the Tribal Chairman, James Kelly, haven't been answered. I'm nervous that he hasn't replied; gone are the days when the anthropologist just appeared, like the Angel Gabriel unto Mary, and the locals, like Mary herself, were surprised but honored by the visit.

"In a few days, we'll find a car for you and send it down so you can get between the two reservations," the professor says. "Now, first thing tomorrow we've set it up for you to go over to the Colony and meet old Delaney

Jack. He knows everything. He'll take you out to the Ranch to the Tribal Chairman, James Kelly. Be sure you go see Mr. Kelly."

Some of the other students will be working in pairs; I want to work alone. Despite the accomplishments of Margaret Mead, Ruth Benedict, Ruth Bunzel, Ernestine Friedl, and many others, the issue of how women will fare in the field still amuses some men. I want to be sure I can do it and prove yet again that women anthropologists are as capable as men.

"You sure about this?" the professor asks, as I contemplate my new home. "Of course."

"You call us, any time, day or night. That goes for the rest of you, too," he says, herding the other students back into the van for the trip to their own field sites.

On my own at last. I already have an "informant" lined up, and I know what I want to ask him: a local "Indian Messiah," Jack Wilson, died here 30 years ago, promising to return. He preached that while people wait for him, they should take up a new religion, although he didn't specify any in particular. Are there intriguing and logical parallels between their old religious beliefs and the new ones? If not, why not? I can almost see the journal article I'll write and the later respectful references to it: "Kane, in her seminal work, notes that..." Neophyte anthropologists who don't know what they're doing are told to make a map, take a census, or collect kinship terms. Not me. I'm on top of things.

THE NEXT MORNING, I make tea on the garage's camp stove, get my notebook, and set out for the Colony. My studies have equipped me to describe every known form of pre-white American Indian habitation, but the image in my head is the tent my sister and I used to make out of damp blankets slung over clotheslines in our backyard, with us hunkered down beneath it eating Ritz crackers. I know the Paiutes won't be living in traditional housing today; in fact, they're among the few groups in the world who never had much permanent housing at all, living as nomads, sheltering in windbreaks or light reed houses in the bitterest winter weather.

Neither my studies nor that image prepare me for my first sight of the Colony: a line of 26 closely packed but very neat unpainted wooden houses along a parched, dirt, tree-lined lane. The houses are tiny; some have trailers parked alongside. I look for the front steps of a respectable widow, Jennie

Mann, which I recognize from the description the professor gave me: dozens of flowerpots, flowering tin cans, flowering tires. Jennie, a substantial lady in her early 60s—short, pillowy, and serene—is waiting for me.

"You are welcome," she says. "This is your man." She nods toward an elegant, silver-haired man sitting alone on the rickety steps, head down. He's about 70, whip-thin, dressed in carefully ironed, faded blue work clothes. A scribbled net of wrinkles outline features that belong on an ancient coin.

"*Ipahwá*," he mutters.

Ah ha! I *know* this word. Weeks of training are already paying off; I can use Paiute greetings with the best of them.

I extend my hand politely. "*Pah wá.*"

He looks up. "No, no, write it down," he says irritably, patting the step. "I was practicin' for you. Delaney Jack's my name." He holds out his hand. "Your teachers said you better start with kinship terms. *Pah wá*'s the Paiute name for the father's sister."

He taps my notebook. "*Pyní?i*, that would be younger sister." He shoots his upper denture in and out reflectively, behind closed lips. "*Pa wá*. Mother's sister. *Pi tu uu.*"

I scramble for my pen, trying to capture Delaney's words in the International Phonetic Alphabet I've been taught. *Pi tu uu*, I write carefully.

Gradually three of what may be Jennie's teenaged grandchildren—a girl and two boys—and three generic yellow dogs join us. They arrange themselves on the steps and stare.

"Aren't you s'posed to be on your honeymoon?" Delaney asks.

"Yes. No. I was on it three weeks ago."

"You left it to come here to us?"

"It's part of my training."

"You miss your husband?" a large, burly girl demands.

"'Course she does," Delaney says, shocked. "Sooner I help her, sooner she'll see him again. *Ha má ? a*, elder sister."

I'm not much good at the Phonetic Alphabet; if I have to list kin terms, I'm more interested in finding out what these kin do, what their roles are. Among Irish-Americans in my town, for instance, sisters live near each other to help cushion the effects of poverty and their husbands' mill strikes, injuries, and deaths. Who is supposed to do what among the Paiutes?

Somewhere in my notebooks I have a set of questions given during training, something called a Role Profile Test. I can remember only a few and ask, "Which relative is most likely to help you if you need it? Who most often comes to you for help? Which relative nags you the most? Which one is most likely to refuse to help you even if you need it pretty badly?"

"Your elder sister'd help you if you needed it." Delaney reflects on this morosely. "And maybe she wouldn't help you at all. I remember the time she deliberately..." His voice trails off. According to the professor, the widowed Delaney lives with his sister out on the Ranch; I hope he lives with the younger one.

"Let's try 'wife's brother's son.'"

"Huh." Delaney mulls this over for a while. He turns to Jennie. "Remind me to tell him I expect that bail bond money back." His teeth slip, and he retrieves them with a smack. "*Na ná kwa, he* certainly wouldn't help you. More like you'd have to help *him*." He thinks, chewing on some tiny thing.

Jennie seems familiar with the antics of this particular *na ná kwa*. She pats Delaney's hand. "Now, you don't be so hard. You remember he cured you that time you tried to kill yourself."

"I *didn't* try to kill myself," Delaney grumbles. "People want to kill themselves, they eat wild parsnip. I was brushing my teeth with a rabbitbrush twig. What kind'a witch doesn't know a twig from a wild parsnip? He was too young, he had no spirit helper." He spits. "Matter of fact, I didn't even have my teeth *in* at the time. Not that many try to commit suicide rubbing their false teeth with wild parsnip."

"Well, I can't speak against him. He cured my mother when its feathers fell out," Jennie says in Paiute. Or maybe she says something else; my ear isn't that good yet.

I'm delighted. *This* is what anthropology is supposed to be about: defeathered mothers and the dignified Delaney besieged like Job by feckless relatives and incompetent witches as he cleans his dentures. Paradoxes, conundrums, phantasmagoria, and completely conflicting accounts of the same event are fine by me—people who grow up in big families are used to them. As a would-be anthropologist, I know that people who are considered mentally ill in one culture can be model personality types in another. As an Ohioan, it makes perfect sense to me that the Mafia runs Youngstown better than the elected officials do and that sometimes the elected officials *are* the Mafia. And, as an Irish-American, it doesn't surprise me that my teenaged brother Patrick is currently president of the local Bosnian Club and its elderly members.

A mounted rider appears suddenly on the dirt road in front of Jennie's, his horse rearing and bucking. From the back, he's the picture of a perfect movie cowboy, Stetson, jeans, chaps, and all. From the front, he has perfect Indian features. My mental elasticity has its limits; I stare in confusion.

"Mickey Kelly," Delaney points with his lips pursed in the Paiute way. I've been warned that finger pointing may invite a good witching, so it's best not to point at all. "One a the best Paiute speakers around."

Delaney loses whatever he was chewing on and fishes around for it under his upper lip with his tongue. He takes a twig and draws a circle in the sand with it. "See that?" He points to some track marks inside.

"Dog prints?"

"Nope." He's pleased. "Dogs leave all four paw prints. See, this is a line of two prints. Old Man Coyote, that's what this guy is."

"Isn't a coyote dangerous?"

"Yes and no. Coyote's as much a danger to himself as anyone else. And a great man for the ladies. I could tell you..."

"Delaney," Jennie reproaches.

"Okay, okay. Well, here's a different one. Long ago, before any people were here, Coyote went across the ocean, maybe to Europe, and he married a woman there." He glances at Jennie, who gives the slightest nod. "She had a litter of children and Coyote decided to bring them back to the U.S."

"The U.S.?"

"Yes. And whoever was over there in Europe told him he should put them into a kind of a willow bottle, and put a cork on it, and not let them out till he got back here. But you know Coyote, he couldn't do that. When he hit the east coast he took a peek inside, and they all ran out and scattered everywhere. He tried to catch them, but he only got two. Those two became the Paiutes and the Shoshone. The rest went all over the country and became the other tribes.

"Same with the animals. I'll tell you that one some other day. But he accidentally let them all out, too."

I was taught not to impose my own cultural interpretations on what I heard but to allow conclusions to emerge naturally from informants, so I wait now, poised to write.

"Just shows you," Delaney concludes. "He was a terrible babysitter."

One of the teenaged boys sniggers.

"Well, next time I'll tell you how a fella from here, Jack Wilson, turned a white horse into a cloud in the sky. Old lady I knew saw it. I know all about it."

"Wuddn't Jack Wilson did that," Jennie objects. "It was The Man Who Became Thunder, thousands of years ago, and that cloud of Jack Wilson's, it was really a block of ice."

"Yeah. Coulda been."

"He called the ice out of the sky and people ate it. A little like the Christian Communion. Some say Jack Wilson's the great Indian Messiah."

"Yeah, and some people, not me, say he was just a great man for being around at mealtimes," Delaney says. Jennie points her lips at my notebook, warning him.

"Well," he says, rising, and now I can see the slight bow in his back, the extra second it takes him to straighten up, "I'll get a fellow older'n me from out at the Ranch to come talk to you this afternoon. Come back around 4:00."

"Shouldn't I see the Tribal Chairman before I do much more?" I ask.

"Oh, you can do that later."

I put the notebook away, relieved and happy. It all seems so easy. Jack Wilson is my man; he's the reason I'm here in this little desert town rather than in any of the other field-training sites on offer. It could be said—and probably will be—that I left Francis for Jack Wilson.

The three teenagers are sitting on the curb in front of my garage when I return from Jennie's.

"Don't you want to write about us?" the girl asks. "Aren't you supposed to write down our names, too?"

"Of course." I've already written some quick notes about them, though not their names: *Girl, large, stocky. Boy, pale, thin, lank-haired, watchful. Boy, Dean Martin.*

The girl hangs over me while I match up the names, shielding the labels from her view. One of the boys strikes a few muscle-building poses; the other hides behind a curtain of fair hair. I take down their stories: Thomasina is 15, hates school, hates her teacher, hates everybody in her class, hates Larry. Larry is also 15 and very pale; he mutters answers to my questions while shyly fingering the books in my bag. Last, draped elegantly against my door, laughing and lazy-eyed, is the boy I dub the Paiute Dean Martin. He could be anything up to 30 years old, but in fact is 17. He impales a lizard with a pen that looks like one of mine. Is one.

"You think you don't need our names," he challenges.

"I do, of course." We're supposed to talk to children because, we're told, children are honest, straightforward, excellent observers. Often they will tell you insightful things they don't even understand themselves.

"Eddie's my name," he announces, flinging the limp lizard in my direction. "My guess is about 34–22–36. Right? Not my type, though."

The other two pretend to be deliciously horrified and run off, screeching and hooting. Not Eddie, though. Somehow, Eddie just disappears.

WHEN I ARRIVE at Jennie's house for the afternoon interview, Delaney and a woman in her 40s are struggling to unload something awkward from the back of a flatbed truck.

"Archie Jim," Delaney announces and orders the woman, "Pull!"

Archie lies spread-eagled and face-up on the truck bed, looking delighted with himself, not seeming to mind being scraped across a floor of grit.

"Now!" Delaney and the woman sling him out and down under Jennie's tree, a big cottonwood, where he sprawls like a starfish. "This here's Archie's niece Doreen, Doreen Williamson," Delaney says. "And Archie here is 90 years old, the man that knows everything."

"Don't know enough to close his fly," Doreen mutters. Delaney edges delicately to block the view and make an adjustment. Doreen shakes her head, swings up into the driver's seat, and roars off, wheels spitting gravel.

Delaney and I sit down under the tree, me with notebook and pen at the ready. I spot Larry watching from the brush, advancing and then shying back like a nervous cub. And isn't his friend, the smooth Eddie, the young Dean Martin, there too? A second ago, I thought so, but he's gone now.

"This girl's teacher," Delaney says, addressing Archie, "told me all about how she's supposed to study Jack Wilson. Good thing, too. Never got the credit he deserved, Wilson."

"No, sir," Archie agrees. He waves a near-empty fifth of bourbon to punctuate his point. Everything on his face is arranged to accommodate his glorious pumpkin grin: cheeks draped in rich folds around it, laughing eyes in soft hammocks. Like Delaney, he's wiry, presumably from a life of hard ranch work. "No, sir. Jack Wilson near wiped out half the western U.S."

"Well," Delaney cautions.

"Well, he coulda if he'd *wanted* to. Take the battle of Wounded Knee. He started that, all by hisself."

"You want this girl to flunk out of school? That what you want?" Delaney takes the pen out of my hand.

"Now listen," he says, then motions to Larry, adding, "You get over here, too."

Larry scoots over, crab-like, without standing up.

"Where's your sidekick?" Delaney demands.

"Eddie? He's gone to collect his mother's pay."

"Well, that's nice. His ma's a good woman; she's killed herself for Eddie."

"He hired her out to pick garlic on the Donateo farm. He gets something for it, I don't know what."

Delaney sighs. "Has he got the old lady out there, too?"

"Who?"

"The grandma."

"Dunno."

"I bet he does." He shakes his head. "Well, about time we got down to work." He waggles an imperious finger—at me? "'Stead of shooting craps all day." So he must be talking about Archie. "Or moping around like a girl." Larry flinches. "All this stuff depends on who you talk to. *And* whether they know anything. Some people think Jack Wilson was a healer, and some say he was a kind of miracle worker, and some others, they think he was a crook, plain and simple."

"It's white people think that—about being a crook," Archie interrupts. He holds the bottle up to the light and squints at it.

"Not only them," Delaney says. "But it's white people usually call him 'the Indian Messiah.' *We* didn't call him that. "

"Yeah, but he brought a horse out of the sky from nowhere," Archie says, "and he called down blocks of ice from the air on a hot day."

"How did he get the name Jack Wilson?" I ask. As a matter of fact, I'm wondering where all their names came from. (And their various color-ings—Larry is nearly as light as I am, and, as a redhead, I'm practically transparent.) "In my books, it says his name is Wovoka."

"He got his name from the ranchers he worked for, the Wilsons. Like most of us did. And Wovoka wun't his name, either, Wovoka don't mean anything in Paiute. It got writ down wrong," Delaney explains. "It's like if I wrote your name down wrong and started calling you something like, oh, I don't know, 'Eyegool' in English."

"Eyegool." I retrieve my pen and write it down phonetically.

"No, I'm just trying to show you. 'Eileen, Eyegool.' 'Wy"kótyhi, Wovoka.' See, somebody wrote his name down wrong. Wovoka's not a real word."

"So that was his real name...Wy"kótyhi?"

"Yeah. One of them. It means a thing for cutting or chopping. Write that down," he orders. "Cross that other stuff out."

Jack Wilson's real legacy, according to the anthropological literature, is the Ghost Dance. That movement, at its height, spread to almost all Indian groups in the western half of the United States. To many anthropologists—and, apparently, to Larry—Wilson's message is simple. Larry says, "He told people to do right, not to hurt anybody. Not to fight."

I'm surprised by his contribution, but it's nice to see young people aware of their past.

During my training program, I copied down a message Jack Wilson sent to the Cheyenne Indians and pasted it on the inside cover of my notebook. Now I read it out loud to the little group:

Do right always. It will give you satisfaction in life.... Do not tell the white people about this. Jesus is now upon the earth. He appears like a cloud. The dead are still alive again. I do not know when they will be here; maybe this fall or in the spring. When the time comes, there will be no more sickness and everyone will be young again.

Do not refuse to work for the whites and do not make any trouble with them until you leave them. When the earth shakes [at the coming of the new world], do not be afraid. It will not hurt you.

I want you to dance every six weeks. Make a feast at the dance and have food that everybody may eat. Then bathe in the water. That is all. You will receive good words again from me some time. Do not tell lies.

"'When the earth shakes,'" Delaney repeats. "That's not right. Wilson said it will split." His dry, cracked hands sketch two horizontal planes, one sliding across over the other, "with the Indians on the top, the whites on...the other one. All our dead Indians and our animals will come back, and we'll live the way we used to." He falls silent, frowning. "Now, the white man won't be harmed," he assures me. "He'll just go someplace else, to a different world." He reaches over, and I think he's going to pat my arm, but he pulls back before touching me. "Someplace nice."

Archie cackles.

"What kind of dance was it?" I ask.

"Oh, an ordinary one—everybody knew it."

"I don't think I know it," I say.

The two older men eye each other uneasily. Delaney lumbers to his feet and hauls Archie up to join him. Archie is distinctly bowlegged and crab-backed, although it isn't clear whether he has these traits permanently or they're a result of the state he's in today. They begin shuffling and then dance silently in a kind of sidestepping, counter-clockwise circle, emitting occasional, quite possibly involuntary grunts. Delaney gives Larry a shove during one go-round, and he joins in, a skilled dancer. With a whole crowd of people, I can see how hypnotic the dance would be.

Jennie comes out. Mortified, all three males look at her and quickly sit down. "I can't leave you a minute," she says to them.

I think I'm going to like Jennie, although she has that reined-in female exasperation that makes people all over the world nervous. Of course, I shouldn't say that; one thing anthropology teaches you is that what you think is universal—behaviors, ideas, practices—might not be. Maybe she just shares this characteristic with my mother back in Ohio. Or maybe in some places it doesn't scare people. It scares this group, though.

"The real trouble," Delaney intones loudly, brushing off his pants with more vigor than needed, "started when them Sioux took it up. The government was still sore over your General Custer at Little Bighorn, so they figured the Sioux was on the warpath, and they sent the Seventh Cavalry—they was Custer's old men—to wipe them out at Standing Ridge and Wounded Knee. Hundreds killed, and their big man, Sitting Bull, and his brother, Little Bull."

I think about this. Today, if the American government hears about an Indian movement—or indeed any movement—based on education, Christian principles, temperance, and nonviolence, it would probably create an absurdly named project to embrace—and control—it. In the Wilson case, you can bet it would be something like "Native Americans Building on Beliefs," which, of course, would be reduced to an acronym. NABOB would provide federal funds for mission statements, facilitators, projects, workshops, breakout groups, reporting-back sessions, strategic objectives, monitoring and evaluation, and plenary sessions.

Back then, though, they just shot Sitting Bull.

"Jack Wilson died in, what—'38?" Delaney asks Archie.

"Thirty-two," Archie answers.

"He told the people he'd come back," Delaney continues, "but while he was gone, we should be good and join a religion. And not drink." He glares at Archie. "Some listened, some didn't."

No one seems clear about which religion Wilson meant, or whether the denomination matters. But a lot of missionaries have passed through the valley since his death.

"What church did they join?" I ask.

"A lot didn't bother, but a few went Methodist," Jennie says. "And a few Catholic. All good people. I went to a couple churches—some made us sit in the back—but the last while I've been with the Reverend Parks here at the Assembly of God. A lot go there now."

"That's the thing you want to do tomorrow," Delaney says. "Go see Reverend Parks, up the road there, right at the end. Ask him how he got the people to come. That should wind it up for you fast, and your teachers will think you're real smart for getting the answer so quick. And you'll get back east to your people sooner, too."

Doreen and the flatbed reappear. Delaney and Larry gently load Archie, still all stiff-angled, back on.

"You come out to the Ranch and see me," Archie says, stretching out on the bare metal. "I know all the old stories. There's the one when Coyote gets his mother-in-law to put her head in a rabbit-hole, and he comes up behind her and..."

"Helps the old lady up!" Delaney bellows.

Archie's eyes widen. "Oh," he says. "I don't know that one. Oh...well, okay. But in mine he catches hell and goes blind."

Delaney carefully rearranges Archie's limbs, pats his shoulder, and signals to Doreen, who drives off at a processional pace. Larry runs after them, waving Archie's bottle.

Delaney's eyes follow the truck down the road. "When he's gone, and I'm gone, I don't know who's going to know anything."

"Well, Larry's young," I say, "and *he* seems very interested."

"Larry's white, 100 per cent. He just hangs around here." Larry's coming back, having delivered the bottle. "No need to bring it up, though."

Maybe Francis's view of me as "oblivious" isn't that far off. At least I haven't made the embarrassing mistake of seeming to think all Indians look alike. Still, I better get the matter straight.

"Well, what about…" and I name two families, who, judging by Larry, now look white to me.

"Paiutes," Delaney says. "You don't want to think all Indians look alike."

I WALK THE FEW blocks back to my garage. My first day of fieldwork! Nineteen pages of field notes! Only a few mistakes! Now I have hours of work ahead, transcribing what I've scrawled into typed, fileable, cross-referenceable notes.

The professor told us to write a personal journal entry every day—I guess to keep our field notes separate from our own subjective reflections. I don't like this idea. The handwritten field notebook requires three hours of transcription and typing for every hour of interview. On the top of each sheet I have to list the topics covered, the informant, the interaction's time and place, and have enough carbon copies to file one for each topic. When time is short or if I'm tired, I know I'll be tempted to ignore the notes and concentrate on myself and my journal, turning the whole experience into "What I Did On My Summer Vacation." And a journal is too introspective for me; the great Ohio humorist James Thurber spoke to the heart of most Ohioans in his book, *Let Your Mind Alone.*

I decide to police my field notes and be 100 per cent objective, saving myself a lot of time.

Under the garage door I find a note from the post office—CALL HUBBY!! BEORE 9!! NANCY—with a New Jersey number scrawled at the bottom. Nancy is the white—or maybe just whitish—clerk who helped me sign up for a post office box this morning.

Has Francis been shot? He's in training in the Rifle Corps and that's bound to be dangerous—all learners, all shooting. It has to be something serious; people don't phone long distance just to talk. Is he calling to break some bad news about my family? Not possible. My mother has the rights to bad-news-breaking. Her style is unique: "Hello? Eileen?…It's Grandma." Or: "…It's the dog." When my aunt was dying, it was: "Hello? Eileen?… It's Lucy. I don't want to bring you home for nothing, but she has a rattle in her throat. Will I hold the phone so you can hear it?" There's no danger my mother would delegate dramatic power like that.

The nearest public phone booth is on Main. I race down Bridge Street, across West, across Center, left on Main. Not enough change, someone in the phone booth—Larry. I pace. Larry keeps putting in more coins. Finally, he hangs up and wanders out. I go in and make a collect call.

"What? What is it?" I shout at Francis. "What's wrong?"

"Honeybunch," Francis drawls. *Honeybunch?*

Larry is slumped on the curb outside, head in hands. I hope he's out of hearing range.

"Are you drinking?" I ask Francis.

"Not now, I'm sleeping," he replies. "It's 1:00 a.m. here. There's a three-hour difference. I wanted you to call me back before midnight here."

"Why before midnight?" But I know: because it's the end of my first full day here. How sweet he remembers.

"It's our anniversary. One month."

Oh. The honeymoon week, the three weeks' training in Reno—one month. I cringe.

"I've been trying to get you all day. I miss you. Do you miss me? All day, I've been thinking of how nice our wedding day was. Remember?"

Of course I do. In the early morning hours before the wedding, I drove out to the woods, into the downy, translucent green of new leaves. I remember thinking I'll never be an ice-skating champion now. I'd never skated, but no matter; that avenue is closed to me forever. I'll never be the spokeswoman for oranges in California. I won't be one of the last female gunslingers or live alone on an island...

Ah, that's where the image of the banana boat came from.

"Eileen? You there?"

Of course I miss Francis. And of course I remember the rest of our wedding day, too, the familiar, worn faces allowing themselves to become romantic again, just for a couple of minutes. At the reception, the jaded stories of married life were trotted out, jokingly, to cover the slight shame of having once had dreams. Francis, calm and gentle, put people at ease, telling an aunt how nice her dress was, holding my crying little sister on his lap, making the dog drink a full bowl of water after it lapped all the slops from the beer keg.

Francis loves to pick up bits of stories and tell them to me when we're alone. For instance, he once heard that some of the old guys were making all the stands for a local church fair out of stuff smuggled out of the mill; another time he learned that his elderly cousin was being treated for scruples—she couldn't leave a store until she checked the receipt to make sure she wasn't cheating. We come from the same place, the same people; we're adding these stories to our own new family's hoard.

"Eileen?"

"I do miss you," I say, suddenly aware that Francis is tapping on the receiver hook. And I really do.

"Good. Gotta go now, one of the guys wants the phone. Bye, Poopsie." *Poopsie?* Is Larry still sitting on the curb? Yes, but there's no way he can hear Francis, thank God.

Now I'm bothered and hungry. I go into Rickett's Diner, right on Main Street, where everyone's white except a short Indian mopping the floor. A long-jawed waitress with tiny, pinched features and a stringy frame eventually wanders over to my table.

"Whatcha want?" she asks flatly, her head turned away toward the Indian. So much for lighthearted repartee with the locals.

When my order is ready, she thumps it down on the Formica table: a dry pork chop, canned green beans, mashed potatoes with a nice pond of pale gravy, and an iceberg salad with a bit of the core in it, all just like my mother's. I nearly cry.

I can't hear whether the waitress is as surly to the other diners as she is to me, but she is certainly rude to the Indian. "Morgan, get your sorry behind over here and clean up the mess the lady's made on the floor," she says when some green beans skitter off my plate. I need to pay more attention to Indian-white relations in this town.

A portly white policeman lumbers in right as I'm getting ready to leave.

"Reenie!" he shouts and stomps across the linoleum, arms wide open. She dances aside, laughing, and he rocks from side to side, pretending to block her. He plunks himself down on a stool at the kitchen end, dwarfing the seat in fat-flaps. She gives him a cup of milky coffee and a big smile.

I set out again, south on Main, scratching out a rough map of the town before it gets dark. Larry's back in the phone booth, but he catches up with me.

"I could help you," he suggests.

"Great." I hand him part of my pad and a pencil. "You get your call through?"

"Nope. I got through but he couldn't talk to me."

"Who's that?"

"My brother. Prison in Carson City. Grand theft auto." He says the charge defiantly, almost proudly, as if at least it isn't shoplifting.

"When will he get out?"

"Three years. They won't let me go see him without my mother, and she's so mad she won't go."

"You must miss him."

"Yeah. I do." He crosses the street and draws the east side of Main, down to the last architectural detail.

"How do you do that?" I ask him when he finishes. His map is nice enough to be framed, not stuck in a notebook.

"Dunno." He shrugs. "I just start the line and follow it."

"Do you study art in school?"

He looks surprised, as if I have some fairy-tale notion of "school."

"I used to draw pictures for my mother. She tossed all my brother's stuff when he got sent away, and my pictures got thrun away, too." He gives me the pad and heads off, shoulders drooping.

Thrun away. There's no better way to put it. That's what Larry looked like a few minutes ago, sitting on that curb.

I CONTINUE MY MAPMAKING until dark. Occasionally people glance at my work, and a few talk to me. Joanne Connolly, who works as a maid for a white family, takes my pad and writes down how to roast pine nuts, the traditional staple, right on top of my Main/Center intersection. Roy Quinn, a young man who says he's living with his wife and her mother, mentions how in the old days a man never spoke to his mother-in-law and what a pity it is that so many of the old customs have died out.

Joanne pulls in a passerby, an older woman, who says she doesn't know anything about Indians, she's only an Indian herself. And a white man with a foxy look, one of a group leaning against the wall of the lounge bar, suggests that I talk to Morgan McBride. "He's the man. Tell him I sent you."

"Morgan McBride," I write the name on a new sheet of my pad.

The man snickers. He gestures behind his back to the group at the lounge, and they laugh. Anthropologists are often used as weapons. Someone will say, "X [the person's worst enemy] told me you would be the best one to talk to about poisons/traditional punishments for adultery/witching/theft," etc.

I put a question mark beside Morgan McBride's name.

CHAPTER THREE

The *Kah' nii*

THE NEXT MORNING, an almighty clap of thunder reverberates off the walls of my sweltering garage, waking me from a dream of…what? Being inside a kettle drum. I wait for the welcome drops of rain. It's the beginning of my second full day in Yerington.

"Eileen? You in there? It's Paulette. Open up." She thumps again on the metal overhead door. Paulette Chapman is a respected, feisty, middle-aged Tribal Council member; last night she walked straight up to me on Main after Larry left and asked me what I was doing. When I explained that I was making a map of the town and that I'd be talking to people on the reservations, she replied, "I wouldn't bother with all that. If I were you, I'd study why the old people around here can't get full Social Security." But she offered to help me meet some people, anyway.

"James Kelly got a pamphlet on you," Paulette says now, as I make her some coffee and fish out khakis and a tee shirt from my suitcase.

Even trainee anthropologists like me try to plan for field problems, such as what to do if no one will talk to me, or if I'm invited to eat maggots, or if someone steals my notes and passes them around, but I'm not prepared for a *pamphlet*. What can it be? Sounds bad, as if there's a contract out on me.

"So he wants you to come to the next Tribal Council meeting," Paulette continues. "Explain yourself."

"Am I in trouble?"

"Not really," she says, unconvincingly. Just then we're interrupted by a boxy ramrod of a man, about 50, who appears just outside the open garage door. He seems to be tracing some animal tracks, poking a stick here and there and muttering.

"Cyril Watkins," Paulette says.

"Lady." Cyril nods to me, but he's distracted, eyeing the tracks. "Single line of prints. I don't like that one bit," he mutters. "That's coyote tracks."

"S'what I told you," Paulette says to him.

"Yes, well, maybe you better come out and stay with me and Maybel a while," he says to me. On the drive into Yerington my first afternoon, the professor pointed out the Watkins's off-reservation bungalow.

Paulette nods to me. "You should." Has she arranged this? "It's a dump, this place. Mice, roaches. And I hear the door opens by itself."

That's true: yesterday morning I woke up in full view of the street, too early, or at least I thought so, for anyone to see. Either the door is faulty, or someone, not me, has the remote control, because I have to hoist the door open myself.

"Them garage door openers," Cyril says. "They're based on the bomb. Remote transmitters, just like detonators. Not enough people know that."

This is news to me, but it gives me the excuse I need to move in with a family. I want to live closer to the Colony or the Ranch, but very few Paiute families live adjacent to either. Delaney told me yesterday a little about Maybel and Cyril, a decorated World War II veteran. The couple keep to themselves, don't get involved in tribal politics; they're modest, careful people, and among the few Paiute Catholics. Maybel had a stroke recently, but by all reports she's recovering.

Cyril tells me to go out and talk to "The Boss," Maybel, about moving in.

"Thanks. I'll go as soon as my car gets here."

He starts to march off, erect as a soldier, then swivels back.

"You got the one about Coyote and his eyeballs?"

"No."

He frowns. He must think I'm collecting folklore and am falling behind. I'm grateful for his concern.

"Coyote and Wolf were cousin-brothers. What you call a first cousin. We call some of ours 'cousin-brothers.' You got a notebook?"

I snatch it from the table and leaf to a new page.

"Wolf was more powerful than Coyote. And more dignified. But Coyote was full of fun, too full of fun, and he wouldn't let anyone get the better of him. One day he was arguing with a bird, and this bird said, 'I can take my eyes out.' Coyote didn't want to be outdone, so he said, 'I can, too,' and did. His eyes rolled in the dust, and when he put them back in, the color had changed. You *sure* you don't know this one?"

"I don't, no."

"Well, then, you really better come out to Maybel and me. She can tell you in Paiute—she knows the whole story. Her grandmother knew a man who was there." He strides off toward town.

There? Where?

"You say you want to know what religion the people took up after Jack Wilson died, you should ask Reverend Parks at the Mission," Paulette says. "Just been here a year, but now he's more Paiute than the Paiutes are. I'll go over with you."

She walks with me over to the Colony entrance: a run-down church, a house trailer, and large piles of cut brush. This is the only church on reservation land; the Paiutes lease it to the Mission, but in earlier days other religions had the lease. Now, some other churches, mainly white, have been built on nearby streets. There's no sign of the Reverend, so we sit down near the church door to wait.

"You know, Jack Wilson lived right on this exact spot. Right here." Paulette pats the ground.

My first connection with Wilson! I study the space for relics, or atmosphere, or *anything* special, but it's the same swept dirt as the rest of the place, except for the pile of cut brush.

"I don't go to this church much any more," Paulette offers. "Too emotional." Apparently some members of the Mission, when spiritually transported, speak in tongues and go into trances. "I like to keep a grip."

Still no sign of Reverend Parks.

"He's around, " Paulette says. "I guess I might as well tell you how the Paiutes got their hands while we're waiting. I got this from my mother; she was big into all this. She only spoke Paiute, and here's me with almost none, really.

"Before the time we live in now, the Indians didn't have hands," she intones, eyes shut. A small wiry man, about 40 years old, emerges from a little trailer beside the church. "They only had stubs where their hands are now. Coyote and Lizard got into an argument about what kinds of hands the Indians should have. Coyote said they should be like his, like paws. 'No,' said Lizard, who had five fingers. 'They need to pick up things, like pine nuts. They need hands like mine.'

"Lizard crept into a crack in the rocks, so Coyote lost the argument.

"This is how the Paiute people got their hands."

"Huh," the man says. "Pity they ain't using them now." Paulette opens her eyes. "You see any Indians helping me build this *kah' nii*?" he asks, pointing to the brush pile. He stretches to his full height and scans the empty land-scape beyond the Colony. He may have been trying to look like a biblical figure, but, at a red-headed five-foot-four, with six or seven generations of wind-seared kinsmen behind him, he looks less like Charlton Heston and more like a walnut on a stick. This is the Reverend Parks.

"This girl needs to know about why we go to your church," Paulette announces.

"God only knows," Reverend Parks answers. "I think it's for the eats."

I need better information than that; I can't imagine how a report built around church eats will be received in my department. Then again, another graduate student, Richard Lee, is currently researching caloric intake and energy expenditures among the !Kung or San hunter-gatherers who live in the African Kalahari. He follows people and observes how they obtain food, measuring the time and energy they use up and the calories that they consume. I can't see myself logging each of Jennie's forkfuls at church sup-pers, and I already know something my colleague discovers: it's the women who are expected to collect most of the food, in this case, from the buffet. Prepare it, too.

"I'm building some shelters for the big Mission Revival and barbecue in August." The Reverend waves at the brush pile. "The *kah' nii* was your tra-ditional winter house, but nobody uses it now. I'm gonna serve the supper in it, maybe some deer and rabbit. Get people thinking about their culture. You need to come to that."

"She can't wait till August, her professors need her report," Paulette retorts. I appreciate her sense of my importance. "If she wants culture, she can talk to Morgan McBride. He knows everything about the Paiutes."

"Yeah, well," says the Reverend. "Talk to Morgan, you'll get 2 per cent about the Paiutes and 98 about Morgan. *And* he's..." He tightens his lips.

"He isn't," Paulette says.

"Is," the Reverend insists. He juts his chin. With that and the lips, his face looks like a hand puppet's.

"He's only *thinking* about it," Paulette says. "Right now all he does is wear women's clothes. Just in the house."

"Is what?" I ask, but they talk over me. Are they implying that Morgan is a witch? A man wearing women's clothes can be a sign of his transformative powers. This is great.

"No boyfriends, yet," Pauline concludes.

Oh.

"Well, he sure is irritating. *And* snobby: he rolls up his nose at people." The Reverend announces this with such feeling I wonder if he has been the victim of one of Morgan's nose rolls. I already like the Reverend; he's a man who makes language his servant, not his master.

"Hey," he calls to Thomasina, the girl I met on Jennie's steps yesterday. She and two little kids skulk through the sagebrush, clearly hoping to pass by unseen. Paulette identifies the boy as Eddie's brother and the doll-like girl as Thomasina's sister.

"Get over here," the Reverend demands. "Give me a hand. Thomasina! George! Wilmalee!"

Thomasina studies the Reverend and the situation: the mound of young willow switches, the heaps of drying *tule* (bulrush) rods, the trailer, the forlorn church. She lumbers over, topples the biggest pile, and thumps off into the brush, giggling.

"Sakes!" cries Reverend Parks.

"Sakes?" little George shouts, delighted. "Is that a swear word? Sakes, sakes, sakes," he shrieks at Wilmalee, picking his nose and pretending to flick boogers in her hair.

"Shoo!" says Reverend Parks, then calls again to Thomasina, "And you, you just get back here, missy. When I'm gone won't no one be left knows how to do this. Park yourself down here and learn something. Tie up these *tules* in bunches so's we can put them over the framework."

All three disappear. "Damned Indians," he mutters.

"I guess I'm not wanted here." Paulette pulls herself up, looking relieved, and leaves, too. "Don't you miss that Tribal Council meeting," she calls.

"Okay, I guess it's you and me, little lady," he says, waving some switches at me. "A traveling preacher and a girl anthropologist. Two red-heads." He tsks.

"Are you just visiting?"

"Well, I'd *like* to stay, but in our ministry we get moved a lot."

He peers at the dusty scene; Eden, his eyes say. Home.

He begins with a brief prayer for the work. When he finishes, I reflexively bless myself. So much for my last five years of well-argued refusal to go to church. I only made an exception for the wedding to keep peace in the family.

"You supposed to go to the Tribal Council meeting?" the Reverend asks.

"Yes."

"Me, too. The Tribal Chairman know what you're doing?"

"I can't get hold of him. I wrote him some letters."

"He ain't exactly sociable. But you better go over and tell him what you're doing." The Reverend's words have the weight of someone who may once have forgotten to do just that.

"I will."

Ain't exactly sociable. Northwest Coast Indian chiefs were so nobly, traditionally aloof that "talking chiefs" spoke for them. The Paiutes never had chiefs of any kind, though, so maybe the chairman just doesn't want to talk to me.

We get to work on the *kah' nii*, sticking the 20-foot willow switches into the ground in a large circle, bending and tying them at the top to form the supports for a dome over which woven *tule* mats are supposed to go. Reverend Parks has big plans for this Revival. He expects that Indians will come from all over to hear sermons, speak in tongues, and eat deer ribs, rabbit, and sage hen. Also, he says, he hopes they'll be eating other traditional foods—pine nut soup, freshwater shrimp, blueberries, buckberries, mint tea, and seeds.

"We're gonna have us some Paiute ice cream, too," he says. "That's their big treat. I got the recipe from Jennie. You roast some pine nuts and put them into the *opýh*, that's their soup bowl, and you mix in a little water and stir it all up with a *pa"tú"*, that's the stirrer. Then you set it on the roof to freeze."

"Not in the freezer?"

"No," he shakes his head. "You gotta do this stuff the right way. Can't mess with people's culture. Remember the oath us ministers gotta take: 'First, do no harm.'"

We work on, sweaty, lacerated by bits of sharp willow, making little progress. According to Driver's *Indians of North America*, which I consult nightly, a *kah' nii* is "a domed affair, covered with thatch or brush, hastily assembled and soon abandoned in the wandering in search for food." I can't see how it can be assembled hastily, though it's clear why the worshippers might abandon it pretty quickly: the framework is already wobbling.

One of the willows Reverend Parks tied springs back out and whips him across the groin. He yelps. Thomasina, from her hideout in the brush, laughs.

"I didn't come here to do this," he wheezes, doubled over. "I came to preach the worda God. But some of these people here don't know nothin' about their own culture. Lookit Thomasina. And little George and Wilmalee don't know the first word of Paiute. *Shit!*

"I'm real sorry," he moans. "I've never…I don't think I ever—"

"It's okay," I reassure him. After all, would it bother a male anthropologist if someone said "shit" in front of him?

"—felt such a pain." His breath rasps. "You know, I do all this 'cause even a Indian deserves a culture. But I end up doing it all myself. Making rabbit traps, building *kah' niis*, boiling *ja pá*, chopping coleslaw." He straightens up, wiping his eyes. "Lord!"

I didn't believe it when some of the local people told me ice cream was a traditional Paiute dish, but that turns out to be true. Now I'll have to ask about coleslaw.

THAT NIGHT, I write to Francis and my mother. To Francis: *missyouloveyouwantyou*, etc. To my mother, about the backlog of mail I collected from the post office: *Please don't send me any more postcards addressed to "Running Water" or "Sitting Pretty."* And, for revenge, I add, *Talked to a really nice Protestant minister today.*

CHAPTER FOUR

Missing Bomb City

UP AT FIRST light, and ready to mingle, I stride into town, a Woman on a Mission. This is real anthropology—meeting interesting people, interjecting subtle questions, taking lots of good notes. I'm almost a professional now. I'll have to be careful; I don't want to look too intimidating.

"You look homesick, Sweetie," Paulette calls from the bus stop on the other side of Main Street.

"I'm not." Our professor in Reno warned us about being homesick, so I'm determined not to be. I also don't have Culture Shock—he warned us about that too, so I have set my mind to not being shocked, come what might.

I reset my face to a more authoritative expression.

Paulette raises her eyebrows and mouths something.

"What?"

She steps into the street and cups her mouth with her hand. "Constipated, then?" she asks. "I know that brand of coffee you use always constipates me." She taps her stomach exaggeratedly to make the point and then waves down the approaching bus.

I ignore some guys leering in front of the casino and march on.

Is there no place I can study that's a little closer to my home, Paulette asked me yesterday morning when we were having that coffee.

Yes, there is, actually. Home itself.

It's not yet academically acceptable for anthropologists to study people who are culturally similar to themselves or to do research in their own communities. John Hostetler's 1963 study of his people, *The Amish*, is unusual for its time, allowable perhaps only because they live undeniably exotic lives in small rural communities—small rural communities near Youngstown, in fact. I would love to study Youngstown, where people live undeniably exotic lives (according to the FBI) in the poisoned air of a gritty urban landscape. But when I suggested this last fall to my supervisor, Professor George

Peter Murdock, back at the University of Pittsburgh, he was horrified. Being only 62 miles northeast of Pittsburgh, maybe Youngstown isn't "primitive" or exotic enough for anthropologists? Of course, if it were, and I were a "native," what did that make the Pittsburgh faculty? ("Subjects," as it happens, because a fellow student, Mel Williams, is working quietly on his account of the department.)

All around me now, anthropology is changing; "natives" even more exotic than Hostetler have become anthropologists. This creates awkwardness, as some feel that their own cultures have been misinterpreted or abused by academic careerists. And ordinary natives feel ethnographies have been one-sidedly analyzed in publications and at academic conferences where they have neither the access nor the professional wherewithal to respond.

I was surprised one day last year to find out where I fit into this scenario myself. After a seminar by the eminent visiting British anthropologist, Raymond Firth, Professor Murdock introduced me by saying, "This is Eileen. She's a working-class girl from a poor mill family. I got her from Youngstown University." They both beamed. I was confused and a little upset. Did my professor really see *me* as one of the department's first "natives?" He seemed disappointed once when I couldn't explain the mill's process of "puddling" pig iron. But did *he* understand the manufacturing process that turns chrysolite into the absbestos that lines our department's walls?

To my logical mind, a study of Youngstown would be fascinating. Historically, steel was central, and the churches were important, but the Mafia has always been key. Understanding the Mafia's role in the town explains a lot about its economic, political, legal, and religious organization, as well as its ethnic relations, waste management, city planning, shopping mall development, and entertainment venues. The Mafia controls the police entrance examination system, so at times its members have made up about a quarter of the police department and even more in the sheriff's office and the courthouse. Business people pay them protection money, and most people play "the Bug," their illegal lottery. Sometimes policemen collect the day's Bug receipts for their Mafia bosses.

Citizens of Youngstown know all the "usual suspects." We know why Cadillac Charlie Cavallero was arrested for blocking the sidewalk but seems free to knock people off as he pleases and why Sandy Naples was let out of jail regularly to take his clothes to a French laundry and to see his young girlfriend. We understand why he was killed on her front porch. After Vince DeNiro was executed by a "Youngstown tune-up," a bomb wired to his Oldsmobile ignition, we wonder why, a year later, Cadillac Charlie wasn't more careful. We understand why local people are enraged that, having been warned, he still took his little sons in the car with him.

And we know why the local people, toughened at the blast furnaces, just now coming out of the longest steel strike in U.S. history, look on the Mafia bosses with some indulgence. For one thing, they aren't the hated steel mill owners; for another, they aren't the clowns in Washington, whose few efforts in relation to Youngstown are pathetic. Even if Ohio creates a state lottery some day, will people trust it? As my mother points out, with the Mafia's "Bug," at least we know where the money goes. And the Mafia makes Youngstown "work," even if only as a byproduct of its own rackets. It sometimes provides accidental "benefits" too, one of them being nationwide color for our otherwise bleak city. We don't particularly begrudge the Mafia its influence.

But when I explained all this to Professor Murdock, he told me I wasn't "objective" enough about Youngstown to use it as my first field experience. So, in its gory heyday, Youngstown isn't being studied by anyone except the FBI, and here I am in Yerington with the Paiutes, and maybe I am a little bit homesick.

LIZARDS, MICE, DARTING things—where do they come from, where do they go? Eddie seems to come and go out of cracks. You see something, maybe, out of the corner of your eye, and there he is. And then he isn't. But here he is in front of me now. "There's a call for you at the phone box." He smiles at me absentmindedly, as one might at a pet.

A yellow mixed-breed dog sidles up to us and brushes a happy wagging tail against him. Eddie kicks it viciously. The dog vomits.

"Why did you do that?" I shout.

"What?"

I don't have time to give Eddie a good talking-to, but I will; that was sickening. I race down Bridge Street toward Main. Why doesn't Francis send me a letter warning me he'll be calling at noon, or whenever? These calls must be costing a fortune.

"Eileen?..." It's my mother.

"Who is it? Who died?"

"Died! No one. Well, let me think, Jimmy Anzivino, from the wedding, but you hardly knew him. Blown to smithereens. By the Usual Suspects—I don't like to say over the phone. You can never tell who's listening, and his mother thinks he was just fooling around with the pilot light in the stove. I'm just calling to see how you are. Did you get my letter?"

"No. What does it say?" I still believe she must be concealing a death.

"Just that things have calmed down a little. We packed up all your wedding presents, and Dad put them down cellar, up on the shelves so they won't get pee on them. He's better now he's been doctored, but you still can't trust him. Next time, Dad says he wants a female."

It takes me a moment to realize she's talking about my father's latest pup.

"Well...thanks. I'll get them on my way back to Pittsburgh."

"I put a few copies of the newspaper article about your wedding in with my letter. I better sign off—I was canning picallili last night until the last dog was hung." I picture my mother in her big old-fashioned kitchen, canning a British/East Indian food, using a phrase that refers to a punishment for Wild West rustlers and, earlier, for marauding medieval dogs. Now it simply means "late." Will the Paiutes have cultural complexities like this that almost defy unpicking?

"Eileen? Still there? Do you think the Indians would like some picallili? I could mail it."

We say goodbye. Nancy has my mother's letter behind the counter when I go into the post office. I don't ask her why it's not in my box; I'm careful how I act around her after a few people warned me she has a tongue like a razor. Thomasina is also in the office; she snatches the letter from my hand, and she and a friend take turns waving it at me, each reaching higher and higher to grab it from the other. Jennie is there too, and, surprisingly for a short woman of her compact bulk, she raises her arm in a single fluid arc and grabs it.

"That's a nice wedding picture," she observes when the newspaper cutting falls out of the envelope. "Looks like you, only better, the way a picture *should* look. Mine always look like me," she complains. "I look like someone sat on my head." Jennie is built on a grander horizontal scale than most of her people.

She and the rest of the group now gathered around are pleased that they, too, are mentioned in the newspaper write-up—if only as an "Indian reservation in Nevada."

"Your dress is beautiful," Jennie says, and the girls, pushing and shoving hard to see it, twitter in agreement.

It was a gorgeous gown: it felt like a cloud of lace as I marched up the aisle on my father's arm towards Francis standing at the altar, calm, grinning.

And then the vision of that banana boat. Sailing away to exotic ports.

And my father's arm tightening as we approached the altar. My father is a quiet man; he must have spoken to my mother during their courtship, but he has said very little since. Even so, I knew he doesn't really like Francis. "The altar boy," he calls him. "Awful religious." Of course Dad has never gone to the drive-in with us. X-rated stuff in the back seat.

I invite Jennie to have a root beer with me in Rickett's. "We don't go in there," she states simply. How foolish I feel. She's put the gentlest interpretation on it; in fact, Indians *can't* go in there. So we sit on the grass in front of the courthouse.

"I didn't get married until I was 23, either," Jennie continues, "but my mother got married at nine. She followed my father around to the farms where he worked, making mud dolls to pass the time. She missed her mother something awful, she said. And she didn't even have periods until she was 14."

"How did they get married?"

"She couldn't remember, she was so young. But she said later on she often saw my father giving blankets and beads to her father. She didn't know why at the time, but that's how people got married—the man gave the woman's family something. If both of the people were grown up, they might just decide to live together and be married that way.

"I was born in a sagebrush windbreak—we didn't have houses—and when I was growing up, my mother and father followed the old customs. When I began to have periods, my father built a little hut for me to stay in on those days. I had to gather wood every morning and evening, to make me ambitious when I grew up. My mother would come before sunrise to bathe me, and pile up and burn the wood I'd gathered, and make me jump over it."

"Did they arrange a marriage for you then?"

"No, my mother didn't want me to get married until I was old, so she told me if I looked at a man, I would get pregnant."

I can identify with that. My own mother said more or less the same.

"I was very wary of men," Jennie goes on. "I tried to pass this on to my own daughters, but you can see for yourself it didn't work." Ten people live in Jennie's two-roomed house, most of them her daughters and their children.

"So, they got no blankets and beads for you?"

"No, but I got a couple doilies from a lady I cleaned house for."

There's a marriage system I've read about that I can't resist telling Jennie, possibly in the belief that all Indians are interested in other Indians. "You know, with the Indians up in the Northwest, a man paid the bride's father in property, but as soon as he did, the father gathered up twice as much property to get her back. Then he held a big feast to show what a great man he was. So the marriage was over until the husband got together twice as much as what his wife's father had given him and held a feast himself to put her father in his place. Now the woman was worth four times what she was when they'd started. A woman could be married and divorced and re-married maybe 10 or 12 times, maybe every two weeks or so."

After a long pause, "That's stupid," Jennie says. "Those people up there lied to you. That poor woman would be on the road all the time. Never even get a wash done. Whoever told you that, it must have been a man. You want to be more careful, look stuff like that up in a book first."

Eddie and Larry arrive as Jennie leverages her ladylike bulk off the grass. "Eddie thinks you're mad at us because we did something, so we're sorry...." Larry says.

"Us?" I look at Eddie. He laughs.

"Asshole," he says to Larry, elbowing him hard in the same place he kicked the dog.

I go back into the post office and send a note to Francis. I miss him. He'd never kick a dog. "You'd like it here," I write. And the people here would like him, I'm sure. He's so easygoing. Freckled. Perhaps that would make a good article for me to write up—"Freckles as an aid to rapport"?

CHAPTER FIVE

Anthropology: A Mirror for Man

ANOTHER DEAFENING DAWN wallop on the overhead door, and I'm out of bed like a greyhound out of a trap.

Eddie again. "Some old guys in the Colony say you need to talk to them."

"About what?"

"Dunno. Maybe they're on the warpath, Maybe they want a nice white squaw."

I look away a second to check the time, and he's gone, but I can still hear the snickering.

Seven a.m. and already nearly 90 degrees. I should go out to visit James Kelly this morning and find out about the pamphlet, but I don't have a car yet, and it's already too hot to hitchhike. I'm looking for an excuse. Perhaps I'll go tomorrow.

I've accomplished a lot in the four days I've been here: I've drawn the main street and the Colony map with Larry's help and, with Jennie's, named the people in the Colony houses and learned something of their statistics. I also have half a dozen pages filled with kinship terms. They're more interesting than I thought they would be. You can use them to predict a lot of things about a group: whom each person can marry, which side has the right to pass on the family line, where a couple is likely to live after marriage, and even—strange as it may seem—how a person treats his father's sister. If I were Delaney's daughter, whom could I marry? I love working these puzzles out; understanding clearly structured systems makes me feel that I'm coping.

People point out patterns to me. I know that the majority of people who took up a new religion in recent times joined the Assembly of God, and yesterday on the courthouse grass Jennie explained why Christianity, in some form, appealed to them: "I think Jack Wilson's message was a Christian message specially for us Paiute people. Our Coyote and Wolf are like your Cain and Abel. And our animal stories are just like Genesis."

I've also been over to the Yerington library twice, searching old newspapers for any references to the Paiutes. There's very little, so I look for information on the town itself. The first reference I find, from Mark Twain, hardly does the place justice:

> The country looks something like a singed cat ... a barren waste of sand, embellished with melancholy sage-brush, and fenced in with snow clad mountains.... Even the birds, when they flew over, carried their own provisions.

"Pizen Switch" was what the first whites called this Great Basin valley between the Desert, Wassuk, and Singatse mountains. Later, it was called Greenfield, after its lush vegetation. The rumor that it was later named Yerington after a railroad magnate in an unsuccessful attempt to lure his rail line through town is likely to be untrue; the railway bypassed the town in 1880–81, and the town and its post office weren't named Yerington until 1894. It seems it was a later compromise, to avoid two other names.

All in all, I decide if things keep up like this, I can be finished in a few weeks instead of the almost three months I signed up for.

I WALK OVER TO the Colony. Three old men huddle together near the entrance, looking neither warlike nor rapacious, just terrified.

"Eddie said someone wanted to see me?"

"Eddie said you wanted to see *us*," they whisper.

Another reason why I want to swat Eddie, frightening old people like this. "I do. Of course. Thank you. I need some help with some Paiute words and people said you could help."

I open my notebook to the pages of kinship terms.

They relax a little, but say they don't speak a word of Paiute.

"*Pa wá*," I ask. "*Py ní ? i*" They wriggle their backsides into the sand and stare at my mouth, fascinated.

"Her Paiute is funny," one says in Paiute. That's one sentence I know by heart already.

"Delaney asked me to ask you," I lie.

"Well, acourse no one knows his stuff like Delaney," he says, pleased.

I spot Archie Jim being unloaded from his niece's truck and ask his bearers to bring him over. We gather together and go over the words.

"*Pa wá*, that's right, that's the mother's sister," Archie says. "And *py ní ? i*. Yep. But *pi tu uu*, now what's that? Don't remember that one. *Pi tu uu*."

"Hold on a minute." The old man who spoke before is grinning. "Say it again."

I do.

"What you got there is Delaney spitting tobacco. That's it, exactly. *Pi tu uu!*"

"Who were those guys?" I ask Archie when the close-mouthed trio creep away.

"Don't know," Archie answers. "The one did all the yapping was a Shoshone from over to Ely. Wouldn't trust a word he said. You put nails in his mouth, they come out as corkscrews." He signals a passing young man, a walking pectoral mass, and issues instructions for being deposited near three guys shooting craps across from Jennie's. "You still here when I get back, I'll tell you a real good one about Coyote. None a this 'helping up old ladies stuff.' Why, one time…" and out comes the story of Coyote eating his own penis and somehow drowning trying to retrieve it.

"But this is not the end," Archie says. "Nossir. Not the end." And he wanders off.

Most Coyote stories finish that way: "But this is not the end." Maybe because he gets himself killed in a lot of them, only to spring up again.

I RETREAT TO THE shade of Jennie's tree. In this heat, just *thinking* wearies me. And I'm not feeling that good, either, a little brackish and sour. I know I'm not pregnant, and I don't have a fever. Maybe it's a reaction to the Rocky Mountain spotted fever shots? And I'm floundering. Already my research focus is shifting, and I'm getting off track. I'm supposed to be studying Jack Wilson's "legacy," but I'm being seduced by Coyote: Coyote changing his eyeballs, his shape, his essence; Coyote managing to be the butt of his own jokes; Coyote and Wolf, Coyote and Eagle, Coyote and Rabbit. The mischievous, sex-obsessed trickster keeps cropping up. People revere the wise Wolf, but they have a weakness for the gossipy glutton, the lecherous liar, the outlaw who is often the comical victim of self-inflicted pratfalls.

My work may have been more structured if I had had more exposure to research methods before leaving Pittsburgh for Nevada. Everything I'd been taught or had read so far was mainly the anthropological equivalent of war stories—close shaves, rat stew, being loved by the natives. I have little idea of what one actually *does* in the field. Sociologists have questionnaires, and psychologists use projective tests, but I feel that I have too few "tools" or "instruments."

What I'm doing in Yerington is watching and asking. I learned the importance of this, and how to do it, during the training weeks in Reno. It's one of the anthropologist's main tools—"participant observation"—but, as a beginner, I'm swamped by its open-endedness. Right now, though, there's very little scope for observation, because it's high noon and sensible people are inside out of the heat. Across the road from Jennie's, the three crap-shooters are asleep or have passed out amid the remains of their ongoing game and a sizeable pile of beer bottles. Archie is also dozing. I write these details down.

Larry wanders down the road. Eddie usually materializes out of nowhere, but Larry is so hesitant about his welcome that I almost have to reel him in. He sits down with me under the tree.

"I saw you in the library," I say.

"Yeah."

"What do you like to read?"

He shrugs. I can see every bone in his neck and shoulders. "Stuff. Sports." Then, emboldened, "What do you like to read?"

"I'm reading old newspapers."

"I could get you today's," he springs up. "Rickett's sells them."

"I need to catch up with the others, first."

The other day, when Larry left the library, I looked at the books he had carefully re-shelved: German Impressionism, new developments in pack-aging and materials, and the life of the inventor Rudolf Diesel, which I sat down and read too. I also saw that he'd found that old reliable, Clyde Kluckhohn's *Anthropology: A Mirror for Man.* Someone, maybe Larry, had turned down a lot of the pages.

A delicious breeze catches my notebook, and some torn scraps, remind-ers, and afterthoughts blow out. Larry crawls around to retrieve them.

"How come you decided to study this kind of stuff?" he asks.

If Eddie asked me this, I might come up with a self-protective riposte, but Larry is serious. I've been thinking about this question myself and about the journal we trainees are expected to keep, the one I've been avoiding. All the others have probably written half a notebook by now. So "Why I Chose Anthropology" might be a good title for a nice essay-style piece; it would please the professor.

"I think I wanted to get the answers to some questions," I answer. "About race, for one. My father didn't have much good to say about black people. It wasn't just him. A lot of white people in my town didn't like them. We weren't as bad as the South, of course," I add protectively.

"My mother don't like black people, either. Or Indians or nothing."

"My dad was always making remarks. It got so bad I stopped talking to him for a year, when I was a little older than you, about 18." Eight of us in that tiny house, and I avoided any room containing my father. I have to give him credit, thinking back. "My dad and I, we had our own civil rights movement going."

Larry is baffled. "Did you have so many black people? Was it like a reservation or what?"

"No, we just had one black family on our street, the McConnells." I wonder if the Irish had a thing about planting their names on people—a lot of the Paiutes have Irish surnames, too. "Mr. McConnell was an important judge. They all had college degrees, but the rest of us, the whites, many were high school dropouts."

No amount of education could spare the McConnells from fear of the dangerously ignorant, though. Mrs. McConnell once told my mother that she ironed every item of laundry—towels, socks, underwear—"in case someone got in." I didn't understand what she meant by this, but my mother, saddened, explained that Mrs. McConnell didn't want to give racist thugs anything to say about black housekeeping.

"One family? And your dad didn't like them?"

"It wasn't because of the McConnells. My dad grew up beside them and used to babysit the boys. But a lot of black families lived down closer to the mills. Then they started moving out street by street toward us. Each time, some of the white people panicked and moved out."

"And your dad got afraid?"

"It was more that he got worried. You lost money on your house when you tried to sell, and if you stayed, life got a lot worse. The city stopped fixing the streets blacks lived on, and the streetlights, and sometimes they didn't pick up the garbage. Businesses shut. You had to walk a mile to get groceries." I remember when the city cut all the lush maple trees lining the street, because of a disease, someone said, although the maples on the few remaining all-white streets were just sprayed. We were left with flayed trunks, about eight feet high, a surreal vista.

"Sometimes I try to talk to my mother. I even took Eddie over so she could see Paiutes were okay," Larry says.

Yes, well, I tried to talk to my father, too, but I didn't do anything as stupid as bringing someone like Eddie around. Maybe my father's resentment came from feeling guilty about the whites' role in black history; maybe a little reasoning would set him straight. I caught him alone on the porch one summer evening, re-reading his childhood favorite, *The Count of Monte Cristo*, for perhaps the tenth time. We couldn't afford many books, and he was usually too tired to walk uptown to the library, so he read the same books over and over, refurnishing them each time with new scenery, costumes, hair colors, and knickknacks.

"Listen," I interrupted, startling him. "Slavery wasn't your fault. If you think about it, your grandfather was still in his freezing patch over in County Mayo, snagging turnips and scratching around for a few scabby potatoes 30 years after the slaves were freed in this country."

My father gave me a wary look and took his book into the living room. Later, my mother told me, laughing, that sometimes he wasn't sure if I was all there.

"So, I don't know talking does that much good," I conclude after telling Larry this story. "Are you listening to me?" He's breathing through his mouth, eyes wide.

"Uh, yeah. I mean no, I guess it doesn't."

"I met black people on the way to school every day, and it was just like it is with the Indians here. They seemed to have the same brains and feelings as anybody else. So what I wondered was how come I was growing up around some of the same black people my father grew up with, and we looked at them in such different ways?"

"So, how come?"

"I didn't know then."

"My ma says the government is going to make the Indians citizens and then there won't be any jobs for us, and they'll take over. She says we're just hanging on by our fingernails."

"The Indians *are* citizens." And Larry's mother obviously hasn't heard yet that Lyndon Johnson signed the *Civil Rights Act* less than a week ago.

"Yeah, but you know what I mean. She says if it don't get better, we're moving to Utah. Indians can't vote there."

Larry's poor mother. Utah changed that law when I was in high school.

"I know she must be worried about her job. My dad was, too. The job and the house are all most people have. You can be out on the street in no time. One of my cousins was evicted with his wife and four kids on Christmas Eve."

Even families with a paycheck were vulnerable. "If that dog bites some-one," my mother would say as our mild pet sat on the front steps, "we could lose the house." We rushed to put furnace ash on our part of the icy side-walk in winter and in the summer repaired cracks with cement because "If someone falls on that, we could lose the house..." You can't blame people for being scared about their jobs. But some really believe black people aren't as smart or ambitious or responsible as whites. That they are biologically inferior. And some think the same things about women—though not my father, thank God.

"I want to be able to prove what I believe," I tell Larry, "so I went into anthropology."

"How's that prove anything?"

I wish I hadn't started this discussion on such a hot day. A delicious little wind blows what feels like a buckeye-sized cinder into my eye.

"Well, say that where I live, people think left-handed people have crimi-nal brains, and the only reason they don't kill people all the time is that we don't allow them to have guns or knives. We think they can't help it, it's in the blood, it's their biology."

"I'm left-handed," Larry says. "I don't kill people."

"Yes, but maybe if you had a gun or a knife, you would."

"I have a gun and a knife."

"Well then, it's only a matter of time."

"That's not fair."

"If it's right, it's not fair to expect much of left-handed people if they have weapons. If it isn't right, it's not fair to discriminate against them when they kill someone."

Larry studies his left hand.

"Anthropology looks at all the groups of people, all over the world. We're all the same species, so if it's in the blood for left-handed people to be killers, we'll find it everywhere. All over the world, people will be watching their left-handed people, afraid their kids will be left-handed, or worried they'll want to hang out with left-handed people. They might even kill the lefties, just in case."

"Is that true?" Larry is shocked.

"No. We don't find it everywhere. In some places, it's even an advantage to be left-handed."

"Yeah! Baseball! Boxing!"

"Anyhow, that's what anthropology does. Looks everywhere to see what's universal and why, what isn't and why it isn't. It's a great thing to know about when someone says black people are naturally lazy or that weaving is women's work."

"Navaho women weave," Larry says.

"Irish men weave."

"Well, " Larry gets up, yawning. "I can't see spending my life on left-handed people." He peers warily at me from under his pale hair. "Sorry. Just joking."

I look around. Nothing moving. No people. Praise be. I go back to the garage.

Now I have something I want to write in that journal. Not about anthropology, but about my father. I want to record that I wronged him when I was talking to Larry. My father is a good man. He has never met an individual black person he doesn't like. He has never met anyone he doesn't like, and how many people can you say that about? The problem is that he has to meet them, first, and he doesn't want the first time to be when he turns up for his shift and someone else's stuff is in his locker.

One of the things my undergraduate college, Youngstown University, did for me—besides introducing me to anthropology—was to re-introduce me to my father. A young labor-activist professor, Vern Bullough, assigned me to write a report on steel mill history and nearly wept when he saw the Bible-sized outcome, two pounds of unsorted facts.

"God, I'm tired of these Good Girl reports," he said. "Did you even *talk* to your father about this? What's his name? What does he do in the mill?"

I told him his name. I didn't know what he did.

"Great," he said. "He's supporting what, six kids, helping you through college, and you don't even know what he does to pull that off?"

The next time we met, I was able to tell him that my father worked at many of the jobs in the mill but was hired as a tool-and-die maker.

"I'll tell you what else he is," Bullough said. "He's the son of a hero. I found out because his father had exactly the same name. He died after being hosed down by the mill police during the freezing January 1916 strike. He was 36."

"I never heard this."

"Did you ever ask your father about the mills, or his father? Or his grandfather?'

"I know that his mother and her three kids moved back in with her parents when her husband died."

"What about the grandfather?"

"After he took her and the kids in, he lost his job in the next big strike. My dad was nine or ten, then. He told me last night his grandfather worked 12-hour days and seven-day weeks during World War I, and when the war ended, the mill owners forced the men to work the same hours, no extra pay."

"Yes," Bullough said, "and when they went out on strike, the owners brought 5,000 southern blacks up take their places. I'd be surprised if your grandfather ever worked again in the mills. If he did, he had to turn up outside the mill with his lunch bucket, like most of the others, for the 8:00 shift, and if the boss didn't pick him, he came again at 4:00 and maybe again at 12:00."

I knew that my father's mother, still in her 20s, had to go out to work; maybe she supported them all. My dad once told me the kids never had Christmases or birthdays again after one of the strikes.

Bullough handed me his file about conditions in the mills and the strikes. That night, I gave it to my father. He was a quietly emotional man; he'd mist over at the idea of a lost spaniel. Later, I found him in the kitchen, red-eyed.

"Those poor devils," he said.

"Your father and grandfather?"

"Them, and the whites that lost their jobs, and the blacks grateful to go into that hellhole for half the money."

Steel and strikes shaped my father's world. In his lifetime, mill owners created ethnically and racially segregated company housing and jobs: blacks in the blast furnaces, cinder plant, and coke works; Irish and Scottish in the open hearths and on the railroads; Italians as bricklayers and masons; English and Germans in the machine shops. I knew almost nothing of this; I wasn't the one who had to compete with blacks in the mill, or with anyone else. Except men, of course. I was hoping anthropology would help with that, too. Were women subservient everywhere, or was my mother one of the few exceptions?

A few days later, when I was alone in the kitchen reading, my father came in, slapping a tightly folded newspaper against his palm. I dreaded this; everyone in the family did. I tried to escape; he was going to read me something about the goddamned buffoons that ran the country, the Mafia's latest caper, the tin cans called cars these days, the police. But no, what he really wanted now was an excuse to talk about the mill; we never talked about it in the house.

"It says here," he said, jabbing the paper, "that the mill management claims worker theft is one of their biggest problems."

"How insulting!"

"Oh, no, it's true. It would be their biggest problem except there's only so much you can carry out in a lunch bucket. I know guys would take out an overhead crane, cabs, rails, and all, if they could. "

"Not you," I said, dismayed.

"Course not. With six kids and a woman like your mother? But you know Dutch Wilkins, that pipe fence he's got all around his property?"

"Yes?"

"Well, he's a pipefitter in the mill." In the next hour, the stories unreeled: tales about guys who converted their attics into rumpus rooms or built second bathrooms with tools and material smuggled out of the mills—wrenches, clamps, pieces of wood, copper, brass, anything that might be useful and small enough to be carried out the gate. The way he told it, the nearby suburb of Struthers was built out of mill supplies.

"Don't they get caught?"

"Not often. The guy on the gate, he usually doesn't want to know anything about it. If it's a new guy on the gate, they wait to see what he's like."

What the men really admired, he said, was an outrageously ingenious caper, something involving intelligence, planning, cunning, and, most importantly, an unmitigated contempt for management. A real poke in the eye. Sometimes things were taken out just for the hell of it, to see if it could be done; the satisfaction came from the elegance of the maneuver, not the value of the items, which might be useless outside the mill. The insult to the bosses is what counted.

He beamed, transported, perhaps, to happier times.

A few weeks later, Dutch was caught and fired. "It was like a wake in there today," Dad said.

I FINISH WRITING AND go back to the Colony. Larry is still under the tree, drawing lizards in the sand. Eddie and Eddie's cousin, a startlingly wavy-haired Paiute boy named Curly, leave the boozy crap game and plop down beside us. "Larry, Curly, and Eddie, like the Three Stooges," Curly says, "but Eddie's the odd one out."

Eddie is certainly odd; something about him has begun to seem faintly familiar, but in a way that eludes me. He has a feral handsomeness, a curious combination of brains, mischief, and a seeming indifference to both kindness and cruelty. He appears to live outside some of the rules and gets away with it. Larry, on the other hand, looks like he has paid heavily for whatever little he gets. Curly's only distinction, other than his hair, is his massive size; he has hands like shovels.

The boys loll under the tree, struck down by a profound teenaged torpor. Once Eddie manages to stir himself to perform a lightning card shuffle for a passing girl, and Curly throws a few rocks at a cat. The inertia is contagious. I've brought Driver's *Indians of North America* to keep flat a Colony map I'm hoping to finish, but my energy is flagging too much even to open it.

Larry politely asks to look at the book. I pass it over, proud that I manage to ignore his grubby hands; I always read it with the paper cover flaps folded over the pages, to keep it clean. Eddie snatches it, cracks the spine, settles back, and flips the pages. He reads aloud in a high, priggish voice: "The aim of this book is to offer a comprehensive comparative description and interpretation of American Indian culture from the Arctic to Panama. It is designed for use as a text in anthropology courses, and as a general introduction for anyone interested in Indians."

"Where's Delaney?" I ask.

"Gone to town," Eddie replies.

We all wilt. Larry falls asleep. It's so hot my eyelids feel pasted open, stuck to the sweaty skin below my eyebrows. Suddenly, someone yanks my hair hard and delivers a dull rap on my skull. It's Delaney's five-year-old grand-nephew, Earl, wearing a Sioux feathered headdress. Delaney stomps along behind, carrying a few things in a torn grocery bag.

"Shame on you!" Delaney scolds. He snatches a little rubber tomahawk from Earl. "Tell the lady you're sorry!"

"See all I got at the store?" Earl shrieks. "Look at me, I'm a Indian! I scalped you!"

Curly rolls his eyes. "We didn't wear that stuff, Earl." He throws a rock at another passing cat.

"We didn't," Eddie agrees, leafing through Driver. "We wore…"

Earl pouts, holding back tears. "I'm a *Indian!*" he repeats.

"You okay?" Delaney asks me. "It's too hot for you here. You want a drink a water?"

"I knew it!" Eddie announces, smacking the book. "Buck-naked. We didn't have a stitch to our names. You just look here at this guy, Driver; he's got something to say about the clothes on every tribe in the U.S. except us. Even got drawings."

"Lemme see that," Delaney snaps, hoisting Earl up onto his lap.

"Hey," Earl says. "Naked ladies. Look, Delaney."

"Nibbynose! You look at your coloring book," Delaney replies. "You need to color Mickey." To me, he says, "I just come from James Kelly. Tribal Chairman. He wants to know what you're doing. I think you better go see him."

"Oh. A couple days ago I thought you said there was no rush."

"Yeah, well, I figured you'd be gone by now."

"Gone?"

"I thought once you got your answer from the Reverend, you could finish up and go. But the Reverend says he don't know what you're talking about, so I guess you better go see James Kelly, tell him you'll be around a little while. By the way, Cyril asked me when you'd be out to stay with him and Maybel."

"The minute I get my car," I say. And it couldn't come a minute too soon.

A pickup pulls up, driven by an ancient white man, turbaned in a dirty bandage. The Indian I'd seen mopping at the diner steps out.

"Morgan McBride," he announces, with a salute. He waves his hand dismissively at the old man, adding, "A colleague." And then to Earl, "Keep that red cray'n inside Mickey's lines."

During our training sessions in Reno, we learned that "outsiders" in a group are often the best observers of the group's culture, because they're usually struggling to be included. Morgan is such an outsider. He's markedly stunted in size, with one reasonably good eye, one good arm, and one good but foreshortened leg. He needs to use a crutch. One side of his head is bald. All these features are distributed randomly on either side. He also has buck teeth and wears something like a sarong over his other clothes. Two or three of these anomalies might be okay with the locals, but the Reverend said he's irritating, too. How well does he fit in, I wonder?

Larry wakes up, sweaty and stunned?

"See?" Eddie shows him. "Looky here. She got tattoos all up her arms and stomach and legs up to her... and oh, boy, not a thing on her titties. See, page 141, 'Southeastern Clothing.' Nothing about us, though," he adds, clearly disappointed.

"Here, let me have a look at that," Curly demands. *Indians of North America.* We're Indians of North America, right? Right, Eddie?... We *are*," he reassures himself when no one answers. "Nobody cares about the Paiute."

"Here," Eddie says. "Listen to this. 'Genital sex activity was the only approved variety, as in our society.'"

"Wouldn't you just know it," Morgan sighs.

"'All other kinds of sex outlet were not only frowned upon but regarded as causes of illness,'" Eddie reads pretentiously, eyeing the crutch that Morgan carries like a club.

"'Chapter 7: Narcotics and Stimulants,'" he continues. "I'd say we're in *there*, all right."

"What do you mean?" Morgan demands. But Eddie skips ahead to page 266, "Premarital Mating," leaving a big smudge on it.

Delaney winces as he shifts Earl to his other knee. "I was planning on telling you the story of Wolf and Coyote."

"Whooeee!" Eddie crows.

"Have some respect!" Delaney booms back.

"No, I meant this chapter."

"Coyote's Paiute name was *Icá?a*, and Wolf's was *Isá*," Delaney begins gravely, settling back against the tree for a good long oration.

"'The Egocentric Northwest Coast Men,' 'The Manly-Hearted Plains People'..." Eddie reads the section headings.

"We're Plains, right?" he asks Larry.

"No, she says we're Great Basin." Larry points at me.

"Don't point!" Morgan says. "Don't you know anything?"

"I thought it was just we didn't point at rainbows," Larry protests.

"We? You're not even an *Indian*."

"Yeah!" says Curly. "Us Indians can't even go into that restaurant where your mother works." He throws a rock at a passing lizard.

"I can't either, stupid, remember?" Larry says. "I got banned until my mother pays for the time I put my foot through the screen door, accidental. Mr. Rickett takes some out of her paycheck every week."

So Larry's mother is Reenie, the waitress in Rickett's.

"And wow, the time you smeared syrup all over the seats," Curly goes on. "She got the fuzz on you, that time."

"That syrup was a accident, too."

"Uh huh."

"Wickham?" says Eddie. "Scuzz Fuzz?"

"Who's Wickham?" I ask, but the other two, quiet for a second, study Larry, who looks miserable.

"Okay," Eddie says. "So there's nothing about *us* Indians in here. You ought to write something for this book, Morgan. 'The Shit-headed Great Basin Man.'"

"Shit-dicked," Curly mutters to Morgan, but eyeing Delaney, who appears to be asleep with Earl in his arms.

"Hey, hey, hey!" Larry shouts. "There's a lady here."

"Show us your tattoos." Curly smirks.

"Boy, I'm getting old." Delaney wakes up, stretching. "Okay, write this down. This is about the time Coyote was going along and he came to a big party and asked if he could dance on his eyeballs."

"All these stories," says Eddie. "They always start out okay, sensible. Like 'A dog and a cat walk down the street.' Then comes the next line, and all hell breaks loose: the dog jumps on his horse, or cooks up a big dinner, or has an argument with his grandfather. It's ridiculous."

I remember one of my own favorite tales about the Inuit girl Sedna. "Sedna and her father lived by the water," I start to tell them. "One day she married a seabird."

This reminds Delaney of another story. He taps my notebook imperiously. "In the beginning, before there were any Indians, there were two friends, a codfish and a rainbow trout. The river was dry, and both of the fish were stranded. One day the trout tried to swim and got stuck and called back to the codfish, 'There is no water.'

"The codfish was making a fire and throwing rocks across the river. He made a big hole with the rocks. Soon, water came up behind the codfish. The big giant from Hot Springs, *Paizó?o*, decided to go over and see the fish; he wanted to eat them. But he'd never seen the river before, and he drowned because he always carried a rock basket on his back and it pulled him under."

"The codfish was making a fire," Eddie mocks.

"You couldn't make this stuff up," Larry says, wriggling himself closer to Delaney.

Eddie puts Driver down in the gritty dust. It's the most expensive book I've ever bought, about half of what my father earns in a day, and if Eddie's father is employed, about as much as he will earn in three.

As he and Curly slouch off, I hear Curly say, "Even if you *can* pronounce the words in that book, you *shouldn't*, man. It looks bad."

THAT NIGHT, I think about Larry. Of course I know now he's white, but the Paiutes' racial and ethnic mix can confuse anyone. Some people look like their ancestors did when they crossed the Bering Strait from Asia thousands of years ago (or, by the Paiute account, when Wolf created them right here), and some—a lot fewer, admittedly—look like Francis. Francis! I was supposed to call him! I'll do that first thing tomorrow.

CHAPTER SIX

Two Italian Towns

FIRST THING THOUGH, before the sun gets too hot, I take a local taxi out to James Kelly's house on the Ranch. Each house is on its own plot, and most have additions, but they're all unpainted, like those in the Colony.

"Not here," an old woman says from behind the screen door.

"Is he coming back soon?"

"No idea." Her mouth is set in a thin line, etched like a seam on her face. She latches the screen.

"I just want to say hello to him and explain what I'm doing here."

"He knows what you're doing here. Writing a book about us and keeping all the money."

"I'm not…"

"Plenty do." She pulls some teeth out of her pocket and puts them in, the better to eat me with.

I have the taxi take me back to my garage. I don't even look around the Ranch; maybe everyone out there thinks I'm making a lot of money by writing about them. But if "plenty" are doing so, their works certainly aren't in the library.

Around 3:00, Delaney sends Eddie to summon me to the Colony.

"Don't get him started," Eddie warns me. "I got some deliveries coming in, some collections to make. I'm a busy man."

"You don't want to be talking to old people all the time," Delaney scolds. He pulls me down beside him with a firm grip. "Sit."

I don't have much choice about the age of the persons I talk to. My census shows almost no one between the ages of 17 and 35. And being 23 myself, 35 to 90 constitutes my "old" category.

Delaney makes himself comfortable. "Where's Eddie?" Gone, of course. "Did you find James Kelly?"

"No, he wasn't there."

"See the Missus?"

"Yes. She didn't seem to be too friendly."

"Huh. Maybe she thought you were after James. Maybe she's jealous."

Great. A love triangle.

"Okay, open that notebook of yours. I'm going to give you some history."

"Good. I need to know more about the history of the two reservations, and a little about Yerington—"

"Wolf is our Creator," Delaney intones.

This is going back a little further than I planned for today.

Delaney continues, "Wolf always found game, but Coyote never found any. He was going along one day and he met Wolf. 'Brother, how do you get so much game?' he asked. Wolf wouldn't tell him, but Coyote begged.

"At last, Wolf said, 'I keep the animals in a hole.'

"Coyote wanted to go to the hole to catch some. 'Take only one, and shut the hole,' Wolf warned him.

"'I will,' said Coyote, but he opened the hole wide, and all the animals, all the ones we know, rushed out. Wolf looked around and saw they were all gone, scattered across the land. He was angry and wouldn't speak to Coyote. That's why we must hunt for food today.

"Always playing tricks," Delaney says. "Always thinking only of himself. But this is not the end."

We ponder the message. Coyote is everywhere, unleashing disaster after disaster because of his carelessness or curiosity. He and his cousin-brothers around the world, the Irish *Púca*, the southern Br'er Rabbit, the Afro-Caribbean Anansi, the Disney Bugs Bunny—they all have a lot to answer for.

Delaney begins another story. "Another time Coyote was going along and he set his eyes on this woman. He was going to have her, one way or another..." and then he stops short. "I think that's enough about Coyote, now," he says, perhaps because this is a famous one, often recounted in books, about how Coyote gets involved with a woman who has inward-pointing teeth in her vagina.

"All right," he continues, making short work of everything between the Creation and now, "we got no sewage, not yet, they say next year but who knows, and no indoor bathrooms and only one telephone here. These houses started out with just two rooms—a kitchen and a bedroom—and most of the houses are only 12 by 18, three feet apart. The idea they had was that old people and the sick and such could live in the Colony, and the rest of us would farm out on the Ranch. A lot of ideas, like your Korean War, for example, are better on paper than in real life, and the Colony didn't work out the way the government thought." He pauses, pursing his lips, working up a spit. "There's two ways of looking at it, and I can see both, because I been living out there but I'm in here a lot. The Ranch people think the Colony people left because they were lazy. The Colony people think too many greedy people came into the Ranch from Smith Valley and drove them out."

"Is that true?" I ask.

"Who knows? Some are no good, some aren't." He spits.

I write it down. "What kind of work did the people do who didn't work out at the Ranch?"

"We did whatever the white people let us do. Ranch hands, potato fields, the women picking onions, garlic, cleaning houses. Anything. Some of us lived here, some lived on the ranches where the work was. That's where I lived from when I started working as a kid. Then I brought my wife there when we got married. The work was hard for both of us, and we hardly got paid enough to live. Couldn't leave too easy, either. Some were sort of tied to the ranch they worked on. Other guys had to move each season. They took what they could get, and it wasn't much. Some got hooked on opium, morphine, for the pain."

"But some of the ranchers were okay, weren't they? I heard someone say they were a little like a family, the Paiutes and the ranch family working together, eating together."

"Some did, more didn't."

I wait. He says nothing more, so I write that down, too.

"What do people do today for work?"

"Ranch hands, some laborers in the Anaconda mine, rodeo workers, some work on farms, a few at the meat-packing factory. The women still clean people's houses, still pick onions and garlic when the time comes. The old people, they just hang on best they can."

I know a little about this kind of work and poverty from Paulette and from my labor union background in Youngstown. Agricultural workers, casual laborers, and domestic workers like my grandmother aren't eligible for regular Social Security benefits. Older people like Delaney and Jennie live in quiet poverty, on the edge of hunger; Jennie does a little housework in town, and Delaney gets light work occasionally on ranches, repairing tackle and painting sheds.

"What would you do if you won a million dollars?" I ask.

"Buy food."

Morgan said the same when I'd asked him. Food first, then help relatives, then maybe buy a car.

Our professors in Reno are wary of our paying "informants," partly because we barely have enough for ourselves. But would I want to see someone like my grandmother, a deserted wife and mother of five who worked cleaning all her life, help a young researcher with her stories and then go home to a dinner that might be less meager if she were paid a little for her help?

I turn to history. "Tell me about when the first whites actually settled here." The first recorded white man to come into the area was Captain John C. Fremont, who camped in the valley for a while in 1844.

"Around my father's time. I remember him talking about all the trouble some of the ranchers got into—they didn't understand the desert."

"From some of the stories I found in old newspapers, I thought it was earlier. The other day I read Italian farmers were here in the 1800s. What about the Guerreros, for example?"

"Oh, no, those were *Italians*," Delaney says. "You asked me about whites." He glares at my notebook. "You want to get this stuff right."

So I put history aside for the moment. I remember that Jennie told me to ask Delaney about marriage customs. "Get the man's point of view," she said. So I do.

"Don't want to talk about that," Delaney grumbles. "You want to talk about *your* marriage customs?"

I certainly don't. Yesterday I had a letter from my mother asking what to do about the three extra wedding present toasters. I fall back on that other old anthropological crutch, Material Culture: houses, tools, implements, clothing.

"What about your homes in the old days?'

"Lookit, we were so poor we didn't even have houses. We had nothin'. Nothin'. Just windbreaks. And even so, all our neighbors fought over us— the Washo, the Pynúk, and all those Saí?i—I always say the poor Paiute would have been wiped out if the white man hadn't showed up."

"I never heard of Indians taking this view before."

"Yessir, ma'am, I thank God the white man came," Delaney says. "I don't know what would have happened to the Paiutes otherwise. We were too small and too poor."

The Pynúk were Apaches. A hodgepodge of Columbia River Indians—the Sahaptin, Umatilla, Walla Walla, and Nez Percé, among others—formed the Saí?i. They and the Washo were a formidable set of enemies, but still, the idea of the white man as liberator is novel.

"There was a fight over my town, too," I offer. I don't like the idea of being seen as part of the great white humanitarian emancipation.

"See?" says Delaney. "Those guys were everywhere."

"No, not the Washo, the Mafia. We were too small and too poor to bother with, except we were sitting right in the middle of the territory they wanted." Youngstown is halfway between Cleveland and Pittsburgh one way, and New York and Chicago the other.

"Same old story. Sa-a-ame old story."

"Whoever got my town might eventually control the whole area."

Delaney's eyes sparkle. "But then, then, some guys like our Horseman or Winnemucca Naci and the others came along and…"

"No. Not yet." The Cleveland Licavolis, guys with names like "Charlie the Crab" Carabbia, took over the north end. The Pittsburgh Genoveses took over the south.

Youngstown has no great heroes like the Paiutes' Horseman, Winnemucca Naci, his son Numuga, and Chief Joaquin, all ancestors of today's Yerington Paiutes. We don't even have a colonial liberator: Bobby Kennedy's first assignment as Attorney General in 1960 was to come in and clean us up, but he failed.

The Paiutes have something else we're missing—witches, although Jimmy Anzivino's mother is said to have the Evil Eye. She denies this, but her next door neighbor wears a little gold horn, a *corno*, on a chain around his neck and grasps it whenever he passes her porch.

A few houses in the Colony have been home, off and on over the years, to a rich brew of peyotists, doctors, and past-their-prime witches; in earlier years, they were feared and respected. Witches and doctors got their powers directly from the supernatural, usually through a vision. They held no office or formal position; what standing they had came from their personal powers and attributes. Each accepted pay for his or her work, and each had a ritual—witches for harming, doctors for curing—although witches could cure, if they chose to.

"Tell me more about witches," I ask.

Delaney keeps silent. Maybe he doesn't like talking about them, or maybe he's still thinking about a strategy to free Youngstown. Finally, he explains, "The men witches were real tall and easy-going, likeable. White people respected them, too. They were more intelligent, educated, and better-dressed than your ordinary people."

"What about the women witches?"

"They were quiet and kept to themselves." He looks at me as though there's a lesson to be learned.

"Was Jack Wilson a witch?"

"Hell, no," Delaney says. "He was *witched* by a witch. Tom Mitchell witched him."

"So he lost his power before he died?"

"Yep. Tom Mitchell told Jack Wilson they should put their power together so they could doctor the people better, and Jack Wilson said okay, but once the powers were put together, Tom Mitchell took it all. Jack Wilson's health went way down after that."

"Paulette says Tom Mitchell didn't take his power, that he had it when he died. She knew him."

"Everybody knew him. Anyhow, Tom Mitchell was Paulette's mother's uncle. She'd say that."

We sit for a while.

"Well," I say finally, "it seems either way, people listened to Jack Wilson—like when he told them to take up a new religion until he returned."

"Oh, yeah. He was an important man. And a very good Paiute singer. Tall, too. Pleasant. They all were. Except Tom Mitchell. And Pu" ku 'kai, Horseman, he could get pretty nasty, even if I say so myself."

"Yourself?"

"He was my grandfather."

If I start to ask about Horseman, I'll be off on yet another detour. "Tell me the story of Jack Wilson and the ice."

"Some people say he got ice to float down the Walker River in the middle of the summer. Others say it came from the sky: It fell into a willow pot and people took pieces and ate it."

"But some say the white Wilson brothers, the family Jack Wilson worked for, helped him by floating it down the river," I object.

"I know. Some do. But don't ever say that to Jennie—her mother saw it fall from the sky, and you know she's religious."

"But what do *you* think?"

"Oh, I think there was ice, fact, I know it; I knew people who saw it, and they were sensible people. Thing is, how did he do it? Maybe he did get help."

I'm indignant. Me, a lapsed Catholic atheist, but still, I hate the magic of a good story spoiled. I want the ice to be real.

"It *was* real," Delaney reassures me, laughing.

I meet Larry and Eddie on the way home from the Colony.

"Francis called," Eddie says. "I couldn't find you. He sounds awful lonely." He draws pretend tears down his face.

"Did he say that?"

"No. But a man knows."

"Uh oh," Larry says.

Coming round the corner is the policeman I'd seen in the diner.

"Scuzz Fuzz," Eddie yells, and, laughing, the two boys run.

CHAPTER SEVEN

Not Worrying

A UNIVERSITY TEACHING ASSISTANT arrives from Reno with a car for me.

"Mother of Mercy," I groan. Funny how the old expressions come back when you're upset. "I'll never be able to use this."

"Best we can do if you want to get out to the Ranch. And we need you to pick up the other trainees for our seminars in Reno."

"But where did the university get this? *How* did they get it?"

"Beats me," he shrugs.

"But—"

"You'll get the hang of it."

"I meant—"

"Gotta run," he says, and hopping into a normal, everyday car that stops for him, he's off. The car is a long, battered, pea-green Ford, with "NEVADA STATE POLICE" in large black letters on the doors.

Anthropologists love to hear about the self-inflicted pratfalls of their colleagues. There's plenty of folklore out there: people getting confused about your work ("I thought you just studied naked people?" or "Everyone says you're trying to recruit our women for the Army"); being mistaken for a spy; having your field notes passed around and read; getting involved, even if only in people's minds, in an inappropriate sexual encounter; paying informants; not paying informants; and a thousand others. But a police car must be a first in anthropology.

Why couldn't the department in Reno give me something a little less obtrusive, like a funeral hearse? Or a pumpkin drawn by mice? I slip around the corner of the garage and pace a while. Well, really, I suppose I should be more grateful; I'm looking a gift horse in the mouth. I pace some more. Actually, I would have preferred a gift horse.

I get in. I have no other options; I have to get out to the Kelly house on the Ranch and find out about that pamphlet. And yesterday, Paulette casually told me, "Someone out there is spreading the word that you're writing a book about sex among the Indians and are going to make a lot of money and keep it all yourself." If I don't straighten things out with the Tribal Chairman, my work will be over before it really begins.

The car drives like a dream, actually, and I skulk along the few back streets of Yerington and out the 10 miles into the desert, where I park behind the Kelly's fence. When I knock on the screen door, the same old woman answers.

"He didn't get any pamphlet," she snaps. "It must be the other people you gave the pamphlets to. And I don't know nothin' about sex. Nothin'." She slams the door.

James Kelly, for whom I'm beginning to feel a little sympathy, is still nowhere to be seen.

I HAVE A FEW hours before my meeting with Morgan, who promised to help me with a census of the Colony, so I go back to the garage to reflect on the morning. I unearth the journal and begin writing.

My work has been very easy so far—not only have I spent a lot of time with Delaney, Archie, Jennie, Paulette, and the Reverend, but I've also interviewed many other people, all of whom have been helpful, except, of course, Mrs. Kelly. I'm not under any illusions about the information they're giving me, even though they go to a lot of trouble. I know very well that everything is filtered through many layers of culture, shaped by my questions, adjusted to my perceived status and level of understanding, obscured sometimes for privacy or propriety. Sometimes, when I'm tired, I feel as if I'm moving through a pulsating tunnel of voices and faces, each approaching and retreating, pulled and pushed by their own forces, interacting with each other, and shifting and coalescing again behind me. The faces and voices have been approachable until now. What would a more experienced anthropologist, or even a different kind of person, do about the Kellys? What would a more experienced person do about this *car?*

Anthropology has myths, just as any culture or subculture does. One is that anthropologists can fit in gracefully and nearly become "One of the People" anywhere. Back in Pittsburgh, when I met famous visiting anthropologists, I longed to ask, "Who influenced you most?" "Where do you think the field is going next?" And occasionally I wondered , "How did this person ever manage to function in another culture when he's such a misfit in his own?"

This is a question every professional anthropologist in the field must secretly wonder about from time to time: how his most ham-fisted colleagues claim to have been made honorary chieftains and been borne around the village in a litter, while he himself, considerate to a fault, cannot find anyone who will even speak to him. "I'm the most sensitive bastard you'll ever meet," a professor once said after a few drinks, "and yet people run when they see me coming."

I've never subscribed to the view that western society's misfits may be the *bons vivants* of another society, but I know some get by because they have a redeeming and invaluable gift: they may be so linguistically gifted that "their" people see them almost as natives, or they have endless patience, or a wonderfully musical ear, or are prepared to eat anything with relish. In anthropological research, since you are your own major instrument, you can never tell what characteristics might come in handy. What special gift can I bring to the situation? I have none of those strengths.

I reread what I've written. That tunnel image doesn't work as an analogy. It explains my thinking, all right, but it sounds like the processing of a turd through the intestinal system. I put the journal back under the bed.

THAT AFTERNOON, I walk over to the Colony for my session with Morgan. However, he's heard of a new cleaning job in the casino and is going off to apply for it, so he can't help me.

"Have you heard anything about me and a pamphlet?" I ask him.

"No. Heard other things, but not that."

Great. "What?"

"Oh, just things."

Now that I have the car, I decide to use the free time to move into Cyril's. I pack up my notes and equipment, my copy of Driver, the hair curlers and girdle, and drive out to his suburban ranch house, which is homey and comfortable. "Paid off," he boasts, ushering me in and showing me everything from the stocked freezer to the chicken coop out back. "Thirty years' work in the packing factory, but it's ours now." I'll have a real bedroom to myself, with a door that closes and stays closed.

Maybel makes coffee. I like her; I'd invited her to have supper at Rickett's one evening after she'd told me she'd never been inside. She was still in a wheelchair from her stroke, so we went in the back door and headed for one of the unoccupied front window tables that were catching the last of the evening light. When Mr. Rickett saw her, he motioned us back to a half-hidden table beside the kitchen. We waited over half an hour in the nearly empty diner to be served. So much for the new Civil Rights Act. As we sit at the table, I mention the pamphlet, which Cyril's heard about. He says he's not too concerned. "Don't you worry," he assures me, but I don't buy his breezy dismissal. I've talked to him often enough now to know that if anyone can be described as a Worried Man, it's Cyril. He worries about everything—Africa, gas leaks, Maybel's poor health, his children and grandchildren, Sunday dinner.

"Maybel here likes to go to two Masses on Sunday," Cyril says, "so I go to the first one and then I sit in the car and peel the potatoes for dinner during the second one."

"He worries about dinner being late," Maybel says.

I figure he's telling me not to worry because he's doing enough worrying for two or three. He and Maybel go off to find a desk lamp for my room.

I worry, anyway. Suppose the Tribal Council decides I should leave? Will my trainers send me to another reservation? Everyone here knows people on the other Paiute reservations and even among the nearby Washo sites. Just the rumors about why they want me to leave—working with only one faction, even accidentally; behaving insultingly toward the chairman; prying into things I shouldn't, driving a police car—may be reason enough for a new community to throw me out or at least make my work very difficult. Will I be the only one among all the other trainees who has to move? Will the professors say it's too late to start over? I'll turn into an Armchair Anthropologist, not able to do fieldwork. This is a death sentence in my profession; you can be eccentric, self-absorbed, a rotten spouse, fixated on some stultifyingly minute area of study, or unpresentable to civilized company, but not doing your own fieldwork is unpardonable. You have to be blooded somewhere.

Cyril returns. I try to explain this. "Don't worry," he says, looking concerned. "No matter, you can just stay right here with Maybel and me. You'll get what you need out of books." I'm impressed by the respect shown to books by the older people around here.

"And Mrs. Kelly doesn't seem to like me," I say.

"She don't know you."

"But I've met her twice, at the door of their house. She wouldn't even invite me in."

"Edith Kelly's out of town for weeks now, helping her sister."

"Who's the old woman out there, then?" I ask.

"Which old woman?"

"The one that doesn't like sex."

Cyril ponders. "Well, that could be most of them."

"She was in James's house."

"Oh, that one, that's an old cousin-sister of James's brother-in-law's grandma. He and Edith took her in for a while." He frowns. "You don't want to be talking to people that don't know nothing. 'Specially about sex."

We go out to the car to get my things. He looks at the car and then at me.

"It's what the university gave me," I say. I wait.

He sighs. "Don't worry," he says, and carries my boxes in.

I arrange my new desk and then, feeling awkward just hanging around, go to the post office, where I find a new letter from my mother. Apparently, the Mafia is after my brother.

Dear Eileen,

Not much to report here. Patrick thinks he's in trouble with The Black Hand. *He got mad about something the way he does, dog licenses or flag etiquette or I don't know what but anyhow his letter got printed in the* Vindicator *and he says it got them up in arms. I said what do the Mafia care about dog licenses and he just gave me that look he gets.*

Anyhow, he's gone to Akron until it blows over. He only had $11.00 in his wallet, but I said don't look at me.

You probably saw that show on television the other night about us being "Bomb City." If they didn't make so much fuss over these things, no one would pay attention. Did the Indians say anything? Ask them if they ever heard about Cadillac Charlie Cavallero. Say it's Mrs. Cavallero I blame—she should have put her foot down long ago.

I'll sign off now. I'm sending your friend Jennie a Simplicity dress pattern # 4196, size 16, for a sweetheart-neck dress with a bolero. I also saw a nice dress pattern with a detachable peplum, but not everybody likes a peplum. You could ask her.

Love, Ma.

Jennie laughs when I go over to tell her. "Size 16? My leg is bigger than that." But I notice that, as she speaks, she traces the outline of an invisible sweetheart neckline on her generous bosom.

ANTHROPOLOGISTS ARE ODD. We fall in love with "our" people long before we meet them. We read something like Robert Heizer's "The Use of the Enema by the Aboriginal American Indians," and we're like rabbits caught in a snare. Month after month, we write grant applications to major funding agencies; we *must* get to these peoples to learn more about their rubber bulb and piston-type syringes and clyster tubes. We point out that we are unquestionably the most qualified person to do this research. We try to make it relevant: "Insight into this should contribute further to our understanding of why World War II happened/the current unrest in Detroit/ how to improve children's learning/sheep grazing on the Anatolian plateau." Whatever might work.

The grant agency wades through the verbiage and realizes that we're interested in the development of technology, the early production of rubber, theories of well-being and illness, and roles of traditional practitioners— and gives us half what we've asked for. The next thing we know, we're sitting on a curb, waiting for the post office to open, roaring out the chorus of "Chapel of Love" with two love-sodden teenaged thugettes.

Thomasina introduces me to her friend, Charlene, a cheerleader ("not really—I stole this skirt from a girl in school"). They're both moony with romance. There's been a rash of weddings on the reservation, 36 over the last few months. Johnny Mitchell was authorized by the state and Tribal Council to perform legal marriages, so people who've been married under tribal law for years have come shyly forward to make their weddings official. They are all over 50.

"How'd you know your husband was the One For You?" Thomasina asks.

In fact, the closer the wedding day came, the less sure I was that Francis *was* the one; according to popular western thinking, that means everything was fine, right on track. Women's magazines provide plenty of examples of pre-wedding jitters and reassurances about them. So do the movies and my friends. The more worried I was beforehand, the more relieved and foolish I would feel after the wedding, I was continually told. I definitely had jitters: I postponed the big day from May 1 to May 8 to May 16; and then Francis, shaken, postponed it from May 16 to May 23. When I tried to postpone it again to May 30, the priest rebelled. "Uncertainty As a Basis of Marriage Decisions"— I could see this article in the *American Anthropologist*.

"*C'mon*," Thomasina demands.

"Well, he's sort of like the Boy Next Door," I answer.

"*Is* he the boy next door?" Charlene asks.

"No," I say. "He's *like* the Boy Next Door."

"I don't get it," Charlene grumps. "If you wanted the boy next door, why didn't you marry *him*?"

"There *wasn't* a boy next door," I snap.

"Well, then," she says, "I *really* don't get it."

"*The Boy Next Door*, stupid," Thomasina emphasizes. "He's not *real*."

"Oh, right. Okay."

Driver noted that many North American Indians do not distinguish between the natural and the supernatural; maybe Charlene feels quite at home with the real and the non-real.

"Charlene has a pretend friend named Foopy. She won't tell me anything about him except that he keeps his teeth in a glass at night. Yuck."

Such a hard-luck kid—no cuddly imaginary friends for her.

"What's your husband's name?" Thomasina continues to probe.

"Francis."

"Don't you have a nickname or something for him? Frankie? Sweetheart?"

Truth is, I don't call him anything at all. My mother's family has an unexplained custom of not addressing spouses by name. My poor father may have to go all the way up into the attic to call my mother to the phone, or my mother shake my father awake without using his name or any term of endearment, as that would seem too…what? Familiar? Affected? Protestant? We Catholics spend a lot of time not doing what we think Protestants do.

"No," I say.

"Does he have a nickname for you?"

"Absolutely not."

We sit quietly for a while, I defeated by the heat, they defeated by the lack of romance in my life.

"I don't think it's True Love," Thomasina says to Charlene. "With the white people, he's supposed to have a nickname if it's True Love."

Charlene is impressed. "You're right," she says, brightening. "Foopy's not his real name."

The mail truck pulls up and Charlene runs into the post office. The girls wrote recently to Paul Anka, the current pop idol, and she's hoping his answer will have arrived. "Paul Baby," they call him, so I suppose it's True Love.

I'm about to go in, too, when a battered, sandblasted car pulls up and a worn, wrung-out-looking woman stumbles out of it. I recognize her: Reenie, the unfriendly waitress from Rickett's Diner. Larry's mother.

"You keep away from my son," she shouts.

I squint at the driver; it's the white policeman I've seen a couple of times before.

Larry's mother has the same sunken, malnourished look that her son has, the kind that comes over several generations of bad luck and worse living. "I don't want him near them Paiutes," she screeches. "Over there foolin' around all day, flunkin' out of school over it. I don't know what binness you got there with them, a white lady like you, but Larry got none."

She rants on, implying that my business is selling my white body on the reservation and that she has higher aspirations for Larry. "'Lectrician. I got him all set up with a guy that'll train him, give him a skill, get himself out of this shit." She waves her hand at the courthouse, the church, the casino; it's not clear which one is at fault or if all are.

"I hear he's on that reservation one more time, or hanging around with you, he's goin' to military school. I got enough trouble already." She glares at me as though I'm letting down the entire white lady movement. The policeman toots the horn once, and she darts back to the car, her bony shoulders hunched, her spine all prickly bones beneath her shabby, no-color T-shirt.

"Wickham," Thomasina snorts. "Scuzz Fuzz. He's only here temporary, replacing some sick guy. Most of the police are okay here, but he's just bad. Reenie, she ain't bad, but don't you fool with her about Larry."

That's enough for me. If Thomasina is in awe of somebody, I am, too.

THAT NIGHT, AFTER the afternoon's mushy talk of love, I think about Francis. Or, rather, I think about Margaret Mead.

Mead didn't have much of a life in my opinion. Yes, she had more than one husband, and female lovers to boot, but was she happy? On the other hand, an unmarried woman academic is called a bluestocking, by definition, a kind of joke. Why can't a woman anthropologist be a robust, happy, ordinary kind of person, like most male academics are, married or not? Well, the married ones seem normal; the few who aren't often look as if small animals could forage in the folds of their clothes.

It hasn't occurred to me until now that when I married Francis I would become a Wife, with a capital "W." I don't want to be a Wife. A man went almost to the moon and not a person in the world asked what his wife thought about it, but his wife can't go to a movie matinee alone without the neighbors asking from their porches if she has the ironing done already. He can spend three months scaling the icy peaks of Everest, but she can't read a book until she has the refrigerator defrosted. Visitors to our house will judge me on my stuffed celery, my Far East Easy Chicken with Peanut Butter, my napkins folded like swans. Francis can pass out on the floor, drunk, and they will wonder why I mismatched his socks.

I drive back into town and call Francis. It's only 11:00 p.m. his time, but he sounds as if he had to get out of bed to come to the phone.

"Is that what you really want me to be, a Wife?" I demand. "You know what I mean, a *Wife* wife?"

"Who is this?" he asks. "Just joking. Okay, I know what you're saying. I just want you, whatever you are. Besides, times *have* changed, you know."

Yeah. Tell that to the bitter woman folding swans.

CHAPTER EIGHT

The Tribal Council

THIS IS THE Day; tonight I'll meet the Tribal Council.

"It's 7:30 at the old schoolhouse out on the Ranch," Cyril says. "I'll be there to stick up for you."

Although Paulette Chapman never calls him that in so many words, every time she mentions James Kelly, I envision a Caligula. Other people tell me the Council has a delicate balance of power: James has been the chairman forever, but a couple of the Chapmans run it, or think they do, or maybe some people just think the Chapmans run it, or maybe, if I check my notes, I'll see that James himself is a Chapman in some way...

What will they ask me? What I'm doing, certainly. Who invited me, perhaps. What I'm going to do with my report. Whether they can see it. And what good, if any, it will do the Paiute people. Cyril tells me someone found an old dictionary that defined anthropology as "the study of savages." ("But don't worry," he says.) Yet again, I can see myself packing to leave soon.

I write out a little speech with all the points I should cover. I put the main headings on a card and then summarize them into three words. I also plan to bring a paper I wrote last year, "Non-Unilineality in Oceania: Review and Alternate Hypothesis," which had won a prize. Or maybe I won't. It's been eight months since I wrote it, and already I can't understand a word of it.

I throw out all my notes except the three words. I'll speak freely from them, taking a natural approach.

Taking the natural approach leaves me time to brood. Maybe the Paiutes never had formal leaders, but since people have elected James as their chairman, they will expect him to do some leading. What will happen if James Kelly disapproves of what I'm doing? The professor told me to contact James first thing, and I hadn't. So if things go wrong, he may say it's my own fault and not send me to a new place.

Will I go back to the University of Pittsburgh? There'd be no point, since most of the faculty are off doing their own fieldwork during the summer or holing themselves up writing papers. I could go to the Army base, except Francis is living in barracks. I'll have to go home. My mother and father will fret about the blot on my academic career, and my mother may even be a little embarrassed by the Return of the Married Daughter. Thanks to the *Vindicator*, half the town knows I'm on an Indian reservation for the summer, and yet now, after just a few weeks, I'll be back, and without my new husband. I have few other options; young women in Ohio don't live alone. And I don't have the money to support myself on my own, not until my autumn fellowship stipend kicks in. I don't dare think about going near Francis's family, given that his mother has been heard to say that I'm "pugnacious."

If I go home, I'll lose what confidence I have. No, actually the worst part is that I like Delaney and Jennie, Larry and Thomasina, even Morgan—in fact, practically everyone I've met. Everyone has helped me—except for James Kelly's brother-in-law's grandma's cousin-sister, of course. I don't want to leave them now.

I DRIVE OUT TO the Ranch. By 8:00, the only people at the old schoolhouse are Cyril, Reverend Parks (clutching a roll of plans for the new church he's hoping to build), and me. Gradually, most of the Council—all people I know—turn up but stay outside in their cars. At 9:30, a slouched, graying man comes in—mid-60s, balding crew cut, bomber jacket.

"James," Cyril mutters.

James Kelly looks neither right nor left. He sits at a table at the front of the room and stares down at a tattered sheaf of papers, which probably includes the pamphlet about me. After awhile, a few people shuffle in from their cars. A little commotion outside, and Morgan McBride arrives in a black and pink fluorescent shirt and yellow cravat, a little drunk and livid at being told nothing about either this meeting or one that he says took place a week before.

"Drive me over to Paulette's," he orders, and since the meeting is still far from having a quorum, I do.

"You're supposed to be an anthropologist," he says, shifting his irritation to me. "Why are you doing your research in a police car?"

"I'm not."

"It says on the side of your car 'NEVADA STATE POLICE' in big letters, can't be anything else."

"Yes, but when I'm in it, it's not a police car."

"Like when Coyote puts on a rabbit skin, he's not Coyote?"

Even I have to laugh: how pathetic! I did try to make it look less official; yesterday, I followed the local female custom of driving around with curlers in my hair, but my hair is red, long, and has to be wound around huge rollers, which made me look like a sci-fi astronaut in a police car. I park it behind things—fences, trees, sheds—and I lean casually against the writing on the side when interviewing.

I have to give the Paiute people a lot of credit: so far, those who see the car take it in stride or at least don't comment.

Morgan is the first to say baldly to my face, "You're doing your research in a police car."

By the time we get to Paulette's house, Morgan has refocused his contempt. "You are a horrible council member. You hold up every single meeting," he accuses her. To me, he snorts, "Indians!"

"You'll get a quorum over there without me, and I got company from Reno," Paulette says. "When *you* have company, I don't notice *you* being out and about. Or your company, whoever *they* might be. I'll come later."

"I'm worried about this meeting," I tell Morgan on the way back.

"I'll handle it," he says. "I did elocution in school."

By now the old schoolhouse is filling up, people sitting on the few chairs, an old bed, an armchair, and some benches. Don Keeley, the treasurer, stands at the front and beside him are the Paiute police officer from Schurz and James Kelly. At 10:00, Paulette and a few others arrive. James bangs an ashtray as a signal for the meeting to begin. He stares at me impassively; I don't know how to read his expression.

"I got the government's 10-year plan for us," Don Keeley announces. "I'm gonna go over the main points."

"Why wasn't I told about last week's meeting?" Morgan interrupts.

Someone groans.

"The government is failing the Indian," Morgan declaims, and begins to recite a list of treaties the government has broken, beginning with the Treaty of Fort Pitt with the Delaware Indians on September 17, 1778. He backs up briefly to the 1763 Treaty of Paris, before American independence, a treaty he describes as "sneaky," before starting to work his way back down to the present.

James, head in one hand, circles the other hand wearily, trying to hurry Morgan along.

"And why," Morgan demands, "are the Navahos taking over everything these days? They're running the school at Stewart, and most of the kids there now are Navahos." Stewart is the brutally strict Indian boarding school near Carson City, one of the few places open to Indian children in the past when they weren't allowed to attend local schools.

"Don't matter if they run it," Miller Chapman, Paulette's husband, says. "Our kids are doing fine now at the public school here."

"Oh, of course," Morgan retorts. "I knew you'd take that attitude, because you only went to ninth grade. I spent nearly 17 years at Stewart myself."

"They only got a 12-year program there, Morgan," someone calls from the back.

"About this plan..." Don interjects, waving some papers.

"That plan!" Morgan harrumphs. "What about this *letter*?" He reads out, elocution-style, a couple of pages from a Mr. Myron Foster over in Carson about the Colony's sewage, a subject that he obviously thinks trumps all other discussion. He folds his arms.

"Where's the middle page of that letter?" James asks. "It don't make sense that way. Says he's going to dump all our solid waste on six puppet shows."

Morgan fishes around for the missing sheet. "The plan calls for six puppet shows to be used to explain solid waste disposal to school children."

"Well, I'd give good money to see that," says Chet Bennett, a neighbor of Cyril's.

"It's free," Morgan says.

"All that don't have anything to do with this plan," Don protests.

"Am I expected to do everything myself? Do the Council members ever do *anything*?" Morgan asks.

The policeman from Schurz invites Morgan to sit down.

"I'm moving on now to the vocational rehabilitation plan," Don says. "The way it works is..."

"How come I'm not eligible for that?" Morgan demands. "I wanted to be a nurse. I was trained as a shoemaker at Stewart, but I wanted to be a nurse."

Don throws up his hands. "I'll write down you wanted to be a nurse."

Everett Mann, a local man who teaches school in a nearby town, comes forward to draw a blackboard diagram of the way the Ranch will look after the government builds the 26 new houses it's promising, each on a five-acre plot. The original houses have only three rooms altogether, but these will be two-, three-, and four-bedroom houses, with insulation, water, and electricity. The only charge will be a small maintenance fee.

"Whatever happened to the Colony's maintenance fund? I suppose the people out on the Ranch spent it," Morgan says. "You got eight families out there living on 1,100 acres, while the Colony's crammed on two, and you spend all our itty-bitty funds on yourselves."

James's head had slipped; it's resting on the inside of his arm, his hand sticking up beyond his ear. I don't want him getting irritable; on the other hand, if he falls asleep, I may never have the matter of my status here settled.

"And how come you're running the meeting?" Morgan asks Everett. "You don't live in either place. Someone local should take over."

Everett hands the chalk to Morgan and tells him to be his guest, but Morgan waves it away.

"It's very kind of him to take all this trouble," Paulette insists. "He's almost an honorary Council Member. Somebody has to do some work; there are some here that sure don't." She glares at Morgan.

"This lady," Morgan announces with a majestic sweep of his arm toward me, "is joining the tribe."

Ignoring this, Paulette asks for a vote of confidence in Everett, and everyone, including Morgan, votes for him.

"See, I can be neutral between the Colony and the Ranch," Everett says, "since I don't live here."

"If you're being so helpful to us," Morgan challenges, "why aren't you teaching here instead of in the next town? You people," he continues, addressing the Council, who were all Ranch residents, "you never bother about what the little man in the Colony thinks."

No one says anything, perhaps because Morgan is about four-foot-ten.

"Will you please introduce the lady?" James asks Morgan, finally lifting his head. "Ask her if she wants to take something up with the Council?"

I'm surprised; instead of being summoned, am I intruding here?

Morgan says that Everett may as well do it, seeing as how he's the one who seems to be running the meeting. Paulette tells Morgan to behave and introduce me. "Tribe," Morgan announces, "this is Eileen Kane, from the

Anthropology Department at the University of Nevada at Reno. Professor Kane, this is the Tribe." He bows; job done.

Everyone stops what they're doing—knitting, fixing a bridle, chatting among themselves—and stares at me, seemingly stunned, even those who know my story and have already spent hours talking to me.

"She speaks better Paiute than I do," Cyril offers. The Council falls silent, digesting this. Courtesy is important to the Paiute people. No one mentions that Cyril can't speak Paiute at all. Nor can I; I can understand a little, but I know two dozen nouns at most, mainly what I learned about *kah' niis* from Reverend Parks. He, meanwhile, had fallen asleep in the lone armchair, still clutching his church plans. The back of his wiry red hair pushes up like a brush.

"Huh," James says. "She should go over and converse with Mickey Kelly. Great Paiute speaker."

I have yet to meet Mickey Kelly, although I've seen him ride by sometimes, his horse and tack gleaming, his immaculate Stetson tilted slightly to the right. He's never spoken to me.

"Mrs. Chapman asked me to come and explain the pamphlet, but I haven't seen it," I say.

"What pamphlet?" asks James. Paulette rolls her eyes.

"The Secretary got a pamphlet there?" he asks. This is the first time I've heard that the Tribe has a Secretary, who turns out to be Morgan.

"Um, I got it all right, but I forgot to bring it."

"Go get it, then," Paulette says.

"I saw it," Everett says. "It's about a conference at the University of Nevada in November."

So the pamphlet isn't about me after all. The conference will focus on all the tribes of the Great Basin. Anthropologists, archeologists, and linguists working among them will come, plus job-seekers and academics hoping to network or party.

"We invited?" James asks, perking up.

"I'm sure people will be happy to see you," I reply. My Pittsburgh professors' "informants" are safely tucked away in places such as New Guinea or Guatemala, and I know the last thing one of them, at least, wants is to have locals turning up, contradicting his stories about being loved by "The People." But the anthropologists at the University of Nevada live among "the people" and seem pretty collegial. I'm sure they'll welcome my friends.

I won't be at the conference myself; if I carry out this fieldwork, I'll be back east by then, in my own university. I also have my husband of six, or is it seven, weeks now who'll be expecting me to stay around for a while after my work here is done, even if only in neighboring New Jersey where he'll be finishing his service.

"She's on her honeymoon," Morgan says.

"You miss your husband?" James asks, showing the first sign of interest in me.

"Nah, women don't miss their husbands near as much as men think," Paulette says. "Let her alone, she needs to study and get good grades."

"She knows more about the Paiutes than anyone in town," Cyril boasts. "She'll get a real good grade for this."

"For what?" someone calls from the back. Here's my chance. I look at my notes; they contain only three words, words that make no sense whatever to me now. I explain as best I can that I'm interested in what religion people have taken up since Jack Wilson left them.

"And we got to help," Cyril says, sounding really worried now, as though the Paiute people may not be up to it. If I flunk out, would the Paiutes be seen as Failed Indians?

"Yes," James says, "you people pay attention to her. About time some of you learned about the Paiute people."

I crumple in relief.

Reverend Parks, pink and sweaty in his sleep, snorts as loudly as if he's trying to inhale a huge object.

"The new Indian Messiah," Paulette laughs.

"What about those new church plans of his?" James asks.

"Okay," Everett says. "Who'd like a new church? Raise your hands."

No one moves.

"We should give him a little encouragement," Paulette scolds. "He really wants this church. He don't do any harm."

"Yeah?" a man at the side asks. "Where's that money?"

"What money?" I whisper to Morgan.

"Oh," Morgan whispers back. "Well. Some say the last preacher went off with some church money. You know how some people are. And he sent it back when someone reminded him."

"And?"

"And some say someone put it in his own account."

I'm shocked; if I can keep the somes and someones straight, is Morgan talking about Reverend Parks?

"I say there never was any money." Morgan shakes his head. Does he really think there hadn't been any money or was he dismissive because he wasn't the first to hear about it?

Reverend Parks sleeps on.

I creep out to let the Council get down to real business. Also, I want to shout or hug somebody in celebration. Unfortunately, the only person outside is Eddie.

"What are you doing here?" I demand.

"One, I'm a Paiute and *entitled* to attend Paiute meetings, if I want to. Two, I was dealing with a business contact out here. Three, Francis called."

"What did he say?" I wish Francis were here now, so I could tell him how relieved I am. I want him to meet Delaney and Jennie and Paulette and the others. And I want to show him off to Cyril, one soldier to another.

"Nothing."

Such disappointment. And I feel sorry for Francis, too, always having to leave messages.

Eddie laughs. "Poor baby," he mocks. "Forget it, I made that up about the call. Nobody called. But my business contact out here's not too happy with me. How about a 'police escort' back to town?"

THE NEXT DAY, I ask Morgan what happened after I left the meeting.

"We elected Janice Juarez as our Nevada Day entrant. She's one of the only Paiutes in this area who goes to college. Then we talked about having our own float in the parade. Chet Bennett is such a snot, he said I should be put on the float. I said thank you, I would be delighted."

"Then what?"

"The subject was dropped."

A few days later, as the Reverend and I work on the *kah' nii*, Paulette comes by to show me the Nevada conference pamphlet, which she finally got from Morgan. She says the Council finished the rest of the meeting when Morgan had to leave for his job at Rickett's. "We zipped right through the last agenda items in no time flat. But no need to tell Morgan," she says. "Don't hurt his feelings."

"Someone told me that James Kelly wasn't sociable, but he seemed sociable at the meeting," I say to her.

"Don't know who said that," she answers. "He works full time at the mine and full time on his farm and full time on tribal business, and his Secretary ignores most council letters, so, no, I guess you won't see him hanging around."

"So it was *Morgan* who was supposed to answer my letters to the chairman?"

"Yep."

Reverend Parks whistles a happy, tuneless air. "The Council said they're so excited about the new church they're postponing the subject till the October meeting. They'll have time for a good discussion then." This has given him a real boost. "I know I get a little down sometimes, but I'm real grateful the Lord's sent me here."

Paulette says they are, too, and sits down to help with the *kah' nii*. A tall, strapping lady, hair tied back in a cowboy kerchief, opens the door of the Parks's trailer, waves a feather duster at us, and withdraws instantly.

"The Little Woman," the Reverend beams. "She's awful busy. No time for this stuff."

Despite what she told me when I first arrived in Yerington, I can see that Paulette *does* have some Paiute. She's counting one to ten under her breath.

CHAPTER NINE

Why Anthropology?

"I WANT YOU TO light a fire under some a them girls," Reverend Parks says. "See if they have any ambitions in life except mooning around over boys."

So, the next time I meet Thomasina in our usual place, on the curb in front of the post office, where she can see boys and I can bump into people casually, I ask her, "What do you want to be when you grow up?"

"Dunno. What about you?"

Well, of course, that was The Question.

I ask others. "Dunno" is the answer I usually get to this question, although when I persist, some of the boys come up with "working in the meat factory," "mining," "ranch hand," "driving a truck," "pilot," "football player," "heavy equipment operator," and "doctor." None of the girls want to do what their mothers do—domestic or farm work. A few suggest "teacher," much to the jeers of the others, or "nurse" ("Oh, yeah, that's what we want to be, too!" their friends echo), "secretary," "medical technician," and "dancer." When I ask Eddie, he replies, "I was born grown up."

What plans do the white kids in town have? Since the local school is closed for the summer, I round up some teens when and where I can—outside the phone booth, in Rickett's restaurant, the local garage, the baseball field. They're the same age as my young Paiute friends but are certainly not a matched sample; there are differences in income, access to local facilities, education of parents, and aspirations. Most of them are middle class, as that's defined in Yerington and in current books on American class. A few may have been at the lower-middle end of the scale; one is at the upper end. They list far more skilled and professional occupations—lawyer, journalist, doctor, artist, real estate developer, accountant. And they're more specific—criminal lawyer, commercial artist, executive secretary, Boeing 707 pilot. Some of them know what I'm coming to ask them—"male model" one says, striking a pose.

What interests me most are the professional occupation choices that overlap—doctor, nurse, teacher, pilot.

"How do you become a pilot?" I ask the white teenagers. They know a variety of specific educational sequences and institutions, including the fact that TWA has a training center in Kansas City. The Paiute teenagers are less definite: "You have to have a good head for heights and be able to fly on one engine." "A nurse?" "You get a job in a doctor's office, I think." For their more common choices—"heavy equipment operator," for example—they know what to do since a respected local man has such a job, and they know exactly the skills and connections that it requires. The same for becoming a barber; two boys are already barbers. Some young Paiutes are beginning to move into professional roles: one girl won a scholarship to nursing school; a boy won a large football scholarship to an eastern university, a coup that in my own town catapulted several boys, white and black, into wealth and social mobility. But this boy turned it down and became a construction worker. No one knows why.

Some of the more modest choices and fuzzy career planning don't surprise me; a lot of kids in my home town are as vague as the Paiutes with their "head for heights" qualification for becoming a pilot. It's difficult for kids in Yerington or Youngstown to consider what careers they might aim for; the reason is not simply lack of money for education but a poverty of the imagination, since they lack role models.

The Youngstown I know has almost no middle class. "Class" usually implies a segment on an ordinal scale, but almost everyone there is working class. In fact, the Youngstown Symphony Orchestra in the 1940s was composed entirely of steel workers, led by a musician who was also a mill timekeeper. The mill owners live in Philadelphia or New York and send their managers from these cities; no local managerial class has emerged.

Small business owners know that their existence depends on steel and manufacturing workers, and so they vote with them in elections. They form another group, too, one singled out by the Mafia to pay protection money. Black people may work in the mills and can form part of a mixed-race work team, but that relationship ends at the gates, not because of class but because of race. Swimming pools are barred to them, they sit upstairs in the movie theater in "the buzzard's nest," and they're roped off in the back of the ballroom at the local amusement park. Both blacks and whites are polite, and children, both black and white, learn about these restrictions only in their early teens when, half-awakened by sex, they find that the houses and yards of their childhood friends are now, somehow, not welcoming.

Most of Youngstown's few white professionals come from working-class groups and are still socially embedded in them. The even smaller number of black professionals often have to take second menial jobs to survive. And they are cunningly screened from many jobs, as well as from house loans or entry to some schools: job applications, loan applications, college entry forms, etc., contain a fill-in blank: "Nationality_____." To write "American" or "U.S." is smart-alecky. People like me are expected to write "Irish" or "English and German." Blacks are expected to write "Negro" because that is the real purpose of the form. Some write "Negro and English" or some other historically likely combination, but it doesn't matter. That one word is enough to disqualify them.

There can also be "class" divisions within a family: most white women who worked outside the home before their marriages—in the past as domestics, now in service or lower white-collar jobs—learned from their bosses' lives how things could be. As wives, they save for good china and wall-to-wall carpets, and they encourage "correct" table manners and social rules for husbands and children. The church reinforces these middle-class ideals. Such a clean, perfect place with its incense, polished wood, linens pressed to perfection, scrubbed men, and quiet children—life can be like this, the building itself seems to say to women, before they go home to too many children, too much work, and a fine film of industrial ash on the windows. But the husbands, ill at ease in dress clothes, thickened, scarred fingers clenched to hide permanently black fingernails, are nervous about eating out, attending anything "fancy." For them, being a mill worker comes before anything else—religion, ethnicity, neighborhood. They form their support groups, if not a class per se, from other workers just like themselves.

Thus, an odd group of non-steelworkers form the slightly higher end of the class scale, with the few "industrialists" at an apex so far removed as to be invisible. Blacks form the lowest end—such voids between the groups are hardly what we learned about in sociology.

Perhaps I could learn more about the true class structure of my town from talking to men like my father, but I never do.

Do the Paiutes form a class, a race, or something else? I interview many white people in Yerington—older men whose families employ Paiute ranch hands; men who as boys had Paiute friends; the sheriff who calls one of these his "brother" (and whose son I list as a Paiute in my census because he's in Paulette's house most of the time); teachers with a deep respect for the shy but intelligent Paiute students; a medical social worker who believes traditional medical practitioners are effective. Many, including some who are very knowledgeable about old Paiute customs, take pains to explain that Paiutes, because of their culture, think differently about things—law, for example—and that this is perfectly acceptable. Most who knew Jack Wilson tell me they respected him as a leader.

The whites also explain that "some people" think the Indians, especially the Colony Indians, are "trash"; generally, however, the distinction is not based on class, or race, but rather between "good" and "bad" Indians. Good Indians don't drink, they work hard and look after their families. Most of these are women, especially female heads of households. "Bad" Indians drink and are arrested often. "Smart" Indians are also respected—Morgan, for example, who sometimes represents the tribe at city council meetings— and good historians, such as Paulette's husband, as well as Jennie, Archie, and Delaney. Everyone I talk to names the same "good" and "bad" people, who tend to correspond to the Paiutes' categorizations as well.

Had the Paiutes been white, they would be considered working class. But their situation is much more complicated: they are poor, a race, and a colonized people. A way of life has been imposed on them. Colonial schools try to make them white citizens, but the more children realize that "ideal," the greater their disappointment when they try to participate, because as a race they are denied full access to Yerington society. They are dispossessed and disregarded on three counts.

I ask Jennie, always dressed in ironed, starched dresses, if women feel able to mix with people more easily than their men do. "Of course," she says. "The men on the ranches, they lived outside with the animals. Some women did, too. But I worked in a white house, and I know how things *can* be."

Can be. Not are.

"I'M WORRIED," I tell Cyril when he has time to sit on his front porch with me and help with the genealogies of the people on my census.

"Me, too. Look at that poor astronaut Scott Carpenter, got his arm hurt on the Sealab experiment."

"What?"

"Now they're wonderin' whether that's the end of his career. I was Army, he's Navy, but I know he must be worried. The pension and all."

I explain my concern about the state I got myself into over the meeting. I'm afraid that I'm so enmeshed in my own culture that either I've projected a lot of frivolous fears onto the Council, which is actually quite benign, or that there's a lot more going on here than I know about.

"Don't worry," he says. "The thing is, you're still looking at things the way you would at home." He reflected for a while. "And," he adds, "there's a lot more going on here than you know about."

That really puts my mind to rest.

I don't expect to see Larry again, but the figure now coming down the road has to be him: thin, jerky, managing somehow to seem small. He stops at the porch steps, arms hanging, looking up from under his thatch of hair.

"You be careful of that bottom step," Cyril says to him. "It's not high enough. You put your foot down, step's not there, and next thing you've fallen up and hit your chin off the edge of the porch. Your teeth go through your tongue, you'll know it."

The boy brightens at this welcome and makes his way carefully up on to the porch.

Cyril and I work a little longer on genealogies. Larry listens as attentively as if we're discussing the finer points of baseball. He's absorbed by the begats: who comes from Winnemucca Naci, who from Horseman, who from the witches (they fascinate him).

"Got to go feed my chickens, now," Cyril eases himself up. When he moves like that, I can see what an effort it is for him to keep his military posture.

"You know," Larry ventures, "you said about picking your subject so you could answer an important question?"

"Yes."

"I like that."

"Do you have an important question?" *About class inequality, hard luck, even maybe child neglect?*

"Dunno." He pauses, twisting his limp hair. "I guess, yeah, I guess why I'm so different from Eddie. He's so...so...." He looks sheepish.

What subject can you study to answer a question like that? Genetics? History? Moral theology? Veterinary science?

I'm a little nervous for him, being seen out here in public with me, Miss Trouble herself. "Your mother worries about you," I say.

He takes a pencil, draws a direct line on my chart from Winnemucca Naci to a little figure, and writes "LARRY" beneath it.

"She works so hard, she can't keep an eye on me," he says. "Two shifts, a lot of days." He pauses and adds, "My ma don't want me here."

"I know."

"She likes Delaney. I think she likes Cyril," he nods toward the sound of Cyril pounding something out back. "It's just Indians altogether she don't like."

He draws some jaggy lines around his name, with stars shooting out. "Maybe I better not be around so much."

"I'll miss you, of course."

Larry shivers and lowers his head to his drawing.

"Could I borrow a book on anthropology?" he asks. "An old one you don't need right now?"

I go into my room and get him the wonderful novel *Return to Laughter*, which I'd read shortly before I came here.

"I just thought I'd come out and tell you," he says, standing at the edge of the porch.

"Thanks. And forget about Eddie. I think you're fine the way you are."

I like Larry.

THAT NIGHT I write in my journal until 3:00 a.m., when Maybel taps on my door to ask if I'm all right. I turn off my light and lie in bed thinking over the day.

Why anthropology, Larry asked. I chose the field because I want facts to bolster my belief that differences in ability among us—men and women, black and white—are cultural, not inherent. But that's all I had: beliefs. And that's all bigots had, too: beliefs.

When I first looked for answers to my questions, I didn't know what subject to study. In my first year of college, I took courses in sociology, psychology, and anthropology. The only way I could distinguish between the first two was to remember that they were taught in different classrooms. My introductory sociology text was excruciatingly difficult; I concluded that the first half of one sentence could be joined to the second half of any other and still make as little sense. Psychology emphasized tests and measures, which seemed designed to identify the blandest beige, upright citizen as the norm and everyone else as slightly dodgy. What had this to do with Youngstown, with people like Charlie the Crab or Francis's cousin who was a martyr to scruples?

But anthropology! Anthropology was a different story. My first professor, Jim Kiriazis, was a vibrant, robust character with an infectious love of all the peoples of the world, and although he was a Rhodian Greek, he tried not to make an exception for the Greeks' historical enemies. He drew friends from every ethnic and racial group in Youngstown. I wanted to know more about a field that produced someone like Jim; it never occurred to me he might have been attracted to the field because he already had these attitudes.

When the sociology and psychology I studied made claims about the universal characteristics of society, or the universals of the human psyche, they drew their evidence almost exclusively from the western world. Surely if you're going to say something like, "Men are natural leaders," you should look across all known societies and back through history to support the statement. And you better know what you mean by "leadership" and its characteristics, because they aren't the same everywhere. If people don't correspond to our stereotypes everywhere, a supposed attribute can't be biological. In the beginning, anthropology taught me to search the whole world for my answers.

Also, I knew where I was with anthropology's porcupine-quill embroidery or the whistle language of the Zapotec, things that could be touched and seen, heard and smelled, like the rules of the Bug or the traditions of the Church. The sociologist's *anomie* and the psychologist's "id" seemed out of place on Youngstown's grim streets, where having an id would be considered a foppish indulgence.

When I told my mother I intended to become an anthropologist, she humored me. "What job do you get with that?"

"College teacher."

That was fine; she thought I was ill-suited to ordinary life. After all, I was the person who, when 10 years old, assured her that rape was nothing to fear—I got this view from reading about Rapunzel, who lived in a field of rape, a type of grain. And a few years later, when she was ironing, I actually asked her, "Is the Pope Catholic?"

"Have I been scrimping for years, no new Easter hat since 1948, to send you to Catholic school for nothing?"

"Well, the *Vindicator* calls him 'the Pope.'"

"Why wouldn't they call him the Pope? That's his *name*."

"Yes, the *Catholic Exponent* calls him 'the Pope' because it's Catholic, but the *Vindicator* isn't Catholic. It's public. He isn't their Pope."

She snatched a piece of crochet work from the laundry basket and started pinning it to the ironing board to dry. Each jab rocked the board.

"The *Vindicator* doesn't call the Queen 'the Queen,'" I continued, although I knew I was living dangerously now. "They say '"the Queen of England.'"

"It isn't the same," she shouted, nearly dancing on the spot.

"Is," I said.

My brother Patrick passed through, ducked his head into his shoulders, and continued on out the back door.

"All I'm trying to find out," I said, after a necessary pause, "is 'Is the Pope Catholic?'"

"THE POPE IS CATHOLIC," she roared, just as old Mrs. Johnson from next door came in, as she often did, to give my mother a hand and have a cup of coffee. Mrs. Johnson was a Protestant, so she and my mother, scrupulous in these matters, never discussed religion. I liked her; she'd gone to Cleveland on a day trip and come back with a souvenir mug saying "Life is Hell." She was going to leave it to me in her will.

"You go have a rest, Margaret," she said, directing my mother upstairs.

Patrick came back with two sidekicks and the dog, and my smaller brothers and sisters, hearing the shouting, crowded in as well, all delighted.

"Howdy do," my father said, home from the day shift with his empty lunch bucket. He looked around at the crowd.

"Where's everybody?"

"She's upstairs," Mrs. Johnson said.

My mother had more to suffer as I got older. Over the supper dishes, her washing, me drying, I took on gender rules, the overpowering self-interest of institutions, religion, and anything else that seemed to me to be on suspect ground. When she got excited, she helped with the drying, too, so that was another incentive to egg her on.

She held fast on some points. "Not all housewives are miserable," she said, wrapping the garbage up in newspaper. "I think it's a privilege for me to be able to stay at home. My own mother had to scrub schools for 40 years to support five of us kids and all the others." These "others" included my grandmother's sick widowed sister, her alcoholic brother and his motherless little boy, her old uncle, and her husband's mother, left behind by the absconded husband. They shared a two-bed-plus-attic house.

I am descended from women like these, my mother and her mother and all our mothers past, generations of Irish farm women who scrabbled on poor, rain-lashed scraps of rocky land, but I was too caught up in Jesuitical argumentation to stop and reflect on that legacy.

Anthropology was right for me for another reason. It was arcane, and if you were destined, as some girls in my hometown were, to be a telephone operator or an addressograph machine operator, its rarefied abstruseness seemed a great safeguard against being expected to work at anything useful. Each time I read something like "The Shoshone of the Great Basin struck stones or sticks together to produce a sound like the clashing together of mountain sheep horns," I felt I was giving myself a new and welcome layer of occupational handicap.

One night after supper, I said to my mother, "You know the Tasmanians." I read from the book, waving the dishtowel. She washed a can opener. I would certainly never wash a can opener when I had my own place.

She looked nervous. "Yes?"

"Ordinarily, both sexes went about entirely naked."

"What?"

"Other mutilations, such as circumcision, knocking out teeth, and cutting off finger joints, were not practiced."

"Come in here this minute," she called to my father. "Talk to her."

"Please," he said to me later. "Let your mother alone. You know she has nerves."

Reading anthropology lifted me up: "Decorative art—and the art of the Haidas is almost exclusively decorative—attains a development scarcely equaled anywhere else in the savage world." And it reassured me: "The process of conventionalization has not led, as has happened so frequently elsewhere, to the development of geometric patterns." All of this was not only making me more and more unfit for telephony, but it also created a bunker into which I could escape while my mother had her arm half-way down a blocked drain.

My brain—furnished as it was with a floor of cow dung and mud, and festooned with squirrel traps, moieties, masticated cornmeal libations, detachable harpoon heads, and bone mustache-lifters—was acquiring, among my family anyhow, the sheltered status of a nun's virginity or a Chinese princess's bound feet.

So I have answers to Larry's question about why I chose anthropology. But they're my answers. He'll have to find his own.

CHAPTER TEN

Crossing Boundaries

"I ADMIRE YOUR BALLS," Eddie says. "Whoops, sorry." He smirks, nodding his chin at the police car. This isn't an old Paiute custom; he's trying to keep his lard-laden hairdo in place. He slips into the casino, while I go into the post office to send my weekly batch of notes to the university.

I use the car more now, since Cyril has been telling me not to be silly. "Worry about your grade, instead." Often with me, uninvited, are three or four of the most obstreperous teenaged Paiute girls, usually including Charlene and Thomasina. Sometimes the girls seem like movie starlet airheads; other times, an unfathomable menace flickers on a face or two. Maybe their elders think a ride in the police car will give them a chastening taste of what may await them later in life—or even in the near future; one visiting girl tells us she kicked an old Indian nearly to death "for the fun of it." I try to probe into this casually, but her eyes widen at my attention and she shuts up. I laugh—she's probably showing off to Charlene and Thomasina. But no. "It's true," Thomasina says. "Don't you ever give her a ride unless we're with you."

I've also been attracting offers of other forms of motor transportation. First, the motorcycle. It belongs to Marv Dawson, a bear-like, middle-aged white man who knows a lot about the petroglyphs and bedrock mortars—prehistoric stone bowls—in the desert outside town. The Paiutes used them to grind food. Marv assumes that, as an anthropologist, I can give him the kind of professional insight into them that he thinks he's missing.

Marv's chivalry is impeccable; since he thinks I can't ride on the back of his motorcycle and still keep my reputation as a lady, a bride, or a macho anthropologist, he lends me his spare Harley Davidson. My challenge is to get on and off without being crushed by the machine falling over on me. Marv sets me in motion, and we fly down the main street into the desert, him racing ahead to catch me when I stop.

We do this trip several times.

"It might be better if you learned to fly," he muses. "I got a little Piper Colt. You could map bedrock mortars from the air." He says this wistfully, as if only a true scientist like me is entitled to do such a thing. "And you could even fly back and forth to the university. Save time for the work."

"I don't think so," I reply. "I don't have a license or the time to get one."

"Nah. The Federal Aviation Authority." He waves a hand dismissively. "Think they're better'n everyone else. Think they own the air or something. But we don't pay much attention to that stuff."

Marv gives me six lessons in all. I know my limitations, so the outcome is inevitable. My lack of coordination and invariable reversal of directions baffle him. (I'm one of those dangerous left-handers.)

"Well, don't say 'left' when you mean 'left,' say 'right' and I'll know you mean 'left,'" I instruct him. "And just say 'that way' when you mean 'right.'"

Eventually Marv glumly resigns himself to my inability to fly. Still, he promises to take me up when I want to look at something of interest, like California perhaps.

The Indian Mission Volkswagen bus is my fourth vehicle. Most people are busy when weekday services and activities are on, so Reverend Parks asks me to drive the church bus to fetch aged and infirm weekday worshippers. As a Catholic atheist, I wonder about the ethics of driving an evangelical bus, but only for a minute: it provides me with a captive group-interview situation.

This arrangement suits everyone, in fact. It gives the elderly an outing, gets them off their children's hands for a while, and fills the seats for the service. It gives me some excellent informants who can expound for an hour on how Winnemucca Naci, Horseman, and Chief Joaquin majestically repelled white soldiers. And, when we get to the Mission, the Reverend can draw on the most elegant speakers of Paiute to refine his reportedly nearly impeccable accent.

The bus has its secular uses as well. On my rounds I become a taxi service for the tired women who never go near the church but like a lift with the groceries or for Jennie when she wants to visit her sisters in Silver Springs and Schurz. Thomasina and Charlene often act as rear-gunners on the bus, firing rocks out the back windows at show-off girls, both Paiute and white—like Betty Ann O'Donnell, whose clothes are *too cute*. The girls admire my own clothes as well.

"Some of your clothes would look nice on us. After you leave, I mean," Charlene says, kindly including the huge Thomasina in the "us."

"Nah," Thomasina says. "You got a few tops that are okay, that batik one, maybe, but the rest look like a schoolteacher. You ever wear a bikini? I'd love a bikini. I'd probably wear it all the time."

Even Charlene has no response to this image.

"You get one next time you go to Reno, and we can all go out driving."

In the Reverend's bus? I wonder. Or the police car?

The girls put peanuts in soda cans and shake them, showering the bus seats with sticky foam.

Charlene is particularly delighted to tag along on these missions because it gets her out of her music lessons. "My mother is making me learn the *connordoreon*," she complains.

What kind of instrument is this? I'm curious, but Charlene can't describe it except by waving her hands to sketch something complicated, saying it's way, way too big and the sound it makes hurts her ears.

"Your mother deserves a lot of credit for making you learn a traditional instrument," I scold. I'm completely amusical. My singing, my brother says, is "like a fire in a pet store."

The girls laugh. I don't dare neglect Paiute musical heritage, though. *Conn-ord-o-reon*, I note, carefully transcribing Charlene's word for the instrument; Delaney can explain it to me later.

Driving the church bus is risky because the brawny Thomasina often tries to wrestle the wheel away from me so that we can drive somewhere to find boys. After one of these hijackings, Reverend Parks reminds me that I'm supposed to be "Doing the Lord's Work," not cruising.

The bus step is too high for some of the older people, and I'm too light-weight to give them much of a hand. Thomasina strong-arms them up and plunks them in their seats like rag dolls, but most are too fragile to accept her help more than once or twice.

Today Thomasina and I collect Archie, a favorite of the Reverend's. He's gloriously drunk but insists on coming. Delaney and a man he introduces as his cousin-brother, Brody, are slumped on the bus seats, but they cheer up when they see someone enjoying himself.

"He's been waiting all day," Doreen Williamson says. "He says no one wants to talk good Paiute to him anymore except the Reverend and Mickey Kelly." Doreen is married to a Shoshone and the family doesn't speak much Paiute at home. I've been avoiding Mickey because my Paiute is still pathetic and people say he can be brusque with learners.

Thomasina gets out and lectures Archie in Paiute as she tries to haul him up the steps; I parse out her words: a tirade about making the Paiute people look bad in front of The Lady. Archie beams at all the attention but winces at Thomasina's pronunciation. "Speak English," he begs. We try various tactics to get him onto the bus, but between arthritis and alcohol, he's as manageable as a half-open ironing board, and not as cooperative.

Doreen says, "If I can't get five tiny minutes to myself there'll be real trouble. I'm already late for my hairdresser appointment." She points to her husband's flatbed. "Here, take him in the truck. Leave the bus here; you can pick it up later." I picture Doreen, a Methodist on my census, on her way to the hairdresser's in the church bus. But there's nothing for it. So now I have yet another form of transport, a Shoshone flatbed.

Delaney and cousin-brother Brody are thrilled; they practically skip off the church bus, although they had to be eased on like fragile meringues only a few minutes before. Between them and Thomasina, they slide Archie onto the truck bed, and Delaney climbs in with him. Archie claps his cowboy hat on his head with a flourish, and they shout to each other in Paiute, with Archie wagging a schoolmasterly finger from time to time.

"He's way too particular about how a person talks Paiute," Thomasina complains, sitting up front beside Brody and me. "Nobody talks good enough for him."

At one point they bang on the flatbed's back window, motioning me to stop. I do, and avert my eyes, thinking they need some privacy for a pee at the side of the road, until I realize they want us to come back and join them. "You want to write this down," Delaney tells me, waving his hand at Archie and Brody. "These two guys, Archie and Brody, swapped sisters as wives. That was the right way to do it."

"I thought Brody was *your* cousin-brother," I say.

"Yes," Delaney agrees. "I got a sister off him, too." They all beam. My understanding from the literature is that Paiutes shouldn't marry cousins, brothers, or sisters.

"And what did Brody get off you?"

Brody's affectionate look fades, and Delaney motions me to get back in the cab and drive on. They never answer my question.

At the Mission, Reverend Parks soon has the men huddled in front of the skeletal *kah' nii*. Archie sorts through the dried *tules* and sets the others to weaving them into the mats that will cover the dome. They all oblige the

Reverend by naming parts of the structure in Paiute; when he's distracted, they try to fix the willow dome supports.

The Paiutes seem unfazed by my methods of transportation. But far from appearing "neutral," as anthropologists are supposed to, I become something else every time I get on the road: I'm now identified with the Evangelical Church, the police, the Shoshone, or the privileged white man, depending on which vehicle I get myself into.

"Eileen?" my mother's on the phone. "It's—"

I don't want to hear. Who has died? My grandmother? My mother's pet canary? The bird's been a little pale, she wrote recently.

"Me. It's a long time since we heard from you."

"Ma, I talked to you three days ago." My mother *never* makes long distance calls, and now she's called me three times.

"I know, but I worry. You've been gone so long." Today is my four-week anniversary—of my time on the reservation, not of my wedding. It's been seven weeks now since I've seen Francis, eight since I've seen my family.

Officer Wickham corners someone on Main Street, but from time to time he turns and glares at me, exposed for all the world to see in the glass phone booth.

"Are you still living in that tipi?" she asks. Nothing will convince her that the whole Paiute population isn't housed in tents. Eddie answered one of her earlier calls and had a little chat with her, so I suppose that's where she got the idea.

"Listen, what I really want to ask you is do the Indians know we're nice people? We go to church and bake pies and take walks on Sundays and all, just like they do?"

I can see Delaney's grand-nephew, Earl, sitting outside the casino with his rubber tomahawk, pretending to scalp a dog. More than pretending, from the sounds the dog's making.

"Yeah, Ma, I'm sure they do."

"Because I saw a program on TV the other night and they said a man wrote a letter to someone here and addressed it 'Murdertown, Ohio' and it arrived a couple of days later."

"Ma, that's true. It was in the *Saturday Evening Post* last September."

"Well, I hope the Indians didn't read that. Do they know we invented the Good Humor Man? Anyhow, that letter was sent to Jimmy Anzivino's mother and she says it took a whole week."

"Okay, Ma. I'll tell them."

"So how are you getting along? What are you doing?"

What *am* I doing? I can build a *kah' nii.* I can lead the hymn-singing on the bus, and I have over 60 stories about Wolf and Coyote.

What I don't have is enough information on Jack Wilson and his work to understand the current role of the Reverend's church. I know, from my obsessive night-time reading, that in the late 1800s, Indians from many tribes traveled hundreds of miles to listen to Jack Wilson.

How could all this happen, nearly within living memory, and yet local people are unaware of it? Or maybe they just don't talk about it? At least not to me.

Maybe I'm being paranoid.

"I have to go," I tell my mother. "There's a policeman watching me."

Wickham's keeping an eye on me, but also lecturing Cyril, who crossed Main Street between intersections. Cyril stares ahead as the tubby Wickham rocks on his oddly tiny feet, jabbing a finger at him. When I come out of the booth, the policeman strides over. "You be a good Injun, hear?" he calls back to Cyril, who stands stone-still for a few seconds before moving off, eyes straight, shoulders back.

You don't have to like everybody you meet during fieldwork. I've heard that Wickham takes polio-stricken white kids on outings. I don't care. The Paiutes say nothing about him to me, but a local white reporter tells me he delights in humiliating them and using them for his own yard work once he has them in jail. His dislike of me is obvious; I hear he calls me "that girl that's messing around with them Paiutes."

"Indian down at the jail wants to see you," he says now.

"Who?"

"Walker Wilson. At 3:45 sharp, he'll be back off the road gang. Passed through here driving drunk and got 37½ days." He sniggers.

The district attorney has told me that drunk driving is the most common Paiute crime, that a lot of the men have been arrested at one time or another, and that they are sometimes jailed for longer periods than whites because "they aren't as used to liquor" and need longer to dry out. Wilson's sentence seems longer than any human should need, but I don't drink much so can't really say. People say that Wilson speaks wonderful Paiute and knows a lot of local history, but I'm unlikely to find him—he's a drifter. This is a real piece of luck.

"You keepin' away from that kid?" Wickham asks.

"What kid?"

He edges closer and lowers his voice. "You don't get smart with me, you mouthy broad. That Larry."

What I ache to say! How I wish I could sic my mother on him, she who can freeze the impertinent to the spot and flay them with her tongue. But if I do speak back, all I'll do is make a stick for Larry's back.

"Of course," I say.

THAT AFTERNOON I go over to the jail, edging respectfully around a bushy-tailed yellowish-gray dog who tracks my every movement, eyes alert, ears twitching. A man watches, amused, from the visiting room window. Tall, handsome, sleepy black eyes.

"Good to see somebody besides that Wickham," Walker says. He waves me to a battered wooden chair, and sits down on an even more battered bench. "How about you tell Delaney and Archie I'm in here, come see me? Nobody knows I'm here yet."

"If nobody knows you're here, how did you find out about me?"

"Wickham told me. Said you wanted to see me."

Is Wickham trying to help me? Unlikely.

Our meeting is short. The prisoners have only 45 minutes between their gang roadwork and the 4:30 dinnertime. Even so, I decide to approach my subject obliquely.

"Do you know any stories about Wolf and Coyote?"

He laughs, a deep rich laugh, and studies me a while, saying nothing. I scribble down a quick description: he's coming up to 50 years old, nearly six feet tall, thick silver-gray mane tied back with a piece of string. Dressed like a cowboy, which he is, in worn jeans and flannel shirt, a pair of scuffed boots, broken across one sole.

"Plenty," he says finally. "But why bother with that old stuff? What're you s'posed to be doing, anyhow?"

"I'm looking at the religions people have taken up here these days."

"Huh. Wickham said you were on your honeymoon. Without your husband."

"Yes—well, no, I had my honeymoon a few weeks ago."

"Where you from?"

"Ohio."

"Ah." He looks off in the distance, or as much distance you can get in a jail visiting room, perhaps trying to conjure up Ohio. "So now you're here all by your lonesome?"

Most people haven't asked me so many direct questions so fast; the Paiutes have elegant manners. Driver has a different interpretation of their behavior: "The scarcity of food in the Great Basin Area of North America must have contributed to the dull unresponsive personalities that fieldwork- ers have so often found there." True, the reservation isn't a madcap hotbed of giddiness, but so far nobody I've met can be called dull.

"Well, I'd'a thought you need to learn about the old religion first. The old doctors and healers. That'd help you figure out why people are doing what they are today." He ponders this. "Or maybe not."

"Yes," I say, resolving to be as enigmatic as everyone else.

"Take Jack Wilson, now, or Tom Mitchell, or Dick Bennett. Jack Wilson was my uncle. There was what … about 15 doctors here between say 1860 and today. Some were witches, too. You should be writing all that down before it's too late."

He helps me make a chart to show the unbroken tradition of some of these practitioners in the local valley and the nearby Bridgeport area between 1860 and now. The dates he gives me are the periods of their greatest power, usually in their middle age.

1860–70	Winnemucca Naci, Horseman, Chief Joaquin
1870–80	Jack Wilson; in Bridgeport, Dick Bennett and Little Dick
1880–1900	Dr. Joe, Dr. Charley
1910–20	Tom Mitchell, Ben Lancaster, Jim Keno, Lillian McCloud
1930–40	Barney Miller, Rosie Quartz
1940–	Maggie Milton

Walker explains that Winnemucca, Horseman, and Chief Joaquin, all cousin-brothers, all invincible in battle, are the ancestors or ancestors-in-law of all the Paiutes living in Yerington today.

"We're children of three heroes." He shakes his head and traces the scars on his bench.

Dick Bennett's son still lives locally, as do Tom Mitchell's grandsons. Enraged survivors of patients who died at their hands killed Horseman, Little Dick, Dr. Charley, and Dr. Joe. Two on the list—Jim Keno, or "Hoppy," and Ben Lancaster, or White Feather, who was from Coleville—helped to introduce peyote into the area and used it as a medium in their curing.

"That caused a lot of trouble, but the Tribal Council here held a vote on it, voted it out over 20 years ago. Lancaster went back to Coleville."

"So no one uses it now?"

"I wouldn't say so. A while back, yeah, and for a while, a lot of opium. Not me, though."

"And no peyote for you?"

"It's the people over in Bridgeport use peyote. That what you been trying to find out?" He laughs. "All those people, they could tell when bad things were coming, disasters, bad weather and all. And if you had a dream that was bothering you, you could go to them and they'd explain it all."

"Did people listen to them?"

"Oh, yeah, most times. And when people got together, in the fall, maybe, or the spring, the doctors might be the leaders for that, and then the people would break up and go on their way again."

Some of those in the chart were doctors; fewer were witches. Doctors cured people, mainly for mysterious ailments for which there was no suitable "white" medicine or commonly known remedy, such as dizziness or insanity. Some also had miraculous/religious powers, people like Horseman and, more recently, Jack Wilson. Today Jack Dalton combines his work as reservation policeman with doctoring.

"Witches could do some doctoring, too," Walker says. "They were really good at helping you if you got witched by somebody else. Trouble is, they could witch, too,"

"What did they do?"

"Oh, man, they could bring a world of trouble down on top of you. Bad luck, evil stuff, sometimes even kill you. And, another thing: a witch could steal a doctor's power."

"Someone told me witches were likeable, though; easy to get along with."

"Depends." Walker frowns. "That was more the doctors that was liked. Take Tom Mitchell; he was a witch and he wasn't that well liked. He had that witch's power to cure people that were witched, and he could fix people who tried to kill themselves eating wild parsnips. But people said he used his power to cause trouble."

"And women witches?"

"Don't get me started. And there are still a couple around. But they're quiet kind of people these days."

"Now," he hunkers down on the bench, "I suppose I'd best tell you some stories about Wolf and Coyote. Just in case."

An anthem of tales follow: The Man Who Became Thunder, The Death of Wolf, and *Cánaho!*, The Monster Cannibal. Walker looks guarded now, darker, somehow older, smaller, closed. And Coyote in his words becomes more mysterious—not just a comic troublemaker, self-centered, greedy, cheating, but a lonesome shape-changer, a boundary-crosser, moving between man and animal, male and female, living and dead, a hopeful creature who is fooled as often as he fools.

"He seems like a sad figure, sometimes. You almost feel sorry for him," I say.

"He teaches us things," Walker says.

"Yes, but now the lessons come through his suffering. If he *can* suffer."

"Oh, he suffers. He knows when his plans blow up in his face. But he keeps on goin'. And he learns—look at him asking Wolf how to do things. 'Brother, tell me...' he begs, and Wolf tells him, but he doesn't understand Coyote's little world and what works for Wolf won't work for Coyote. So Wolf's afraid of Coyote, he's like a wild card, and Wolf needs to keep the world running his way." He shakes his head. "Oh, yeah, some people think Coyote never learns, but he does, man, and then he outsmarts himself and ends up in new trouble." He pauses. "Believe me."

I write as fast as I can. The stories fill my notebook.

"And he helps each of us to think about things, but in different ways. Take me—what I learn from Coyote is not the same as what Archie learns, or Jennie. We need different things. So write this down: Coyote tells you more about the teller than the tale."

I underline that.

"Know how to call a coyote, if you want to hunt one?" he asks after a little while. "You make a sound like a rabbit that's hurt: '*Waaa.*' Remember that, not too long, just: '*Waaa*'."

I write that down too, although I don't think I'll be calling any coyotes.

"Dinner, Walker," Mrs. Bennett, the cook, calls through the doorway.

"Gotta go, Missy, Missus, whatever you are." Walker stands, stretching. He unfurls to nearly six feet, lithe, self-assured, amused.

"The people from Ohio," he drawls, looking at me with a lazy, ironic eye, "they got any other strange honeymoon customs?"

At the front door, the gray dog's ears stand rigid, alert, his yellow eyes wary, searching.

THAT NIGHT, I dream of coyote and all his appellations and titles: clever fool, self-serving schemer, sly deceiver, scourge of the current order, limitless sybarite, lazy inventor, tower of ivory, house of gold, refuge of sinners, comforter of the afflicted, cause of our joy, Gate of Heaven—no, wait, some of those are something else...the Litany of the Blessed Virgin. The words, the rhythm, they never leave you. "Give me a child for seven years, and I will give you the man," the Jesuits say. Still, Gate of Heaven's not bad. Coyote lives between boundaries, carrying messages between worlds. But I still feel a little sorry for him.

CHAPTER ELEVEN

The Murder

"Your mother called," Jennie says. "At 6:00 a.m. Must be something."

A guy just off the night shift, trudging by the booth when the call came, left a note on Jennie's porch. Jennie's house and the curb in front of the post office are becoming my known *loci operandi*. I phone my mother back at 10:00.

"Ma, you called at 6:00 a.m."

My mother holds no truck with time zones. "All I know is it was 9:00 here. Dad wants to talk to you," she says. " Don't let him run up my bill."

"Eileen, how ya doin'?"

"Fine, Dad, how're you?"

"Fine."

Silence.

Then, "Here's a good one for you. A guy, carpenter in the mill, goes to confession over at St. Pat's. 'Father,' he says, 'I been stealing lumber out of the mill for the last 10 years. I've reformed now, and I'm sorry. I won't do it again.'

"'Good,' says the priest. "That's a serious sin. Now, for your penance, I want you to make the Stations of the Cross.'

"'Oh, jeez, Father," the guy says, "I can make them for you, no problem, but I think you'll have to steal the lumber yourself.'

"You tell that one to the Indians," Dad says, laughing at his own joke. "They'll like that."

Back in Jennie's kitchen, which is so searingly hot I can hardly think. Jennie looks as crisp and fresh as a spring dawn in a blue dress my mother made and sent to her. Jennie and my mother are real chums now; Jennie herself happened to be passing the phone booth a few weeks ago and had taken her call. She thanked her for the dress pattern she'd received, and they discovered they had a common interest in sewing. Jennie had made up the *Simplicity* dress pattern # 4196, complete with bolero, and we sent my mother a photo. My mother replied with the blue dress and a new pattern, *Simplicity* # 667, a pink dress with a polka dot lined wool cape. In this heat.

"Tell me again what this subject is you're studying?" Jennie asks.

"Anthropology is the study of savages," according to the dictionary floating around the Colony. I mentally sort through more recent definitions, which are changing rapidly.

Any answer I can offer, such as what I told Larry, is much too long-winded for a snappy reply in this heat. I'm nearly halfway through my time here, and I wish I had ready answers to the repeated questions: "What's anthropology? Do you miss your husband? Aren't Ohio and Iowa the same place?"

"Anthropology is the study of man," a professor reminded us in a seminar last spring, translating its Greek roots, *anthropo* and *logos*. "And what the misguided historical materialists fail to acknowledge—"

"Man?" Marina, one of the older female students, barked. "*Man?*"

The professor looked baffled. It was rumored that he believed that Marina was a lesbian, because of her outspoken views on women's rights. "All right," he retorted, producing the hoary anthropological saw, "Anthropology is the study of man, embracing woman."

But anthropology's "embrace" was tenuous. "Anthropology holds up a great mirror to man and lets him look at himself in his infinite variety," Clyde Kluckhohn had written. (When that was quoted in another seminar, Marina sneered, "Well, if he moved it two inches either way, he'd see the little woman behind him. Isn't gender part of the infinite variety?")

"When we heard you were coming, we thought you'd be a man," Jennie says.

It's true that the majority of anthropologists are male, and also true that the societies in which they work are unlikely to let them embrace their women, either intellectually or physically, so we are taught little of what women think or do. In classes, we heard more about the sexual roles of women than any of their other activities—and then only the features titillating to western ears: women breastfeeding pigs in New Guinea, being lent to visitors at night among the Inuit, being married to a set of brothers among the Todas of India. The prevalence in mythology of that toothed vagina is a favorite topic, too. Funny that male subincision, the custom of splitting the penis lengthwise, is a topic one had to ferret out for oneself in obscure texts. Marina was not one to let this anomaly go by. In yet another seminar, she sniffed, "I notice we don't hear much about *that*."

The professor crossed his legs tightly. "The male member…" he began.

"In my opinion," she said, "the male member leaves a lot to be desired."

Although there are some eminent female anthropologists, they are as hobbled by gossip as nineteenth-century equestriennes were by their skirts. Any quirk of appearance or personality takes precedence, in our lecturers' accounts, over their accomplishments. "Baggy Maggie" is one professor's name for Margaret Mead. On the other hand, the eminent Ruth Benedict, one of her lovers, is always referred to as "the beautiful Ruth Benedict."

"It's a hard job for a woman. Leaving her husband and all," Jennie interrupts my ruminations.

"I haven't left my husband," I protest. But in his last letter, Francis complained that everyone was asking where he was hiding the little bride. Is anyone asking him why *he* isn't *here*, I'm tempted to ask?

"Have you talked to Delaney about our marriage customs yet?" Jennie asks.

I wipe sweat from my eyelids. "He said he didn't want to talk about it. He said to ask you."

"Hmm."

"Did the Paiute women change their names when they married?" I switch to one of my sore points. In my opinion, changing your name as a grown person makes no sense. Malcolm X has the right idea: better an "X" than a slave name, which to me is the same as a "married" name.

"We didn't have names to change. Not last names. The white ranchers gave us names. And if they didn't, the Indian school at Stewart did. Do you think any of us would have called ourselves 'John Smith' or 'Big Mouth Bob'?"

"I guess not."

"When we got married, sometimes our parents picked someone, but sometimes we just decided to live together, and we became married. The relatives might give a little push; they didn't like you going around together. It was shameful for the family. Sometimes, you didn't feel like getting married, though."

"Well, why would you, then?"

"To get out of the house. Well, we didn't really have houses, but you know what I mean."

"Yeah, I do."

"Our mothers were very strict—our fathers, too. If they saw you walking around with someone, they'd be watching you all the time. Your family might say, 'You'd better get married.' If you went around with a cousin-brother or -sister, it was even worse, because both of you disgraced the family. In the old days, Delaney married his cousin-sister; his grandmother told them not to be sneaking around and making her ashamed."

The Paiutes have what anthropologists call a "Hawaiian" system of naming their kin; all brothers and male cousins are called by the same kinship term, as are all sisters and female cousins. Since they're grouped together, cousin marriage is discouraged. Delaney, Brody, and Archie obviously ignored that. Maybe True Love intervened.

The heat is killing me. I should have been able to remember my definitions a lot better; I'd just taken my end-of-first-year exams and practically had them tattooed on my brain. Okay, anthropology is the study of culture, and the definition of culture that makes the most sense to me is one the anthropologist Ward Goodenough offered recently. Basically, he said, culture is in the head. It's a group's way of thinking about things, deciding what to do about them, and figuring out how to go about it.

I like that—it's a way to escape the everlasting yurts, cassava squeezers, and bladder-membrane windowpanes. Anthropology studies how groups of people use their particular idea systems to live their lives. What influences the idea systems is still in contention.

"An anthropologist studies people's way of life, and their ideas," I finally come up with, as an answer to Jennie's question. "Like you might come to my town and study my people."

"That would be nice," Jennie says. "*You* could tell me about *your* marriage customs."

Well, put that way, I guess I should.

"My mother is strict, too, like yours," I say.

Jennie settles herself more comfortably in her old overstuffed chair. Her fingers sort quickly through some willow twigs. "I'm making a new sunshade for my grandson's cradleboard," she says.

"I could never phone a boy, for instance" I add.

"No, we couldn't, either." She nods, obviously thinking how alike we are. But in Youngstown, we had phones.

"If you wanted to talk to a boy, you had to wait for him to phone you." What a thrill it was, though, to be poised between the phone and your Catholic mother, hoping the next ring would be your hot-blooded boyfriend wanting to talk about what he intended to do with you next and not your aunt wanting to talk about the new linoleum in her dining room.

We had all kinds of rules for women, both married and single.

"You don't want to have long hair or wear shorts after you're about 18," my mother told me once, when I was about 13. She was ironing, as usual. I was trying to read a book.

"I *do* want to."

"You don't," she said. "And you don't want to waggle your behind like that when you walk down the street."

"Ma!"

She picked up her old bottle with the sprinkler top, dampened my good white dress with it, and rolled it up tightly. "You'll get one more wearing out of this before next summer," she announced. It was late July then, and one of our social rules was that you couldn't wear white after August 15. Until then, we were free to sport gouts of industrial soot and grime on our white dresses and gloves.

"When you reach 14 or so, you'll want to wear a girdle, too."

"I won't."

"You will."

As I recall, we also had a go-around about tampons, too, although the word was never used. They were sinful, apparently. Also, I'd be sorry, later.

One of the most important rules was that a boy had to pick you up and bring you home after a date; in the summer, most of the family would be sitting on the front porch, brothers hurling catcalls and mother making little jokes with an undertone of nonchalant menace, the idea being that the boyfriend should know you had a nice respectable family, one that could kill.

Jennie shifts in her chair, bringing me back to her hot kitchen. That front porch ordeal is wincingly real.

"Why didn't he want to talk about it?" Jennie asks.

"Who?"

"Delaney. Why didn't he want to talk about our marriage customs?"

"I don't know. Should I ask him again?"

"Yes."

"Wickham's looking for you," Morgan announces.

I've driven over to the Colony for help on his specialty, a history of who witched whom. Sharing alarming news is his other specialty; he often tells me he finds Colony life dull.

"He can't come onto the reservation, so he's waiting for you on the road." Wickham can't be bringing news about my family—Morgan is such a dramatist that he'd want to tell me bad news himself. He's torn between glee at surprising me with potential calamity and annoyance at not knowing what it is.

Wickham is waiting at the settlement boundary. He, too, seems annoyed, perhaps because I can drive on the reservation (courtesy of the Paiutes) and, by federal law, he can't. My police car doesn't help, either; it's bigger than his.

"You know an old Paiute fellow's been found dead in the Colony?" he barks. "Willie Jackson? Killed? Last Wednesday?"

I shake my head, stunned. He's surprised that I know nothing about this. I'm surprised, too; people committing murders without telling me? It probably happened while I was learning the difference between mother's sister's daughter and younger brother's wife.

"The suspects claim they were with you the whole time. So—you with them when it happened?"

"Me? Who are the suspects?" I picture the sozzled craps players under Jennie's tree. It's hard to imagine them as killers; even if they're inclined to kick people to death, they're usually too uncoordinated to do it.

"Kids. They say they were with you."

Thomasina? Charlene? What about their friend's offhand comment that she kicked an old man around? But that was weeks ago. "Girls?"

"Huh-uh," he says, naming the kids, whom I do know, but vaguely. I've never met Willie Jackson, though. He comes from someplace else. Where was I on Wednesday? I can only tell one day from another now by checking my notes.

And why has nobody said anything to me? Are people—Delaney, Morgan, Jennie, everyone—hiding all kinds of data from me?

"You need to come over to the station, make a report."

ANTHROPOLOGISTS' PARANOIA. IT'S been creeping up on me. In the first days of fieldwork, elation, fear, and hubris keep you going. After months or even years of preparation, you've arrived at the place you've been reading, thinking, and talking about, and people are actually willing to speak to you. You might even understand a little of a language most other people think is extinct, and, as yet, no one has threatened to kill you or throw you out.

Delighted, you begin to imagine the first lines of your thesis: "As Murdock has noted in his seminal work, bilateral kinship is the norm among North American Indians, but recent research among the Paiutes suggests an alternative interpretation...." Or you picture yourself back home saying, "When I was living in the jungle/in the desert/in the slums of/in a little village in...."

But as the weeks pass, elation fades. Surely people are concealing supernatural beliefs, sex practices, bug-roasting techniques, or names of handy medicinal roots. How do other anthropologists produce such detailed monographs on subjects such as menstrual taboos or recipes for poisoning neighbors, when you can't even collect basic census information because people are going on with their lives without informing you? Or prepare yourself for police questioning because no one even mentions a suspicious death?

"Why didn't anyone tell me about Willie Jackson?" I ask Morgan as soon as I return to the Colony.

"I suppose they thought you already knew," he says. "You seem to be everywhere, asking questions, writing stuff down."

"But people here in the Colony don't really think I had anything to do with it, do they?" Actually, I'm more worried about the impact my supposed involvement may have on my local rapport, if I have any left. Respectable girls in the town I come from fret about having hairy legs or a Kotex bulge under their skirts; being associated with a murder suspect, or even the victim, is not the concern there it might be in a place like, say, Cleveland. Only a few years ago, Leo "Lips" Moceri gunned down another Mafioso outside the *Tots n' Teens* shop while I was putting a blouse in layaway. I told my mother later, but all she wanted to know was how I thought I was going to pay for the blouse.

"Of course they don't think that," Morgan brightens; it's clear he hopes they do.

I GO OVER TO the jail in the hope that Walker will have stories to distract me.

"The police want to talk to me."

"Yeah, tell me about it," he says.

There's something different about him today; I'm here earlier than the first time I visited because the jail has no work detail on Saturdays. Maybe the light is different. Amazing how sometimes you can look at a handsome man's face and see how, with his bone structure, he could have been a beautiful woman as well.

"Don't worry. They don't know nothin'," he says. "It's not about the murder, it's about you. Who you are. Just like it's not about my drinking. It's about me."

"You mean because you're a Paiute?"

"Nah. Well, yeah, you could say that, I guess."

"Doesn't seem logical."

He laughs at me. Not with me. "So what? Not everything's logical. Not logical for nomads to be cramped into tiny wood houses. Not logical for witching to work, but take it from me, it does. Not logical for the smartest kid in town to sit at the back of her class and never say a word. I could give you a thousand examples, but c'mon, you're educated, you can figure these things out for yourself." He sighs.

"The smartest kid in town?"

"Thomasina, who else? So she fooled you, too." He laughs again. "They did an IQ test on her once, she came out somewhere around Einstein. Not everybody was all that happy."

Tired and worried, I have enough riddles to deal with already; I can't think about Thomasina or who is against her. Or why.

"Tell me about Wolf and Coyote," I ask. I can't believe I actually said that.

"You know, Wolf isn't all that interesting, not to me anyway. Coyote's my man. Even his disasters are funny. Even *my* disasters are funny." He grins crookedly.

"So he's more like us."

"Yeah. See, Wolf sets the world up, real careful, all perfect, rules and all, but who can live that way? Somebody's got to take the rough edges off. I think Coyote's working out how the little man can live. He breaks out of all the rules so he can get by, see what might happen, see if he can get something he wants, anything."

"All he seems to want is food and sex."

"And a little fun out of life. Sometimes it works for him, most times it don't. And he knows that better than anyone. He's his own worst enemy. But he won't give up. He can't—there's bosses and high and mighty people with money and power that just push the little man around. So? That's what I'd like to know—*who's* the trickster?"

I've got an answer at my fingertips for once: last week Professor Murdock sent me a copy of Radin's *The Trickster*, and I've read the whole thing. "The Trickster is a creator and a destroyer, according to a book I have. It says he's a creature who tricks others and is always tricked himself."

"Does anybody ever write about *why* he does what he does? What he's thinking?" Walker demands.

"I don't know. I haven't read anything like that so far."

"Well, someone ought to. They need to get to the bottom of things. Why are these white guys so interested in what Coyote does?"

"I think they're trying to figure out what he *is*. These days, we don't have characters who are gods and not gods, good and bad together, so full of opposites."

"Opposites like what?"

"Well, he teaches people things, but he's a bad example himself; he creates things and smashes them; he's clever and a fool; he can invent things and then he's so immature.... I don't know. He only seems to do good by accident, while he's doing something completely selfish."

"Those ain't opposites," Walker laughs. "I guess there's their first problem right there."

OVER AT THE post office, I find a sweet card from Francis and a letter from my mother, addressed soberly to Prof. Eileen Kane.

Your brother's being challenged for the presidency of the Bosnian Club. And Ronnie "the Crab" Carabbia got convicted for racketeering. A few months ago, it was the other brother, Charlie, for assault. (These were two of the most notoriously dangerous gangsters in Youngstown, both middle-aged.) *Thank God my children never had any doings with the police. I blame their mother.*

Just to be nice, though, I told her Ronnie'd probably beat the rap on appeal.

Love, Ma

CHAPTER TWELVE

Drawing Lessons

"You want to do something about that car," Eddie says.

I'm lounging in the swing on Cyril's porch, reading. Eddie's dropped by with Curly, apparently to throw some rocks. He certainly doesn't have my copy of Driver, which I've begged him to return.

"I couldn't agree more."

"Flames would be nice. I could get some decals."

"Where's my copy of Driver?"

"Dunno. Somewhere. I don't bother with it."

"Oh, sure," Curly says. "You should hear him. He can't shut up about some stupid people up somewhere on the coast. He's read about them in your book, and now he thinks we're just nothing."

"We're boring, boring, boring," Eddie says. "Up there, now, if you're a chief, you need a daughter because you'll have to pass your chief's hat on to her husband. So if you don't have one, you get your son to pretend to marry another guy. That guy becomes your son-in-law, and when he has kids with a wife, one of the kids will become the chief." He conjures the book out of nowhere and gives it to me. I put it behind my chair.

"Up where?"

"On the Northwest Coast. I was half thinking of going up and having a look. They burn stuff—cars and expensive stuff like that, just to show off in front of their neighbors." Then, as usual, his focus changes in a flash. "What kind of job will you get when you finish studying all this crap about us?"

"Probably teaching anthropology." I've already done a little of that, as a teaching assistant.

"Yuck."

"Yuck," Curly repeats, hurling a stone at one of Cyril's chickens.

"Okay," I say. "Tell me this, then. Does magic work? When a man has three wives, are they jealous of each other? Do men wear face make-up anywhere? Why would an Inuit leave his mother to die out on the ice? What if you were accused of a crime and the way they decided if you were guilty was to put your hand in a pot of boiling oil?" Geography with its schist and gneiss, history with its multilateral treaties cannot *begin* to compete with this stuff.

Curly looks to Eddie, expecting that he will know the answers.

"Is that in Driver?" Eddie asks.

"No," I answer. "I guess you'll just have to take my class." I try to shoo them away. I'm behind on everything.

Teaching Anthropology 101 is probably the only job I will get. I *can* be an "applied anthropologist," using what I learn to be of some practical use to people; for example, women are the farmers of Africa, but often agricultural aid and technology is designed for and given to the men, who don't use it. I could work on adapting programs to women farmers' needs. Or I could look at something else that has intrigued me recently: government-subsidized light industry in rural Ireland, created to augment poor farmers' incomes. But the farmers won't work in the factories—why not? I *could* be an applied anthropologist, but anthropology departments aren't encouraging that discipline much yet. Soon, though, with so many of us training, university teaching positions may become scarcer. And now, with all the civil rights issues and the war in Vietnam, anthropologists may get more involved in practical work, and it might lose some of its stigma. But not so far: these days, the message to students is clear, if implicit. If you're any good, you'll get your PhD and enjoy a tenured life in the academy, where you'll teach and write for other anthropologists about the exotic peoples of your field research.

"You know, this isn't a bad book," Eddie picks Driver up again, "but sometimes I wonder if he's writing in English. Lincoln wrote this way, we *still* wouldn't know the slaves were free."

An anthropologist has to pass many tests, just like the princess and the pea. Never show surprise—even if someone consumes his own vomit or uses his daughter as a packhorse, for example. Have an encyclopedic knowledge of objects you'll probably never lay eyes on, like squirrel traps. But mastering the passive voice is one of the most critical *rites de passage*, so I know what Eddie means.

Anthropologists write things like "The newborn child is licked clean by its mother." If we use the active voice, we do it in a Victorian style: "Vanity found rich expression in personal adornment." We festoon our work with equivocating clauses to cover our asses: "While this [information] leaves much to be desired, it seems probable that young couples normally lived with relatives.... This is not meant to imply that there were no exceptions to the rule." Or: "Only men were allowed to drink jimsonweed juice in some locations, but both men and women imbibed the concoction in other regions." Who can argue with that? We're partial to the verb "notes" as in: "As Herskovits notes in his seminal work..." and the adjective "seminal," and we espouse the word "espouse": "Those structural-functionalists who espouse this position..."

"As a matter of fact," I say, "I can write like that. I'm helping an important person write a book." Professor Murdock has asked me to help him in drafting the chapters of his latest project, to be called *North American Indians: From the Eskimo to the Maya*.

Eddie struts around the yard, imitating my voice, "An important person! Gosh!" Curly joins him, jeering.

Cyril comes out. "Get!" he orders, and to me, "You need to do your work."

The boys wander off behind the house, wiggling their hips. I guess that's supposed to look like me, too.

"And stay away from that shed," Cyril calls after them.

This thing with Professor Murdock is both a gift and a curse. The idea is that he'll develop a new, more useful way of regrouping the various Indian tribes into "culture areas," and he'll give me some notes on each area. I'll do the research, picking out a tribe to represent each culture area, and draft the chapters. It doesn't sound too bad until I realize he has identified 23 areas, and each has between six and 40-plus tribes. I'll have to read up on about over 700 different groups. But it's a privilege to be working with him; I know how lucky I am.

To help me develop the correct style, Murdock has provided copies of two of his previous works, *Social Structure* and *Our Primitive Contemporaries*, with instructions to follow them closely. Thus, I've learned to write by studying his words:

It is here postulated that the process noted by Spier as incipient among the Havasupai had actually been completed in pre-Columbian times among the river Yumans, who had presumably adopted agriculture at a considerably earlier date.

Eddie and Curly return from behind the house, hauling some stuff in a sack. Larry's with them. They disappear around the other side of the house, obviously trying to avoid Cyril, who has just left to go to the store.

I need a break. When I'm not talking to Delaney or Jennie or Walker, I'm sorting through photocopied articles for details of North American Indian material culture in the form of objects such as tools, weapons, housing, and clothing. Skin tumplines, poggamoggans, dog travoises, cedar wicki-ups, leisters or fishing spears, candlefish, shredded bark raincapes, mouse skin blankets, buckskin overshoes, greasewood fishhooks, four-pointed bird arrows, pigeon nooses, obsidian lip plugs, filed incisors, grizzly bear neck-laces, rod and slat armor, cattail flag mats, bearskin skirts and the use of warm baby urine for earache—all cycle endlessly in my brain as I sleep. One day recently I walked into Rickett's and leaped back, thinking I'd stepped into a willow hoop squirrel trap, cunningly disguised, as they always are; in fact, it was a raised crack in the linoleum that nearly tripped me up.

Maybel's ironing in the kitchen so I give up my work and go in to give her a hand; she's still a little weak from her stroke, and the heavy iron tires her. She says she's a day behind in her housework, so it must be a Thursday: she irons on a Wednesday; people in Youngstown iron on Tuesday. I'm glad to help, though; I can nearly iron the Grand Canyon, courtesy of my mother, who seems to iron every day.

The clothes are ready in their individual baskets: one for the rolled and dampened boiled-starch whites, another for colors, another for the jeans that have to be ironed under newspapers. Whites have been extra-whitened with *Mrs. Stewarts's Bluing*, which is not the brand my people use, but I don't say anything. I spit on the iron, Maybel nods, and we zip through the work. I pin her few crocheted pieces to the ironing board when we're done. She learned that from me, and from her I learned that you should keep your rolls of dampened clothes in the freezer for a day or so before ironing them.

Refreshed, I decide to go over to the Colony to see if I can find Morgan and get back to the witches. I go out back to get the car.

"Ta da!" Eddie sings, bowing and pointing. Larry has painted interlaced flames through the letters "NEVADA STATE POLICE."

"No decals, so we used paint."

They lope off, slapping each other on the back. My copy of Driver has disappeared again.

LATER THAT EVENING, after a futile search for Morgan, I drive home along Main Street. Paulette flags me down. Francis phoned at 6:00 and will phone again at 7:00. Funny how when Delaney or Paulette answers the public phone, they can always find me. How I long to talk to Francis, tell him how I felt when I left the Tribal Council meeting, how he's the person I wanted to celebrate with.

"Eileen? It's Francis," Francis says about 20 minutes later.

I'm ashamed. "You don't have to tell me who you are."

"Sometimes I wonder. Do you miss me? I'm calling from the Officer's Club. All the guys here think I'm making you up. It does sound pretty ridiculous, you know." He chuckles nervously, but I can hear the scolding undertone. I have to admit that Francis has some really irritating mannerisms.

"Show them the wedding announcement."

"I want to show them *you*. I want to show you off here to Captain Schwartz and the gang," he says. "They're here every night. *And* I want to have a party and show off your cooking. I want you to wear that pink Jackie Kennedy dress."

Aha! He *does* want a Wife. I've been right all along.

I can hear men baying something footballish in the background. "Those are the guys," Francis says, proudly. "I'm involved in a court-martial. I've been appointed to defend this guy who's accused of deserting."

"But you aren't a lawyer."

"That isn't the way it works. You get appointed and you do your best for the guy. It's a lot of work but I feel honored to be asked and …."

I spot Morgan and try to keep track of him while still listening to my husband. I wind the phone cord around and around my index finger until it turns white, then let it spring open. A surge of blood burns.

"Anyhow, when the trial is over and I have more time, I think you'd like it here," Francis says. "It's nice and modern except for the photography section of the signal school; that's still an old-fashioned two-storey barracks…"

Damn! Morgan disappears. It may take days to find him again.

"And we have a nice company of WACS," Francis goes on, as if he were throwing down a glove. "Secretaries, assistants." His way of saying he might find other company if I don't come to live with him?

"Huh."

"They come in to the Officer's Club, too—just their officers. Some cute ones."

"Are you drinking?" I demand.

"Sure I'm drinking," he says. "I'm in the Officer's Club."

"Wait a minute." I cover the mouthpiece with my hand and call to Doreen who's just parked her flatbed in front of my car. "Can you see where Morgan's going?"

"Who are you talking to?" Francis complains. "I'm calling long distance. I want to know what you do all day. I'm trying to picture it. Today, for example?"

"Today I spent a good part of the day ironing."

"I mean seriously."

"I'll write you a good long letter tonight, Francis. I really do miss you. It's just the sooner I get this done, the sooner...."

"Yeah. So we can have some time for *us*."

We listen to each other breathing. We're so far apart, it's hard to remember when we were close. That *"us"* sounds strange to me now.

There's Morgan! If I run right now, I'll catch him.

THE NEXT MORNING, I'm back at the church.

"These girls gotta learn something useful, something to hold their interest." Reverend Parks is still dissatisfied with the little band of teenaged girls. He watches Thomasina and Charlene kick the guts of a baby buggy around the scorched churchyard. "You know, that school system up at Stewart was cruel, but they did teach them some skills."

"Morgan learned shoemaking." He told me all about this after I caught him on Main Street last night.

"Yeah. Well. Morgan."

"I heard the kids didn't come home for years from Stewart."

"Most of them were allowed home in the summer for a few weeks or so, but I don't know how easy it was." Reverend Parks's eyes mist up. He's a little like my father that way. "Everybody here between 35 and 60 went there, but I don't know how much they want to talk about it."

"Don't ever mention things like orphans or children in iron lungs to him," Mrs. Parks warned me a few days back when the Reverend was away and she could venture out without fear of being dragooned into the *kah' nii* work. "Or little kids without gloves, homeless pets, or starving children," she added. Mrs. Parks is such a big woman, she can probably carry the Reverend under her arm, but her tone made me wonder if she too might welcome some tender concern from him and whether she ever gets it.

"You could teach them some little thing, couldn't you?" Reverend Parks asks.

I taught 60 Catholic sixth-graders for a couple of years back in Ohio, when I was 19 and a lot more patient.

"Just some poetry or songs or something?"

The only song I can remember is "Old Zip Coon,"– too racist to sing to anyone here or anywhere for that matter. One of the few poems I recall opens with the lines "Where we go to school each day/Indian children used to play," which is pointlessly obvious in this setting.

"Or maybe drawing? I see you drawing those hats in your notes." He points to my sketches of the stone bowls in the nearby desert.

In the end I agree to teach cartooning.

My pupils are members of the Missionettes and Junior Missionettes, aged seven to 16, who have joint meetings over the summer because so many members are either away visiting relatives or helping their mothers pick garlic out on the farms.

"There'll be a prayer, then a business meeting, then the drawing lesson," Mrs. Parks explains when she greets me at the church door. "Will you run out to the Ranch and pick up the Williamsons?"

Roberta Williamson, Doreen's daughter, is the president of the Missionettes. Fortunately—since I saw Thomasina put sand into the bus's gas tank the other day—I don't have to go. Doreen shows up in the flatbed with Roberta and baby Clarence strapped into a cradleboard. Lying in the bed of the truck, as usual, is Archie.

Archie rolls off and stretches himself out on the unshaded dirt of the churchyard.

"Lord's sake," Doreen nags him, "will you stop disgracing me and come in? We won't be *praying* or anything."

Archie ignores his niece, struggles to his feet, and hobbles off in the direction of Jennie's house.

Ten girls wrangle and wrestle; little Marion Jackson is using the altar rail, or what I take to be the altar rail, as a hurdle, improving her clearance with each leap. Mrs. Parks doesn't notice; she asks the girls to settle down and calls the meeting to order.

"Sister Parks, when are we going to take our trip to Reno?" Charlene pipes up.

"You can ask your question during the business meeting, Charlene."

"But we want to know *now*," Charlene whines.

"Ask it during the business meeting. Roberta will now get us started by reciting the Pledge. Get up here, Roberta. Come on now."

Roberta climbs into the pulpit and puts her hand over her heart. "We are privileged to be children of God. We promise to serve the family, the church, and the nation." She tries to lead the others in repeating the Slogan ("We care") and the Motto ("Because We Care, We Serve)."

Two girls shoot paper wads at Roberta, and a guest, brought by Marion, tears covers off the hymn books. The rest coo to Clarence in his cradleboard. The only people reciting the Pledge, the Slogan, and the Motto are Mrs. Parks, Doreen, and me.

Next, Mrs. Parks offers a prayer and then plays a hymn on the organ; this time only Doreen joins in, since I don't know the words and Roberta is firing back at the shooters.

"Okay, we'll have the business meeting now. Charlene, do you have a question?"

"No."

"Reno?" Mrs. Parks prompts.

Charlene looks at her as though she were demented.

"The Secretary will read the Minutes," Mrs. Parks snaps.

Charlene steps forward and reads what she can of her own writing, which is very little.

"Where are the rest of the minutes?" Mrs. Parks demands.

"No idea," Charlene thumps herself down.

"Well," Mrs. Parks says. "Marion, why don't you introduce the guest you've brought with you?" She nods at the hymn book ripper.

Marion says nothing.

"You can just stand up and tell us her name."

"No."

The girl herself refuses to give her name, so we move on.

"Let's close with a reading from Revelations," Mrs. Parks suggests gaily. "Charlene, note down some points from the reading."

Everyone turns around in the pews to watch Charlene write; only the mystery guest listens. The meeting closes, we move to the back of the church where a long table is set up with paper, pencils, chalk, and a small blackboard. I outline the basics of drawing cartoon faces—angry, surprised, babyish, old—but only the two women pay attention. The rest set to drawing whatever they like.

"A house doesn't look like that," Charlene says to the guest, who is drawing what looks like one of my stone bowls. "Does it, Eileen?"

"It could," I say, ever the neutral observer.

"What would she know?" Marion asks.

"Draw us a picture of your house, Eileen."

"Maybe next time we'll do houses; today we're drawing faces."

"Come on, show us what your house looks like," a few of them beg.

I show them a photograph of my family standing in front of our house, a picture I've started carrying in my notebook. I miss them.

They pass it around, quietly, one or two glancing at me and back at the picture a couple of times. My family's two-storey house is modest, but perhaps it seems like a mansion to these girls. Have I been insensitive in showing them where I come from? Will they resent me?

Eventually, I get them to draw faces.

When I look at their drawings, it's my turn to be shocked. They've followed all the rules I taught for drawing baby-like cartoon faces—the proportions of upper to lower face, the placement of eyes, how to change expressions, etc., and yet....

"*Your* faces look like *you*," Charlene explains, comparing her own drawing to the ones I drew on the board. Mine look like kewpie dolls or the faces on baby Disney animals. Their faces look like Indians: rounder, straighter eyebrows, less exuberant smiles. There's some variation: while the younger girls and the darker-skinned older girls have drawn baby Indian faces like Clarence's, who's perched in his cradleboard at the head of the table, the lighter-skinned older girls have drawn pictures like mine, which I now realize are "white." Thomasina, though, has ignored every instruction; she's clearly an artist in the making and can draw anything she sees, including Mrs. Parks from behind.

It was hard to tell, but I think the girls liked the lesson until I find a note in Charlene's tortured handwriting: "I HATE TO DRA."

Class ends. Archie returns to the truck, and Clarence is passed around one last time to be admired. I can hear the girls muttering.

"Did you see her *family* in the photos? Did you see them, Marion? Could you believe it?"

"No!" Marion said. "They're *white*."

"Yeah. I didn't think they'd be white."

"*She's* white."

"Yeah, but still."

CHAPTER THIRTEEN

Kinship Patterns

ABOUT SIX WEEKS into my fieldwork now, and I've finally figured out why I've felt queasy since I arrived. I hate turning up on the reservation every morning and grilling people. I hate the anthropologist's desperate neediness, cloaked as it is in friendship.

I like the people—who wouldn't? But in this field you have to make friends with people to get information, and you often make enemies by publishing it. Who else works this way? Spies, for one. The safest way not to make enemies is to work with people who can never read what you write. That might have worked in the past, but it doesn't now.

I'm getting a university grade for a fieldwork course. I'm learning, developing, working toward experience and self-fulfillment. The Paiute people get nothing. Most of them live in substandard houses, are underemployed, underpaid, with poor health care, no security in old age, and little respect from their white neighbors. Yet, they're generous, decent people, like a lot of the people I know at home.

What use will my material be to them? A Paiute citizen's existence is barely recorded; from my time in the library I know their births and deaths don't even appear in the local paper. The University of Nevada will hold my notes, which are not to be used without my permission. I'll write a report, but who will read it except other anthropologists? Some aspects of the Paiutes' traditional way of life won't pass unnoticed, but their current way of life—the one they live now—is not of any great interest to anyone else at the moment. And certainly nothing I am capable of writing or doing will help.

This isn't Culture Shock. The only thing that has shocked me so far is myself—my relentless pursuit of people to help me, ignoring things that don't immediately concern me, evaluating people too much in terms of their utility. Are the other trainees like this?

Something else that's bothering me, now that my work has become a little more manageable, is my carelessness about Francis. Why don't I phone him instead of making him ask strangers to track me all over town? At night he's in a barracks or, more often now, in the Officer's Club, but whoever answers the phone there just has to yell to bring him running.

I'm looking forward to seeing him when he flies out to join me in Reno after I've finished writing up my notes. But then what? What do other people feel after they get married? Maybe this is what "settling down" means—you just get comfortable, God forbid?

I look at what I've just written down—another reference to the Almighty. I have to police my writings for religious references. I can't be an atheist and use the other side's facilities as often as I do to express myself. It's not fair.

SOME FAMILIES ARE cursed by fire, floods, tornadoes, but in mine, it's just dog pee. Furniture, rugs, photographs: our leaky spaniel spares nothing. So it's nice to see the newly restored photos my mother sent this morning. I take them over to Jennie's; she, Maybel, and I are going to the neighboring town of Shurz, where both of them have sisters.

Thomasina is lounging on the top step when I arrive. "I'm going, too. Maybel's still over at Paulette's, getting some pine nut ice cream for her sister."

I pull out a picture, one of my grandmother at her wedding in 1905. Jennie reaches for it, smiling.

"They're white," Thomasina warns. Jennie shoots her That Look. Despite my mother being white, she and Jennie are a lot alike.

In the picture are four women – two younger, two older – and two men. They're formally posed, the men in dark suits, the women in long white dresses, pigeon-breasted in their corsets and cinched at the waist with wide embroidered sashes. All six wear Edwardian high collars, with sumptuous, pomaded hair. They're posed before a photographer's painted backdrop of ruined columns—Rome? Athens? Certainly a place they'll never see.

"Who are they?" Thomasina points to the seated couple.

"My grandmother and her husband."

Maybe Thomasina will think this is what all Irish-Americans call their grandfathers—"my grandmother's husband." But only my family has that tradition.

One of the older women, the bride's mother, had already lost her husband to the mill; my great-grandfather was killed by a shifter, a small mill train, in 1904. "His body was horribly mangled," the *Vindicator* reported. The groom's mother had also lost her husband, in her case to the St. Louis World Fair a year earlier, which he attended and then kept going. The bride's sister, matron of honor rather than bridesmaid, was abandoned the day after her shotgun wedding, and the bride herself would be deserted in a few years. One of the men, the best man, was soon to be blinded in the mill. The other man, the deserter-to-be, was my grandfather. Men disappeared. "All they ever found was his bicycle" or "Years later, a woman calling herself his wife, if you please, turned up."

I explain this to Thomasina.

"They all do that," she states.

"Who? The Irish? Or all men?"

"Yes," she said.

No one contradicts her. I smooth out the letter that came wrapped around the photos.

Dear Eileen,

Glad to see the photos of the reservation you sent us, and I'm enclosing a few from here—my mother and her husband. Look at the hair-dos on them!

Who's that man with you in the pictures you sent? Why have you got your arms around him? You need to be careful out there. (The man is Archie Jim, and in the photo I'm propping him upright for the camera, his legs dangling, a long-legged wispy puppet.)

Dad got laid off again. It seems like just when you get a little bit ahead, it's all gone again. You know, you could live if they'd let you. Your Aunt Mary is helping with the electric bill, and Ma and old Aunt Kate are coming to give me a hand with the fruit canning.

"You could live if they'd let you." I heard that often at home. "What's that in Irish?" I asked my grandmother once, thinking it was an expression she'd brought over with her on the boat.

"*Nil a fhios agam,*" she replied. *I don't know.* "It's from some other people's language."

The "other people" were the Jewish family, the Camens, who owned our corner grocery. They stood by us and our neighbors in bad times, letting our bills run up until after the men went back to work. "Worries go better with soup than without," Mr. Camens always said.

Who wouldn't let you live? The mill owners, the local and mill police, even the National Guard at times, especially during strikes when their harassment escalated from using massive quantities of riot gas to beating and sometimes killing workers and union supporters.

My memories are interrupted by Maybel, who arrives with two pots of ice cream in a bag of ice, one for her sister and one for Jennie.

We settle into the car and head towards Schurz. Eddie waves us down on Main Street and hops in; he has to "see a man" there. He looks odd in the car. It's too prosaic a setting for such a feral spirit, a little like Coyote in a bonnet.

I keep thinking about my mother's letter, about her reference to how her sisters are helping her. "Do your sisters help you when times are bad?" I ask.

"I help *them*." Maybel reflected a moment, waving away an offer from Eddie to hold the ice cream. "But yes, sisters and cousin-sisters try to help each other. When Cyril was away in the army and I broke my arm, my sisters took me and the baby with them to Schurz."

"So sisters and cousin-sisters? Did people help like that in the old days, too?"

"Not so much," Jennie joins in. "Because we moved around in little groups, maybe just mother and father and kids. Never enough food in one place for a bigger group. It was how we survived. "

Working-class Irish-Americans in Youngstown survive by grouping, not separating. Women trust that their mothers, aunts, sisters, and sisters-in-law will help them survive mill layoffs, strikes, and work injuries. My mother's family are typical Irish-Americans. Her mother, her two sisters, and several great-aunts are a domestic production unit. My mother does laundry for her employed sister, Ellen, who in return contributes toward the cost of my younger siblings' school uniforms or Easter outfits. Her widowed aunt helps with the spring cleaning; her mother gives her furniture and rugs from her spare rooms. An invalid sister, Anne, who lives close to the primary school, makes lunch each day for the other sisters' youngest children, who can't make the long trip home and back at midday. In the afternoon, Anne types invoices for the *Vindicator*, a job Ellen, who works at the newspaper, arranged for her. She also irons Ellen's laundry. My mother, the only one who drives and the best at interpreting medically reserved language, takes them all to doctor's appointments and helps them for days afterward through endless rehashings of what the doctor said.

This "sister" pattern may be more common among Irish-Americans because of Irish male land inheritance customs and a belief in good education for women. Women were often the first to emigrate from Ireland to the U.S.; they weren't sent-for brides but an independent vanguard who used their wages to send for their siblings. Sisters often worked together: my grandmother and her two sisters are listed in the 1900 census as living in the same boarding house and working for the same employer as servants. They lived near or with each other for the rest of their lives, married or not.

"You don't want to turn here," Jennie says. I nod absently, my mind still busy with thoughts of kinship patterns in Youngstown.

Husbands were absorbed into these units, at a slight remove from their own kin; what they needed most were the trusted close-knit group of work-mates to help them survive the molten iron, the rollers, the hot ladle car, the 3,000-degree roaring and spitting steel. One unlucky move and a man was dead; a woman still faced a lifetime of piecing together meals, clothes, a respectable house from shared scraps. So women tried to live near female relatives. On my street, families in 10 of the 24 houses were related; on the next, a string of six houses, side-by-side, held families whose women were related by blood. I asked my father once if he minded living among all my mother's sisters and aunts. "No," he said, baffled. And then added, "You know, it's them that lets the men be men. How else could we go out on strike when we have to? We couldn't."

Sisters living near and helping each other was not just an Irish-American custom—my classmates Marietta Agostino and Frances Voinovich lived in little family enclaves too. I haven't thought of Marietta in years; all I can remember now are her pink poodle barrettes.

"I had pink poodle barrettes once, too," Thomasina says.

Dear God! Have I been thinking out loud? Maybel is staring at me. Eddie, cackling, is pretending to write in a notebook. I turn back to the road, my mind drifting again.

Some other ethnic groups have different residence priorities, though, such as organizing themselves around their church. Associations such as the Greeks' Kalymnian and Philoptochochos Societies, and pastors of the Ukrainian, Slovak, and Lebanese Maronite churches provide social assistance, especially to lost new immigrants, who find comfort at Holy Trinity in the city center or at St. Maron's on the east side. Greek children attend "Greek school" in the late afternoons to learn the language, so being close to a church, such as Archangel Michael in Campbell, where the classes are held, is important.

Even so, few neighborhoods in Youngstown were ever single-ethnic, except some black communities. Two generations earlier, my Irish-speaking grandmother shared the Westlake Crossing neighborhood with the young Yiddish-speaking Warner brothers (who became the Warner Brothers of movie fame), as well as with Germans, English, and some black people. Within little more than a lifetime, though, most of the earlier residents left the Crossing entirely to blacks. The Italians in Smokey Hollow went too, everyone moving from the mill-side streets to the boxy suburbs, away from the European craftsmanship of their old homes to lower-quality, black-free housing developments. Slovaks, Swedes, Croatians, English lived side by side, perhaps not marrying each other but exchanging recipes. Irish women learned to make kolache and kolbassi, the English made Swedish meatballs, the Slovaks ate capicola; no one borrowed the Irish or English dishes.

"I don't know where we are, now," Jennie says to Maybel, jolting me out of my reverie. "I've never seen this."

"She's thinking about Francis," Thomasina jeers. "You need to go back to where you turned. Back there where they told you not to."

I go back.

So. Eventually, black people moved from the mill-side streets, too, to our old streets, areas west of Hillman Avenue, previously embargoed by realtors and banks. That's what it's like now. The downtown neighborhoods have drifted into decay, and the suburbs smooth out ethnic distinctions, so that the feast day of Saints Cyril and Methodius is forgotten, as is sauerkraut on New Year's Day. Roman noses are straightened, Hungarians are blonde, and everyone talks of their common festival, Turkey Day.

We finally arrive in Shurz with the ice cream almost perfect, the sisters delighted to see each other. "I thought you'd be here ages ago," Jennie's sister says. "I was out on the road worried, looking."

We discuss Maybel's stroke, and then they tell me stories: how Coyote retrieved the pine nut from the wicked eastern tribes after they'd stolen it, distracting them with a hand game while Mouse squirreled the nut away; how cottontail killed Coyote. "But this is not the end," Jennie says, hugging her sister as we get up to go.

Maybel's sister stands in the road watching until we're out of sight. Maybel keeps looking back. "We never know at this age if we'll see each other again," she sighs.

Later that evening, I see Thomasina in front of the drugstore, hanging out with some kids, who look familiar, and Larry. I think I gave some of those kids a lift to a baseball game a few days ago, before I picked up Maybel for our supper at Rickett's. Now, Thomasina signals them to stay behind and crosses over to meet me. "I have a sister, too," she says. "Wilmalee. She's six."

"I know. Remember you put her on the chart I drew?"

"I love my sister more than anything. Anybody ever hurt her, I'd kill them."

CHAPTER FOURTEEN

Game Playing

"OFFICER WICKHAM SAYS you owe him a statement, down at the station," Cyril looks worried, of course.

Now what? I hoped Wickham had decided I wasn't involved in whatever happened. I haven't looked for my notes from the day the elderly Indian died. I rummage though my file boxes, can't find anything for that day. They have to be in here somewhere, because I always lock my files. My paperwork is breeding under the bed: field notebooks, typed notes, carbon copies, journal, diary, census, maps, genealogies, kinship charts, photographs, budget, newspaper cuttings, notes from my mother, letters from Francis, Professor Murdock's work...

I drive over to Wickham's office. Larry begs a ride into town; he's been helping Cyril take his Army photos out of an old mouse-eaten album and stick them, in little corner brackets, into a new one. Maybe I'm more vigilant, but it seems to me he's around even more than before, listening in, digging out folklore to present to me, teasing out connections for my genealogies. It makes me nervous. I rarely go to Rickett's Diner anymore, even though I'm desperate for green beans and mashed potatoes. When I do venture in, Reenie ignores me; Mr. Rickett waits on me himself. Once Wickham was there, talking loudly about how a military education might bring even the worst kid around.

I hope no one notices us and tells his mother that Larry is hanging around with me—a military school, almost a reform school, will kill his soul. Certainly no Paiute will tell anyone outside, and no other whites come onto the reservations, but now we're driving into town, in my very distinctive car. I make sure he gets out before we reach the station.

"I might see you over at the Colony later," he says.

"If I don't get there, send someone over here to spring me." I mean it as a joke, but he straightens his shoulders and gives me a thumbs up.

Wickham is outside, his bulk spilling out over a plastic chair in front of the station. If he's seen Larry, he says nothing, focusing instead on the flames painted on the sides of my car.

"I don't think I can tell you anything," I say, trying to sound apologetic. "I don't have any notes for that day."

"You know," he stands up, more than twice my width but only a little taller, "I could subpoena your notes. I could also get you for defacing State property." He kicks the chair over and goes inside.

LARRY IS IN the Colony with a few other boys when I arrive.

"Okay?" he asks.

"Yeah," I answer, "but he really doesn't like me."

"Me, neither."

"What has he got against you?" I don't really need to ask: Larry hangs around with the Paiutes and with me.

He says nothing. He turns back to his friends. He's learned a traditional hockey game from an old man, and he's throwing a deerskin ball at Curly and the other boys.

"You missed some of the rules, Larry," Eddie laughs, surveying the group from under the shade of Jennie's tree. "What you're doing now, it's impossible for either side to win." They take his word for it and start using sticks to play golf. If Eddie were playing, he would not only have assessed the situation instantly but also invented some rules to make it impossible for any but his own side to win.

But Eddie is in the shade, playing barbut with Thomasina, little Wilmalee, and his tiny brother, George. Barbut is a Turkish dice game that, more recently, has become a favorite of the Youngstown Mafia, who run barbut rings. If, some day, another anthropologist writes an article on "Similarities and Differences between Turkish Barbut and a Traditional Paiute Dice Game," it will be my fault, because I've taught Eddie to play it.

Exchanging information with Eddie on games is only courteous; after all, he taught me some Paiute mole-pelt magic used in hand games, which he got from Delaney. It's pathetic, he claims, and used only by suckers. But I'm trying to build rapport, be participatory, and see myself as a partner in the process rather than as a high and mighty interrogator. Maybe some of the people who introduced smallpox to defenseless populations felt the same way, imagining they were just mingling and being sociable.

The problem is that Eddie doesn't see himself as an honorary anthropologist, nor does he view our exchange as a professional courtesy. He believes that he's a world-class croupier and has set up barbut rings all over the Colony, with plans to extend to the Ranch. He's the "house" and watches while other players bet against each other. The house doesn't gamble; it only provides the facilities (a patch of dirt in the shade) and handles the dice. In exchange it takes a good percentage of the winnings, and the younger and more mathematically challenged the player, the higher the percentage it claims. The players discover soon enough that they, too, can offer similar facilities and roll dice, just as people in Youngstown have, but of course anyone in Youngstown foolish enough to act on this discovery is now dead. Only the Mafia can be the house. Eddie doesn't seem to me to be a killer, and I haven't told him anything about car-bombing, so his power at the moment comes from the fact that he's the only one who has some dice.

"The winner!" he crows, raising George's arm triumphantly. "Gimme $2.00, please."

"But I only won $2.00," George protests, handing it over.

Eddie ignores his brother and pockets the money. Maybe family means nothing to the serious gambler?

Larry brings me a miserable scrap of gray kitten he found huddled by the porch. He shields it from Curly, who reaches for a rock. Curly hates cats, I don't know why.

Delaney appears with a wadded rag pressed to his face. "Archie just pulled a tooth for me with a pliers." He rubs his swollen jaw. "Here, you, pass me that cat."

Larry, horrified, clutches the dirty kitten.

"Let him see the cat, stupid," Eddie orders. "He's not gonna eat it or nothin'."

"He's gonna bite its ear," Larry whimpers. "He's got a toothache, look at his face. You're gonna bite its ear, aren't you?"

"Ooh," Eddie mocks, snatching the cat and tossing it to Delaney. "Big bad man's gonna bite your ear!"

Delaney bites the cat's ear. It squeals, wriggles out of his grasp. Larry scoops it up and races off. Eddie recoils.

"You boys don't know nothin' about your own culture," Delaney complains. "Only cure for a toothache." He spits out a little blood. "Mine," he assures us.

"You want to be an Indian doctor," Delaney addresses Eddie, who's counting what looks like about $20.00 in singles, "you gotta go over to the big rock at MacLeod Hill and no matter how scared you are, you have to stay there all night and listen to everything. What you hear will tell you about your power, and you'll get something to help you with your power. It might be a feather or water or tobacco or something."

"So far, it's dice," Curly says.

"'F I want to be a doctor," Eddie says, "I'll go to medical school."

"*We* had dice in the old days," Delaney retorts. "Paiute dice."

Eddie perks up.

"We had sticks with a mark on one side and we tossed them on a skin and bet on whether they'd land on the painted side."

The sheer primitiveness of this stuns the boys.

"And we had hand games, too. We had teams, and each team hid bones in their hand, and the other had to guess who had the bone and which hand." Delaney sits back, beaming. "Hand games come up a lot in our stories. I remember...."

"Somehow, I feel a Wolf and Coyote tale coming on," Eddie sighs. "So, c'mon, tell us about how Coyote used to carry his thing around in a heavy basket."

"What thing?" Curly asks. "What basket?"

Great. Now I'll find out if the Paiutes have lore about Coyote carrying his huge penis in a basket, a common tale in some other cultures. More likely, Eddie found this story in Driver or Radin's *The Trickster* or one of my other books he's always leafing through. If so, some future anthropologist will waste a lot of time trying to find a lost connection between the Paiutes and, say, the Shuswap of British Columbia.

"Matterafact, I was thinking I'd tell you about a very brave girl over near Bridgeport who got into trouble."

"What kind of trouble?" Eddie is interested again.

"Well, a giant cannibal killed her baby and stuck it in his belt. Later, when he got hungry, he ripped it up and ate it."

"I call that trouble, all right," Curly says.

"It was because she was a good girl. She was brave and always thought of other people," Delaney continues. "She heard the giant *Cánabo!* coming and tried to warn the men in her house, but they were playing a game and just laughed. And they threw her and the baby outside."

"And?"

"She hid but *Cánaho!* killed the men and left them like statues in position in the game. She ran away, but while she was getting food, *Cánaho!* stole the baby and killed it. So she went to the ocean and met up with *Cánaho!'s* mother. The mother said she'd kill *Cánaho!*."

"I knew it!" Larry has crept back, minus the cat. He has a fearful respect for mothers.

"She boiled up a lot of Indian blood and put sharp arrowheads in it. *Cánaho!* got some wings, and when he flew to the ocean, his mother gave him the drink. After a while it killed him, and the girl and his mother cut off his wings."

Larry wraps his arms over his bony shoulders.

"All the Paiute land became covered with water. Then she made a boat and paddled to Europe, to an island, where she met European Wolf."

"I knew Wolf and Coyote would get in here, somehow," Eddie says.

"No, no Coyote, only Wolf. This one was bigger than our Wolf. She sat outside his house, and he began to cook, and kept saying, 'Whoever is outside, come in and eat.' Finally, she did. Then they slept, each on one side of a door, and each night they moved their beds closer together. Finally, one night, they ... got married."

Delaney gropes for "got married." I assume this reticence is for my benefit.

"They had four children, two boys and two girls, and they married each other. The couples fought, so one pair came here, to the Walker River, and their children became our ancestors. The other pair went to the north and their children are our enemies, the Sáiʔi."

"See," Eddie says to Larry, "U.S.A. I told you that's how you whites got started here."

"Sáiʔi, stupid. Your traditional enemies."

"S'what I said," Eddie says, eyeing me.

I VISIT WALKER, WHO'S still in jail. He looks different, deflated, small, neither the handsome cowboy nor the dark, coiled storyteller, just an unremarkable scrap of a man.

"I can't talk to you about Jack Wilson anymore, Hotshot," he says.

"But you've been helping me so much..." Every time I ask Walker, I have a clearer and more complex picture of Jack Wilson.

"Yeah, but. . . .," he sighs, looks away.

"Someone asked you not to?"

"Yeah. And I said okay. No point in talking about it, it's not a big deal, that person ain't got much, maybe thinks they'll get paid a little something, but later I got to thinking, who has a better right than me? But I said I wouldn't, so … ah, Walker, Walker, Walker." He spits into the corner.

"Might as well tell you the story of *Paizó?o*," he continues. "He was a cannibal like *Cánaho!*, but he was ours. *Cánaho!* lived over in Bridgeport, so I suppose we needed our own cannibal, had to keep up with the Joneses. You hear this one before?" he looks at my closed notebook.

"Sorry." I'm still disappointed.

"You know what?" he suggests. "*You* tell *me* a story for a change. Cheer me up. Got any cannibal stories?"

"No."

"Monsters?"

"Well, I have a monster story my grandmother used to tell me."

"She isn't a Paiute, though?"

"No, she's from Ireland."

"Well, c'mon, tell me the story."

"You know, I never heard it in English. It's in Irish, about a *dearg diabhal*, a red devil. I could translate it, maybe, and tell you some other time. My grandmother showed me one once when I was little."

Walker sits up. "What did he look like?"

"He was green, with long legs and wings, and he came walking up to our house one day. . . ."

Walker nods. A green red devil is not a problem for him.

"How big?"

"Not very." In fact, now that I'm older, it occurs to me the "devil" may have been a praying mantis. But in the story, he's colossal.

"You could tell me in Irish now and give me the translation tomorrow when we got more time."

So I begin. "*Fado, fado—*"

"What's that mean?'

"Long, long ago. . ."

"Oh, yeah, same as Paiute."

By the time I finish the story, Walker is nodding, dreamy. "That was real nice. I could almost see it. That what they talk in Ohio?"

"No. Not even much in Ireland any more. My grandmother speaks it, and I grew up next door, so I learned some Irish. *Beagán.* A little. But the language is dying out."

"Ours, too," he says. "Know what? I'll tell you the story of *Paizó?o* in Paiute. I know it in Washo, too, but my Washo ain't as good, you'd miss too much." He curls into himself and begins. I can almost feel *Paizó?o's* malevolence, even if most of the individual words mean nothing to me.

"You getting on good over there at Cyril's?" he asks, once the story is over.

"Yes, great. I went out there because Cyril thought I should—"

"Coyote found you at that garage, he'll find you at Cyril's, too."

I don't like the sound of that. "Why would a coyote want me?"

"You're on the edge. Coyote goes for the edge, sees what he can get up to."

"Edge of what?"

"Well, you're on an edge between your people and my people right now. And between being single and being married—you just got married, but now you're here alone. And you know Coyote likes the ladies."

I like the sound of that even less, and we sit in silence for a little while.

"Got any more stories?" he asks.

"Well, I sent my mother some Coyote stories about two weeks ago..."

"Your mother?"

This is hard to explain. My mother is not just the demure scold she sometimes seems to be. In fact, like Coyote, she has a number of opposing characteristics. She's a prim matron with a barely suppressed risqué sense of humor. Perhaps, as I've learned from Walker, these tendencies are not opposites. When I sent her some Coyote stories, she immediately sent back a batch of Irish stories about the *Púca*, Coyote's Irish cousin. "Just so they'll know," she wrote, "we have traditions, too." But *Púca* certainly has less sex, or else she cleaned that part up.

"I only sent nice Coyote stories," I lie, although I *had* excluded the one about Coyote hauling his penis around in a basket and also the one where he penetrates his mother-in-law while she has her head stuck in a rabbit hole.

"I'll tell you one nice one she sent back. When her mother was a little girl, she was bringing a cake of bread to her grandfather's house when she met him on the road. He told her to give him the cake and said he'd be home soon. She went on and when she got to his house, she learned he'd been dead for hours. Everyone told her it was the *Púca*. He can take any form, even human."

Walker nods again. I tell him a couple more, *Púca* and the fairies, *Púca* and the *bean sídhe*—the banshee.

"You know what?" he says as I pack up my notebooks. "I did say I couldn't talk to you about Jack Wilson, but there's nothing to stop me telling someone else, and *they* can tell you." He stretches up and out and looks like himself again.

A LETTER COMES FROM my father. I've never seen his handwriting before; it's a beautiful copperplate.

Dear Eileen,

How's the work going? Thanks for the birthday card and the cowboy handkerchiefs. Your mother's got me a gift of some new steel-toed work boots and a fancy wrench. Not much use right now, I'm laid off, but all your aunts are here, helping, putting up enough zucchini to feed the Russian Army. I said I hope that's where it's going. They threatened to send some out to the Indians, so beware. Anyhow, we're going to be okay, because a couple of us guys got a job converting a lady's cellar, so don't worry.

Arthur L. Kane

CHAPTER FIFTEEN

Two-Thirds of the Way

IN BED, PICKING fluff off the blanket. Eleven p.m.

One of my Pittsburgh professors told me a secret a few months ago. It's common knowledge, he said, that many anthropologists have a breakdown, usually temporary, about two-thirds or three-quarters of the way through their fieldwork, whatever its length. The excitement and certainty wear off, they begin to understand how complicated things really are, and they see how little they know. They're more convinced than ever that people are hiding things from them.

I'm about two-thirds of the way through my fieldwork period, and this is the day I can't take it anymore. I've fallen pretty badly behind in transcribing my notes, and I've started mixing up what I'm learning from the Paiutes with the material I'm reading for Professor Murdock's book. One night I dreamed of filing and misfiling my notes and passing them out as handkerchiefs on Main Street. A comment in Driver's book circulates in other dreams: "Fortunately, the fundamental construction of the moccasin falls into two major types." Why fortunately? For whom? And where *is* Driver's book? I dream Eddie and Curly are behind the house, painting flames on its pages.

Most of my dreams are a mixture of ethnographic trivia—split-sinew sewing thread, agave wine, single-note whistles—and Francis. I dream again, as I had before the wedding, that Francis is standing at the back of the church as I walk down the aisle with someone else. He's so forlorn, standing there in a squirrel-skin outfit. Then I dream that while I'm sitting in Rickett's eating pine nuts, he rides in on a black horse and demands that I come home with him. I pretend to be someone else.

I'm not sleeping well.

Over and over I review my notes, recalling the words I typed that day and how useless they seem. That's probably because some of them are. Some of the Paiute folk tales I've been so carefully recording, cross-filing, and index-ing are being supplied by my mother. I know what this sounds like—as if

I'm one of those people who claim they're receiving the local radio station through their dental work. But it's true.

For instance, I'm taking down more Coyote stories from Delaney. Some are very familiar. Have I already heard them from Archie or Paulette? Read them in the articles I'm reading for Professor Murdock?

"Last one today," Delaney says. "Now, Coyote can take any shape—horses, birds, children, old people, anything. One woman, her old mother saw this when she was a child. Her grandfather died, and she didn't know about it, and when she was going to see him, she met him on the road. She was carrying food and he took it from her. When she got to his house, her people knew right away it was..."

"... the *Púca*," I say.

"... Coyote," he finishes.

"Who told you that story?" I ask.

"Walker, I believe. Yeah, when I went over to the jail to see how he was doing."

"Walker heard that story from me. The old woman is my grandmother."

"Oh, I don't think so." Delaney studies me curiously. "Way I heard it, it was Walker's grandmother. Her father died from being witched."

Coyote helps us to think about things. If that story helps Walker, fine. But evidently the barbut game won't be my only contribution to the Paiutes. What next? Leprechauns? Fairy forts?

"You're wearing yourself out." Delaney shuts my notebook gently.

When I finally manage to get to sleep, I'm wakened early, to find Cyril tapping on my door with a message from town that my mother has phoned and will call again in half an hour. It's important.

I rush into town, exhausted. I don't care if I look professional, or intimidating, or even fully dressed. I double-park beside the phone booth. My grandmother *is* old, after all, and anything can happen.

"Who?" I demand when my mother calls.

"Patrick. He's just got re-elected President of the Bosnian Club," my mother announces in a Cleveland accent. She'd been to Cleveland for the day about 10 years ago and her accent has never been the same since, especially when she's recounting something momentous.

Eddie comes out of the casino and bangs on the phone booth door.

"Even though he's only a Class B Member," she continues. "He isn't Bosnian."

"I *know*, Ma. Do Class A Members have special privileges, or what?"

"Well," she lowers her voice so discreetly I have to strain to hear her. I wish I had some stories about Coyote throttling his mother that I could send her. But she would only write back that *Púca* wouldn't dream of doing such a thing. Of course Coyote didn't have an Irish mother.

"Patrick says Class A Members have the right of way into the men's room. I don't know what all that entails."

Thud! Eddie's next bang shakes the phone booth.

"But Patrick says they never abuse it. 'After you,' they always say."

"Ma... Haven't you got any manners?" I scream, opening the door. "And don't you have to be older to get into the casino?"

"Eileen?" my mother says, faintly. Or discreetly, or whatever.

"Sorry, I wasn't talking to you, Ma. I was talking to Eddie. Gotta go. Bye."

"Who's Eddie?" I hear as I hang up. Imagine my own mother not knowing who Eddie is! I hope that she and I won't drift apart now I'm getting so much education.

Eddie laughs at my outfit of voluminous nightgown stuffed into jeans, with a wash-shrunk mini-poncho topping it all. "Yes, Madame," he says. "To answer your question about the casino. And have to be white, too." He blows imaginary dust off his nails, like a magician who's pulled off a trick. "Pretty good, huh? Now please. I'm a busy guy, things to do, contacts to make." He ushers me out of the phone booth, bowing.

I don't know why my mother bothers me so much. She's a Class B irritant, Eddie definitely a Class A.

LARRY SUMMONS ME from the library. My mother's on the phone again, annoyed that I cut her off yesterday. "Not all the Mafia are Italian, you know," she starts right in. "You want to be careful—some Italians have feelings, too. There was that Hogan fellow. Don't try to tell me Hogan's an Italian name."

"Who's Hogan?"

"He died a few years ago in the State Pen. Handsome, very humorous guy he was. Ice House Horvatich and Chicken Shit John knew him real well."

I'm not used to this much underworld familiarity from my mother. When did she start referring to her sister's husband as Chicken Shit John?

Everyone else does, but still. John, my uncle, a church usher, godfather to dozens, and a popular pallbearer, was nicknamed this years ago for his method of fermenting hooch.

"Hogan? Horvatich?" I ask.

"Oh, yes, they were enforcers for the Mafia," she says. Not a word about John. "Your grandma said Hogan was the guy who brought barbut to Youngstown. She knew his people. They were awful disappointed in him."

So it's Hogan and I—two Irish-Americans—who have spread barbut across the continent.

My mother doesn't pause for a breath or change of pace. "Your dad wants to talk to you. Just don't let him run up the phone again."

"Eileen? Here's a good one. Guy was going along, out through the mill gates every day with a wheelbarrow full of hay, and the day he retired the guard says, 'I know you've been stealing something all these years, but it can't be hay...'"

Here we go with the old wheelbarrow-stealing story, told wherever there's a mill or factory. But wait: "A guy was going along..." That rhythm: what is it?

"How are things, Dad?

"Okay. I'm still laid off, but some of the other guys are in there. They're real mad, though, they don't get any coffee breaks when I'm gone." He laughs. Each area of the mill, each team, has its own "coffee club"—members put in so much money a week for a thick brew that a mouse could trot on. My father is the only one who belongs to six clubs.

"Why don't they?"

"Oh, we don't have breaks, except our 20 minutes for lunch. So couple times a day I fix one machine, different one each time, so it slows things down. Gives us all a bit of a rest."

"You break it? On purpose?"

"*Calibrate* it."

"And now? Can't the others calibrate a machine?"

"One or two, maybe. Not enough to rotate the system, keep the supervisors from copping on. Well, your ma's at me to sign off. Tell the Indians that story."

❁

A man was going along… Coyote was going along… I've heard this phrase, this rhythm, so often this summer. And the story elements are so alike: someone with little power but plenty of brains and inventiveness, sometimes foolhardiness, uses the system he's presented with to thwart the interests of those who control him.

Over to the Colony. Delaney promised to ask some old men who knew Jack Wilson if they will talk to me. I can't find Delaney, but Eddie is lounging under Jennie's tree, putting some flashy touches on his barbut moves.

"You really should visit my hometown," I tell him.

"Nah. Sounds like a shit place, from all what you've said." He shifts his attention to my car. "Wonder if I could install glasspacks on that."

Glasspacks, modified mufflers, are specially designed to infuriate anyone over thirty. I can just see myself roaring into the colony.

Jennie leaves her house. She's wearing a smart blue pillbox hat with a light veil and is carrying a paper bag. I make a note.

"Did you just write something about Jennie?"

I don't reply.

"Why do you bother? You see her every day. Only difference today is she's wearing her church hat. There something wrong with her wearing her church hat? Or carrying a paper bag?"

"No."

"Since when can't a person carry a paper bag?" He thumps his hand on the car. "Do you think she's got something in it she shouldn't have? Stole it, maybe? Or what?"

"Calm down."

"Why shouldn't she wear her church hat? Maybe she's going to church. Or even if she isn't, what business is it of yours? She can wear what she likes on her head. Delaney says that witch, old Dick Bennett, he used to wear a dead cat on his head."

Eddie spits on a rag and polishes the hood, breathing hard. "Matter of fact, she's got a 3:30 appointment to get her new lower teeth. Been saving a long time. Wants to show off, coming back."

EDDIE'S HANDED ME a good topic for the journal. "What trust do we break when we watch and record what people do?" Especially when they've almost forgotten that's what we're doing? When they think we're just "seeing," when we're really "watching"?

Researchers have been killed doing fieldwork. William Jones, for instance, was a colorful hybrid: a cowboy, an Indian, and a native anthropologist as well. The Illongit of the Philippines killed him in 1909, apparently because he was too fussy and hard to please about their craftwork. They got fed up when he rejected their offerings because they weren't "museum quality." I can't take much of a lesson out of this. Craftwork must have played a much more volatile role among the Illongit of those days than it does among the Paiute now, and cowboys must have been a lot prissier than John Wayne has led us to believe.

A sure way to offend local people happens when field notes are lost and someone finds and reads them. Non-anthropologists might not understand the gravity of this unless they have some idea of what goes into our notes. We write everything down: the seemingly inconsequential, the boring, and the ordinary, as well as the wondrous and the unexpected. In an unfamiliar culture, you don't know what's important until you've experienced a lot of it. It's all too easy to impose your own cultural interpretations on what you see, partly because it's a human imperative to impose order on things and try to make sense of them. If you start processing and making judgments from the beginning, raw clues will be missed; for example, what if I recorded what looked to me like a vagrant waving a dirty handkerchief, when in fact what I'd witnessed was the historic last-ever use of a moleskin pelt by an elder skilled in Paiute magic?

So I'm taking notes on exactly who attends the services at the Indian Mission. If I write generalizations—"Thirty-five people attended the Mission. It seems to appeal mainly to the younger middle-aged people"—it will be difficult to figure out, without the names, that attendance is based on comfort in English and that this age group has the best English. Perhaps most of them married in from outside the community and are more open to new ideas. Being younger is also a reflection of their recent greater mobility. Maybe the attendees are lighter-skinned and mix more in non-indigenous settings; the lighter-skinned are more common among younger people, since Indian-white intermarriage is increasing. If I "process" what I see ("the attendees are younger middle-aged") rather than *recording* what I see (who the attendees are and their specific descriptions), I won't be able to test any of these possibilities in the future.

"Emulate the Norwegian anthropologist who died before he could write up his study," Professor Murdock once advised us. "His notes were so detailed and dispassionate that another anthropologist was able to write up his work."

I don't believe this; I suspect this Norwegian anthropologist was created for didactic purposes, like the good little boy who held his finger in the dyke. I also know a few Norwegians, and being dispassionate comes a lot more naturally to them than to me. But it's a good beginning principle, because within weeks of starting research—after the initial shock wore off—I *have* become someone else. I am now so conscientious about recording data I even took a lot of notes on the shape, color, and location of some trade beads I found outside town. Delaney gently explained, after I declaimed on them to him at some length, that they were deer droppings.

It's not possible to write everything; screening does occur. I'm guided somewhat by my research topic, the religion the people in Yerington chose after Jack Wilson died (with various interruptions by Coyote). But some days I hope I won't see or hear anything at all, because the recording process is so exhausting.

Having so much detail on paper is necessary but dangerous; if it gets into the wrong hands (almost all hands except yours or that anthropologist who reads them when you're dead), people who help you may be embarrassed, ridiculed, or even incriminated. For example, you may have notes about a community member widely suspected of an old murder by the Indians, but not the whites, or about drug-taking, philandering, misuse of funds, car theft. Some of my notes are about mundane events that may seem sinister or intrusive to a local reader only because I take the trouble to write them down at all—notes on the everyday, the prosaic, like Jennie's hat.

The ethical issues don't end with these raw notes. How will I write up my study? Changing names, occupations, and other facts to protect identities isn't going to make any difference when a community is as small as Yerington. I'm aware of what can happen to the "subjects" of anthropological studies. The communities become "types," endlessly analyzed by others ("As Foster has shown, peasants are likely to... "). It's also impossible to disguise identities of individuals, or even of communities. Everyone knows that Vidich and Bensman's *Small Town in Mass Society* is Ithaca, New York, where the authors are no longer welcome. And in small places, even unnamed individuals are instantly identifiable. After all, how many primary school principals or police sergeants are there in an Irish village of 300 people? How many sheriffs in Yerington, for that matter? And in Youngstown, how many parish priests are linked to the Mafia? I know of at least one, so is referring to the phenomenon a matter of potential libel? Or even a matter of someone's life? So, I have a lot in my notes that is troublesome by any standards. The thing, therefore, is not to lose them or be careless about their security.

I write these concerns in the journal. Then, turning to a new page, I jot down a few thoughts about Francis. He's such a sweet guy, in great demand as a pallbearer. He took my great-aunts to bingo. When we were in college, he was always at our house, helping my sister with arithmetic ("Don't worry, A and B *don't* get tired swimming upstream and down") or Patrick with his presidential campaigns.

"Francis must really like you," my mother said. (She never uses the word "love" in any romantic context, only in reference to things like piccalilli.)

"Yes, he's madly in like with you," Patrick cackles.

But he really was in like with me, and still is—I know that.

CHAPTER SIXTEEN

Who We Are

"Miss! Lady! Psst! Here!" The three guys are still drinking across from Jennie's house. Now one, Junior Russell, described by Morgan as a man with a great future behind him, beckons me over. "Listen," he says with the pained earnestness only a drunk can muster, "you want to be real careful of those half-breeds in town. Stay away from them."

From collecting local genealogies, I know of only a few "half-breeds," and three of them are there under that tree. Two have white fathers, and the third's father is Mexican.

One of them escorts me across the lane to Jennie's front steps. "You can come back over when we're sober and we'll show you how to build a *kah' nii.*" He invites me, with a grand sweep of his arm, to sit on the steps. "Jennie will tell you the story of Wolf and Coyote."

"Peter Mastramico and Sylvester Guerrero," Jennie calls out from her seat in the old armchair in the corner of her kitchen. She invites me in.

Various Indian tribes have different names for Wolf and Coyote, but these are certainly not among them. Jenny has a different story to tell.

"The half-breeds in town." She points her lips toward town.

I've met Peter and Sylvester. They're prominent local professionals, law-yers, descendants of two of the wealthiest and most powerful settler families in the Valley. They often appear, louche and swashbuckling, in the murkiest bar in town. They're both amused and irritated by the fact that I want to work with the Indians when I could be spending time with the two of them, and Sylvester delights in confusing anthropology with palmistry.

"Are they half-Indian?" I ask.

"Nope. Half-Italian."

Even though I've heard it said before, I have a hard time remembering that the Indians classify Italians as non-whites. Later, when I tell her this story, Lisa Domenico, a reporter for the *Mason Valley News* ("The Only Newspaper in the World That Gives a Damn About Yerington") elaborates: "They look down on a 'white' woman who marries an Italian. It's not so bad if an Italian woman marries a 'white' man." (Lisa, a Perkins at birth, had obviously gone the wrong way.) "Junior must have been really drunk when he gave you that warning, because normally the Indians don't like to embarrass us. Not, of course, that we agree with them."

My mother shares this view with the Indians. Like other Irish-Americans in my town, she believes it's disastrous for an Irish-American woman to marry an Italian-American man; not only would she lose a glorious surname, but her wifely status would be lower. An Italian-American woman who marries an Irish-American man, on the other hand, walks with queens. This view is particularly impressive because women like my mother, who actually marry Irish-American men, don't change their minds. It strikes me that this, plus the fact that the Italians have a big hand in running both Youngstown and Yerington, might make an interesting comparative academic study. Since I now know less about everything than when I arrived, though, I stick to my original research plan.

The Paiutes often took their "English" names from their employers, and although a few worked for Italian ranchers, many of their names were likely to be more Irish than mine: Maureen Conroy, Mickey Brady, Johnny Kelly. I'm not the only "Eileen" on the reservation. A Paiute cowboy with a County Donegal name seems as wondrous to me as the magical water babies and monster cannibals I'm hearing about, until I reflect on the miserable circumstances that led to this situation: colonized indigenous people who were given their white employers' names. So today, the glorious Winnemucca Naci, one of the Paiute's three great heroes, has a great-grandson named Johnny Kelly.

Corbett Mack* is a good example of the stew that produced today's people and names. Delaney introduces me to him. He's named after the boxer Jim Corbett, although I doubt he knows his first and last names are Irish.

Corbett's last name is even more loosely tied to him than most other local people's names are. His father was Big Mack Wheeler, an Indian man of monumental size who lived to be 105. "So you probably wonder," Corbett

---

* Unlike many other characters in this book who are fictional constructs, Corbett Mack's real name and persona are used here because he later became the subject of an anthropological study (see Hittman 1991).

says during my third interview with him, "why I have blue eyes. I had yellow hair as a little boy."

I hadn't wondered: his hair is now silver, the kind of silver that dark-haired people get, and I've been thinking his eye color was caused by cataracts.

"Well, let me tell you about my first day at school," he says. "I didn't go to school until I was 15. I can't remember anything before that because I couldn't speak English. Once I learned English, I was able to think.

"My uncle took me over to Stewart to make the arrangements. I was glad to go, and I think my school days were the happiest days of my life; they must have been, because I stayed there until I was over 20. I only left because my mother got hurt in a buggy accident.

"But on that first day, it was all new to me, and I was looking around and they asked me my first name and my last name, and my uncle said my name was Douglas. He said it was Douglas because my real father was a white policeman, Douglas, over in Smith Valley in the 1880s.

"I didn't know this, but after a while, I learned to write and I wrote home to tell my father. Someone read Big Mack the letter and he was angry. He knew about my mother and the policeman all along, but he was mad that the school was using the name Douglas and he said I had to be called by his name. You didn't fool around with Big Mack Wheeler, so we never talked about it again."

We're interrupted by Delaney's pal Brody, who wants to introduce yet another cousin-brother, so Corbett and I never talk about his name again, either.

Mixing with whites has affected bloodlines, as well. Among the Paiutes themselves, who is a true full-blood is clear: 75 among the 373 people claim to be full-blood, and since everyone is interrelated and all are experts on ancestry, claimants can easily be challenged. "Half-breeds" are more interesting. Some are considered all Indian, some are "white" to Indians, and "Indian" to whites. A woman who legally marries a white man loses her right to live on the reservation but her children may still be "Indian." "Blood" and "breed" have to do with language and how a person lives. Delaney's father was white, but Delaney lives as an Indian; Cyril's father was Indian, but Cyril lives a "white" life in the suburbs. Delaney prefers to speak Paiute; Cyril can barely get by in the language. One of my trainers in Reno, the Swedish linguist who spoke fluent Paiute and Shoshone, was partly Paiute in people's eyes. Paiute speakers like the famed but elusive Mickey Kelly could talk to him, while they couldn't speak Paiute to some of their own neighbors on the reservation.

This becomes only slightly clearer one day when Thomasina and I are in the church bus, having driven Archie home from a stint of advising the Reverend on the *kah' nii*. "You ever think about becoming a Paiute?" Thomasina asks.

"No."

We have plenty of discussions like this. What would you do if the pop star Bobby Darin asked you to run away with him—no discussion there, actually. Or, what if you were all alone in the house and *Paizó?o* came in? Or, how would we look as blondes? Instead of answering seriously, I focus my attention on avoiding hitting the Colony dogs.

"You could. You'd have to get a divorce, first."

"Um."

"I'm thinking of becoming white. Mary Juarez did, and Lily Martin."

Mary and Lily look Paiute to me, and so do their kids. Thomasina finally has my attention.

"How do you become white?"

"You marry a white guy. Not you, you married a white guy, but you were white already."

"If you marry a black person, do you become black?"

"We don't marry colored guys," Thomasina states. "There are some at the base, but we wouldn't. We hardly even marry Italians."

"So how does this work?"

"If I marry a white guy, the white law says I'm not really an Indian anymore. I can't share in the tribal lands, 'cause the guy can't. Can't even go to the Indian hospital. My kids, neither."

"So if that happened often, there'd be no one left to use the land?"

"Yeah. But *your* kids could."

"*My* kids?"

"Yeah, if you married a Paiute, Walker, say, your kids would be legal Paiutes. Redheaded Paiutes." She giggles.

Coyote changes from male to female, young to old, human to animal, and crosses all kinds of boundaries, so I suppose such transformations were pretty mundane to Thomasina.

And maybe it's not so odd. According to Irish law, anyone with a grandparent born in Ireland is an Irish citizen. I've finished the last of my genealogical charts and learned that Thomasina's long-disappeared white grandfather was born in Ireland. Thomasina is an Irish citizen.

LIKE THOMASINA, I was never likely to marry an Italian. My mother wouldn't stand for it.

We established this fact pretty quickly one afternoon a few years ago. I was at the kitchen table drawing on a paper napkin, and she was ironing. My freshman-year anthropology professor had given us an assignment based on a relatively new approach, called ethnoscientific analysis. We were supposed to ask a series of questions on a topic of our choosing to create a typology of "folk" categories. This method was quite contentious in anthropology, with various senior "silverbacks" hurling articles at one another. Did it work? And if so, for what? How it would end, I didn't know, but as with many things, I wasn't able to decide for myself whether it worked or not until I tried it on my mother.

I wrote "Ethnic Marital Preferences" at the top of the napkin and braced myself.

"Would you rather your child married an Irish person or an Italian?"

"I wouldn't rather anything," she said, thumping the iron down. "You get up, you, and get back to your books. Or else pin these to the ironing board. Do something useful." She waved a crocheted doily at me.

I continued writing.

"Irish," she sighed.

"Irish or Chinese?" Perhaps exoticism counted.

She gave me That Look. Only a daughter can gauge that exquisite line, that achingly delicious moment right before the explosion. And prolong it.

"Chinese or Hungarian?"

"Depends on the Hungarian."

I sketched the rest in quickly: Irish, German, other northern European, southern European, central European only from certain areas and only if they changed their names to something less foreign. Lebanese Christian, Lebanese Maronite, Greek sponge divers—we went through all the local groupings.

"Okay, would you rather your child became a Protestant or was gay?"

"Gay, of course."

"I mean homosexual."

"Oh." She paused. I scratched that one out; it wasn't fair. She flowered in the company of the few courtly, attentive gay men we knew, but was half-convinced their reputed preference for men was "only kidding," and anyhow, mechanically, it couldn't possibly work.

"Would you rather your child became a Protestant or married a black Catholic?"

"Black Catholic, of course." Did this woman sleep in the same bed as my father?

"Would you rather your child married a Catholic with no sense of humor or a Protestant with a great sense of humor?"

"Would he convert, do you think?"

"Would you rather..."

"All right, all *right*. Who is he? What's his name?"

"Who?"

"The black fellow or the homosexual or whoever it is you want to marry. What parish does he belong to?"

"I'm not getting married. Ever," I protested.

"Well, I hope not. Would you rather lie awake at night, sick over $10.00 a month more on the mortgage? Or how to feed your kids when your husband's laid off? Or what happens when he gets hurt next time, or gets crushed like an animal in that hellhole? Or maybe you'd rather just watch him get smaller and more battered each year? Never see his hands really clean until he's laid out in his coffin?"

"I..."

"Or would you rather read books? And would you rather read books or write them yourself? Would you rather..."

"*Okay.*"

I guess the method works. But still, I got married.

"WHAT'S THAT YOU got there?" Walker asks when I stop in at the jail. Today's mail. Included in a food package from my mother ("Do they like pirogies out there? I could send some") is an old photo of my third grade class, each of us eight or nine years old, performing a St. Patrick's Day play. ("You don't want them to think you're All Work," she wrote.)

I want to ask Walker about local history; Morgan is supposed to be the expert, but since he got the cleaning job at the casino, he works all hours.

"Hold on, lemme guess which one is you," Walker takes the photo and studies the happy children, finally putting a weathered finger on a surly little face, eyes glaring into the camera.

"Oh, there you are," he beams. "Haven't changed at all. That what kids wear in Ohio?"

Hardly. I snatch it back. In the photo, I'm wearing a plumed headband and a shamrock-festooned cape. Some of the boys, kilted, hold shepherds' crooks.

"I wanted to ask you about the history of the reservation here in town," I say formally, rearranging my face to the sunniest expression I can muster. "How did it get its name? 'The Colony'?"

"Who knows? Good name, though, huh? I looked it up once. It said a colony is a place ruled by another country. What's the other country here? The British? The Spanish? I said once to this guy I knew, I said 'Don't tell me it's the U.S. government, we're part of that.' He said, 'Nobody likes a smart-mouth Indian.'"

"I guess technically it's not a colony."

"Coulda fooled me."

According to a deed I tracked down, the government paid a local white farmer, Frank Bovard, $1205.64 for the Colony land. There's no record, of course, of any earlier government payment to the Indians for the millions of acres on which the tiny colony now sits.

"Before the colony," Walker says, "people lived in windbreaks, three sides, sometimes square, sometimes round. They were outside town, northeast, where the old slaughterhouse used to be, and southeast in the old Missouri Flat. A few lived in Army tents. Then they moved into town, but the government didn't build houses until the early 1940s."

"Did you live there?"

"I like to move around."

We discuss the history of the Ranch, too, and then some of the places he likes to pass through on his wanderings.

He reaches for the photo again, smiling.

"Every St. Patrick's Day, the priest at home says everybody loves the Irish because they never had colonies. They're the brave underdogs," I offer.

"Well, Kelly, Conroy, and Riley ain't Indian names. Ever hear of any

Murphys at Little Big Horn? Not on our side, anyway." He turns the photo toward the light. "Do you remember any of these little kids?"

I do: Jimmy Mastramico, Roger Ascione, John Holzbach, Ruthie Friedhof, Jerry McCabe.

Some people in Youngstown—Greeks, for example—have kept many of their customs; even down to third generation and more, their spoken Greek can be traced to particular villages when they visit Kalymnos, Corinthia, Rhodes. Others, like ourselves, have not only lost many of our customs but also press our ersatz ones on others.

We do this because, in the mid-1960s, about half the priests in the U.S. were Irish-born, as were three-quarters of the bishops. For Catholic children on the east coast, unless you attend a minority-language church and school, you're likely to go to an Irish-run school. My primary school put on over 20 plays on St. Patrick's Day, one for each classroom or so, and stoic parents in steaming wet coats sat through them for three or four hours. Look at this photo of my third grade play, for instance. Its theme is "MacNamara's Band," an immigrant, stage-Irish song. Antonetta LaCivita plays a fake harp. Nancy Udovicic, in a green shamrock-trimmed cape, holds a cardboard pot of gold. Barney Kopchak, Johnny Batory, Ray O'Hara, Eddie von Shulick, Jimmy Wilson, and Sean Murphy are all in kilts or green pants. My mother saves to buy cloth for our St. Patrick's Day costumes; once the nuns made her return it to the store because it wasn't "Kelly green," a color unknown in Ireland.

We are colonized, even those of us with Irish ancestry. A few weeks ago, I saw little Earl in a Sioux bonnet, shouting, "Look at me! I'm a Indian!" We share a history of manufactured identities, the Paiutes and the Youngstown Irish-Americans—theirs from cowboy films and fast-fading memories of nomadic days, ours from homesick priests who'd entered Irish seminaries at 12 or 13 and were soon shipped to America, knowing little of their own country; or from scenes from the pseudo-Irish movie, *The Quiet Man*; or from locals' dreams of never-seen ancestral Irish villages, which were now, in fact, just grim suburbs of Dublin. Many Irish-Americans believe that the Irish language is simply English spoken with a brogue, that people still dance at crossroads, that any self-respecting person in Ireland won't speak to an English person. But this idea of "Irishness" binds us together, us and some of the more flexible Croatians, Italians, and Slovak children in my school plays. And what harm do such legends about the "old sod" do? Not much, until you land in Ireland and discover the Irish feel far more at home with the English than with you.

"Well," Walker says when I finally calm down, "You must have *some* of the old ways left."

"Irish step dancing—a few girls learn that and enter dancing contests. And my grandmother has a custom on New Year's Day. In the old days in Ireland, she says they'd bake a loaf of soda bread and bang it on the neighbor's door, saying 'Put the bad luck out of my house and into yours.' Then the neighbor passed it on to the next house. They had a lake at the end of the lane and the last neighbor threw it into the lake. Grandma still does it in Youngstown. Her daughters live in the house beside her."

"Does she have a lake near her?"

"No."

"So who's the neighbor at the end, now?"

"The Stivanskis."

"So, they get all the bad luck?"

"I guess."

"Umm. I can see how *that* tradition will die out."

BACK IN THE Colony. Back under Jennie's tree. It's more than 100 degrees, and we're all competing for the same small patch of shade. Eddie's two little brothers, George and his twin Mike, are busy smashing empty beer bottles with rocks.

"Here! Stop that! You want The Man to come and get you?" Delaney shouts his generic threat.

"What man?" George asks.

"You know the man," Larry sneers. He glances at me, hesitates. "The Man that likes little boys. And girls."

"Listen you, stop that," Delaney says. "That ain't the man I'm talkin' about."

"Well, you should be," Larry snaps back. "They need to know this stuff."

"They'll know when they need to."

"Huh. I wonder how come *I* didn't."

Delaney winces. "I don't know why you're here all the time, anyhow, Larry. Why ain't you ever in school? And ain't you got any white friends?" he asks rather gently, probably knowing Larry doesn't have many friends of any color. His closest friend appears to be Eddie, who has gone to "see a white man about a dog" and has left his little brothers with Larry, dismissing all three as "turkeys."

I want to ask Delaney some questions about the Paiutes' history with the white man. "I read last night that the mail failed to go through only once in the history of the Pony Express, in 1860, and that was the work of the Paiutes, who burned down their relay stations and killed 16 of their workers and 150 horses."

"Yep." Delaney glows.

"What was that all about?" Oh God, I sound like my mother, irritated over some childish fracas. I'm too hot. I bulldoze on. "And the last major Indian war before the Civil War was the Paiute War of 1860. In the first battle, 75 of the 105 white militia who showed up were wiped out, but the Paiute lost very few. What do you say about that?"

"Oh, yeah," Delaney straightens up. "Well, sure. That was Numuga did all that. It was a terrible winter, 1859, thousands of Paiute people starved and froze. The mining companies cut down our pine nut trees, and the whites took our water."

"Numuga?"

"He was a great leader, he was *Mupi'tawá'ka*'s boy, probably. But he was different; *Mupi'tawá'ka* didn't care for the white man, didn't trust him, but Numuga, he tried everything to save us going into battle. People even said he was a coward, that he wasn't a real Paiute." Delaney sniffs.

"And who," I ask, scrambling to write names phonetically, "was this *Mupi'tawá'ka*?"

"You'd call him Winnemucca. Winnemucca Naci. He was Numuga's father, I think, and Truckee was *his* father. Truckee was a peaceful man, too, like Numuga, a friend to the white man, but he died right before the war. Winnemucca, he didn't put up with too much. But he was smart—maybe he put Numuga up to it. I know Numuga fasted and prayed for three days and finally said okay, he'd lead the battle. So he went in and knocked the daylights out of him."

"Out of who?"

"The white man," Delaney says, torn between pride and a dainty concern for my white sensibilities. "Of course, about a month later, the federal government sent out a lot of troops, way too many for us, but we just disappeared into the desert. We didn't sign no treaty or nothing. The troops built Fort Churchill after that to keep an eye on us." Delaney is proud of Fort Churchill. "My grandfather, Horseman, Pu" ku 'kai, teamed up with Winnemucca Naci and Chief Joaquin to kill a few soldiers there. The U.S. Army give Winnemucca a uniform, because he was such a great soldier. Only right. And he was over 90 when he died, in 1882. These are our three soldier heroes."

"So you were telling me a few days ago if it wasn't for the white man the Paiutes would have been wiped out by their neighbors?" I wonder if all this battling had simply been a display to scare the neighbors. "And what about the horse-stealing song Paulette was teaching me? She said it was about some young Paiutes stealing horses from a tribe in Arizona."

"You gotta look at the long term and the short term here. The neighbors woulda wiped us out. The white man didn't. Couldn't. Just took our water and our food."

"But my book here says the people in the Great Basin didn't have definite warfare, 'there was no government to carry on a true war.'"

"Well," Delaney grunts, "we did the best we could."

The twins pretend to duel with the broken bottles. Mike falls down and shrieks, "I'm dead!" According to Driver, people in the Great Basin believe the death of one twin brings the death of the other, but George isn't perturbed.

"Sit down! If you're not good, I'm going to..." Delaney searches around in his head for what he was going to do. "I'm going to tell you a story. About brothers like you."

The twins and Larry mess around at the base of the tree, but are quiet.

"Coyote and Wolf were brothers," Delaney begins, eyes shut.

"Ahhh," Larry stretches out comfortably.

"I was talking to these boys," Delaney says, but continues. "One time, Wolf was out fighting his enemies, and he told Coyote to stay in the house and not to look out. 'I will be killed in the battle if you do,' he warned Coyote. But Coyote started crying inside the house. He knocked a hole in the wall of the house and looked out. So Wolf was killed. Coyote took his brother's body and every night, when he traveled, he'd bury Wolf's body and soak it in some way; we don't know about these things anymore. Every morning, he dug it up again and moved on."

George pretends to gag. Mike, looking sick, claps his hand over his mouth.

"But every once in a while Coyote would hear a little voice saying, 'Get up and make a fire.' He thought this sounded like Wolf and he was excited. He would get up and look around, but he couldn't see anyone. He was very sad."

The twins, huddled together now, sigh. Larry kicks at the tree roots.

"He kept burying Wolf and digging him up. One day he heard a voice, but he looked around and couldn't see anyone. He heard the voice again. 'My brother,' Coyote called. But no one was there. A third time, he heard the voice, and he cried, 'My brother, my brother,' and Wolf came to life. Coyote and Wolf were so happy they were together again."

Larry sniffs. The little boys are bug-eyed, waiting for more.

"So you better be good," Delaney concludes.

"Okay, c'mon, Wolf and Coyote," Larry says, wiping his eyes furtively. "Let's go wait for Eddie. Where is he?"

George points down the road.

"Don't point!" Larry snaps. "We don't point, remember? It's very bad luck."

Delaney smiles. But he doesn't correct Larry's "we."

"So," I persist, "going back to the white man..."

"'The lesser of two evils,' as you say in English."

Yet here is the Colony, with its unpainted houses, almost sheds, jammed into a space less than a millionth of what the earlier Paiute nomads thought of as a small stretch of territory.

"You could say it was a poor end. But it could have been worse," Delaney says.

The Paiutes are a polite people.

LATER THAT NIGHT, Larry comes out to Cyril's to bring me a phone message from Francis. "He says he's number one in his platoon!" He's beaming as if he'd won the award himself.

"In what?"

"Oh. Everything, I guess. And he won some big Army court case. He saved a soldier from going to jail."

"Are you working with Eddie in the phone booth now?"

"No, I was trying to get through to my brother."

"You get him?"

"Yeah."

I remember how sad he was when I first got here that he couldn't talk to him.

"What does he have to say?"

"He says he's turned his back on the past. Doesn't want to hear from anybody here. Going to Mexico when he gets out."

I don't know if you're allowed to hug informants, but we're out behind the house, shooing Cyril's scattered chickens into the coop, and no one else is around. I put my arms around the thin shoulders and squeeze. And later I think of Francis, alone with his two big accomplishments.

CHAPTER SEVENTEEN

The Rabbit Net

"You want to give me a hand here," Reverend Parks announces. He's enmeshed in a dirty gray mess of hemp. "This here is the *wi há?* plant. I'm making a net for the rabbit drive."

"Rabbit drive?"

"How we gonna hold a barbecue without rabbit? I got a promise of a deer carcass from Chet, but we need some rabbits. Acourse you're 'sposed to cook them in a basket, on a pine wood fire—you best write that down—but I ain't got time to be making any baskets. It took me an hour to make a foot of net."

"How much do you need?"

"About 50 yards." Reverend Parks is ever optimistic, it's one of the nicest things about him. Even Rapunzel would be dismayed at the awful prospect of 149 more hours at this task.

We sit down in the dust to make a rabbit net out of the hemp. I'd rather classify some more trade beads I'd found, or cross-file my notes, or redraw my stone bowls so they look less like toilet seats. I set the trade beads carefully to one side and take up the scratchy *wi há?*.

"My book says rabbit hunts are in the late fall, not now," I say.

"Hah!" he scoffs. "That book don't know we had an early spring, so everything's a little earlier now." Is this just bravado, or is the Reverend an acute weather observer, as well as being fluent in Paiute and a pretty good ethnographer?

About 20 minutes and many papercut-like injuries later, I offer, "In the old days, people must have saved their net from year to year."

"Nope. Nomadic. They're not gonna haul stuff like that around."

"Well, they must have kept it someplace, then." I'm sweating and itching from the *wi há?*.

"Nossir. Didn't even have houses. No place to keep it."

"Well, maybe a big group got together to make it each time."

"Nope. 'Cording to your book, they lived in tiny groups." Eddie must have lent Driver to the Reverend; I certainly haven't seen much of it the last couple of weeks.

"Okay, they brought in two redheads dumb enough to sit for nearly four weeks, maybe a little less with time and a half."

I can tell this seems implausible to Reverend Parks, so we drop the subject.

"Thomasina's looking for them beads you got there," the Reverend finally says. "She bought them at the Five and Ten, and the string broke when she was messing around behind Rickett's Diner with some white fellow. Acourse she says she lost them on the way to the Missionettes. I said to Rickett, I says, 'You should prolly change that name to Sodom and Gomorrah Diner.' Said he'd think about it."

What a great excuse to get away from the hemp! I go over to Rickett's, not to check on the name change, but to meet Paulette and her Aunt Edna, who has come over for a few days from Bridgeport. When I'd brought Maybel here for our one attempt at supper, we hadn't been treated well, but nobody fools with Paulette. We go in the front door and Reenie glares at us, but we take a corner booth and settle in.

Edna remembers Jack Wilson; she was a little girl when he died, but her mother and father saw him at work and often told the tale.

"A lot of Indians got together at Nordyke," she says, "and danced for five nights. On the fourth day, Jack Wilson said a big snow, a white cloud, was coming the next day. An old man from Schurz asked if a white horse was coming, and Jack Wilson said yes. On the last day, Jack Wilson laid down two cowhides. He called out, 'Come horse, Indians want to see you.' A white horse came down from the mountains on the other side of Nordyke. Wilson called, 'Hurry up,' but the horse came slow, slow. A big cloud came then." Edna spreads her arms wide. "Jack Wilson called out, 'Snow come down.' The horse cried because the cloud was close to him. 'Good water is coming,' Wilson said, and something cold sprinkled on the people. Two people grabbed the cloud and set it in an old tub. Everyone drank from the tub. The people prayed. But they were afraid of the horse, so Jack Wilson sent it back into the mountains. My mother said it was the prettiest horse she'd ever seen. It flew into the air, cried once, and went away. All the people at the meeting took a bath in the river."

We reflect on this story.

"You ladies all set to order?" Mr. Rickett asks. "We got Marshmallow and Pumpkin Surprise today."

"Last time I had that Surprise it ran right through me," Paulette complains. "I like some kinds of white cooking, but in the old days we didn't have any surprise dishes or alcohol and so we got a low tolerance."

"Some people are crazy about white cooking," Edna says. "My grandmother, she was white, and one day about 15 Indians came into her house and ordered her to cook for them. She gave them the best food she could find. They didn't say a word while they ate, but when they left, each one of them put a dollar bill beside their plate."

"Same thing happens to me most days," Paulette says, "except for the dollar bill part."

"You know," Edna went on, "Walker's father was Jack Wilson's brother and he used to see this same horse later on. Same one."

"I think I'll pass on the Surprise," Paulette tells Mr. Rickett. "I'll take a plain hamburger."

"Me, too," Edna says.

"Why isn't Wickham doing more about the old man who got killed?" I ask Paulette.

She waits until Reenie, who's serving the next table, moves out of earshot. "Wait till payday comes and he gets a few drinks in him. Then we'll probably all be called in."

I'm back helping Reverend Parks, but this time Morgan, Paulette, Thomasina, and Charlene are lending a hand, too, twisting *tule*. Archie sprawls beside us, done in from giving Reverend Parks a grammar lesson.

"I loved my time at school," Morgan announces. "I got a good education, but the teachers were awful cruel."

"Wouldn't know," Archie says. "Never bothered to go, myself."

"They forced us to run between two lines of teachers who beat us with belts. I remember two boys fell down and really got beaten."

"You prolly deserved it. Whadja do?"

Morgan pauses. "I don't really know," he says, bewildered. "I don't think we ever did anything, not that I knew about, anyhow."

"Musta done something. Teachers don't hit you for nothin'. "

Paulette frowns. "If you'd ever gone to school, you'd know how stupid that is. They told us we were dirty Indians. We couldn't go home, and they didn't want our parents to come see us. We couldn't ever speak Paiute. We had to march everywhere. They made us work in the laundry half of every day, ironing clothes, even when we were six or seven. If you didn't do it right, you got a beating."

"And the uniforms." Morgan covers his eyes. "Hideous. The girls wore striped ticking drawers...."

"Drawers!" Thomasina hoots. "Morgan, you want to see my *drawers?*"

"I saw *yours* when they got delivered from the Tent and Awning Supply. Anyhow, they wore striped ticking dresses and thick black bloomers...."

Thomasina explodes in laughter.

"And we boys wore bib overalls on weekdays and white shirts and brown wool knee pants on Sundays. Later on," he remembers, "they changed the uniform and we wore long black stockings with garters and knickers."

"They beat my cousin because he couldn't keep his stockings up right," Paulette says.

"Of course, the older boys wore suit pants and two-piece suits for Sunday."

"Do you have any pictures of that?" Thomasina asks, tears of laughter running down her face. "I'd give good money for some pictures. How many Indians you seen wearing bloomers and drawers and garters? Sure don't see that in the cowboy movies. Tonto in knickers."

"I'm gonna smack you good if you start again," Paulette threatens her.

"We couldn't take food out of the dining room, so the girls hid sandwiches in their bloomers," Morgan says.

Paulette sits straight up. "How do you know that?"

Morgan ignores her. "On Sunday, the girls wore a white dress, a red and blue cape, heavy Army shoes, and long black stockings. Very uncomfortable."

"I'd forgotten that."

"I held a lot of high offices at Stewart. I was elected because I was so smart and popular, and I did a lot of good works for the less fortunate. But I left in my last year. In your last year you had to buy your own pencils and paper and clothes, and I couldn't afford it. What child could pay out money like that?"

"You were over 22 by that time," Paulette points out. "Anyhow, you had money. I remember you used to buy cigarettes and light one and throw it on the ground to watch the poorer kids fight for it. Actually, the other kids hated you."

"I got very good grades," Morgan defends himself. "I got As on every test. And I took the exam for the WAVES every time the girls did and did very well."

"The WAVES were the women's branch of the Navy," Paulette tells the girls.

"Yes," Morgan sighs. "They had *wonderful* hats. Little turned-up brims. The Women Marines had a, I don't know, a *saucier* kind of hat, but we didn't get to take that exam. I took a different one, Negro Ladies' Hairdressing, but I never practiced."

Thomasina snorts helplessly and pounds Charlene on the back.

"This is *not* funny." Paulette, suddenly livid, swipes her hand at them. "I was sent to Stewart on the back of a truck as far as Wabuska when I was six, after my father left and my mother got real sick. Then I went the rest of the way on a train. I didn't know where I was going, none of the kids on the train did. It stopped right at the school. I didn't know anybody there; my brother was sent there the next day on the train, but I was never allowed to talk to him the whole time I was there. Boys and girls couldn't talk to each other. Even your own brother.

"We stayed there nine months a year. Some had to stay all year. In the summer I came home and worked all day on ranches, helping my grandmother pull weeds for $2.00 a day."

"Funny thing," Morgan says, nodding toward the main street. "The local school was right over there. We could almost see it from our houses. But we couldn't go to it."

"They scrubbed me with a stiff hard brush when I got there," Paulette said. "My uncle, they made him carry a railroad tie to punish him for a stupid little thing. Another time they put him in the stockade—a little kid, not much bigger than George." She hunkers down over the *tules*, small and sullen, and says nothing more.

When I get home, I look up a quote I remember reading before I came here. It means much more to me now.

"I do not believe that Indians ... people who for the most part speak no English, live in squalor and degradation, make little progress from year to year, who are a perpetual source of expense to the government and a constant menace to thousands of their white neighbors, a hindrance to civilization and a clog on our progress have any right to forcibly keep their children out of school to grow up like themselves, a race of barbarians and semi-savages." (Thomas Jefferson Morgan, Commissioner of Indian Affairs, letter to the Secretary of the Interior, 1892.)

"To grow up like themselves"—gentle foragers, spirited defenders of what little was theirs, teaching their children, in their own language, to honor the earth—that would never do. Stewart was the answer.

I CAN'T STOP THINKING about the school or rubbing the sores on my hands from handling the hemp. For a break, I go visit Walker.

"You need any more kinship terms, Hotshot?" he asks. He's trying to repair his broken boot by nailing a piece of leather across the crack in the sole. Outside, the gray dog paces.

"I think I'm missing 'wife' and 'brother's daughter.'" I rifle through my notes.

"I think you're missing 'husband,' maybe?" he laughs.

I blush.

"Tell me something," Walker continues. "How come you got married?"

"It seemed ... like the right thing to do. It seemed time, I don't know ... it...."

"Wanna know what I think?" He doesn't wait for an answer. "I think you just decided to do it to see what'd happen. You crossed the line just for the hell of it."

"I didn't."

"Maybe at the last minute you did. Not a nice thing to do to the poor guy, though."

It's true something happened at the last minute. After we postponed the wedding too often and the priest refused to postpone it any more, I went ahead with it. Maybe I've seen too many movies where people are seduced by exotic lovers only to discover in the end that the freckled "boy next door" is not just the sensible choice but the truly deep, romantic love of a lifetime. How many exotic Youngstown Italians have I discounted as a result? Not many, really; only one Italian had ever had the slightest interest in me and

I know now that my mother would have quashed that. Getting married to Francis is the only calculatedly level-headed thing I've done in my life. From this distance, level-headed no longer seems all that it's cracked up to be. Maybe I'm misreading my motives. Who knows, maybe I got married to irritate my mother.

Despite the restrictions of marriage, though, here I am, alone on a Paiute Indian reservation, as planned.

"Anyhow, now you're *noty' kwa*, wife. What do you call wife where you come from?"

"Wife."

"I meant in Irish."

"*Bean chéile.* Means 'The woman together with you,' more or less. *Bean* means 'woman,' and it can mean 'Mrs.' Mrs. Murphy would be *Bean Uí Mhurchú*, 'the Woman of Murphy.'"

"So what's your name, now you're Mrs.?"

How annoyed I was about the wedding announcement in the *Vindicator* where my photograph was captioned "Mrs. Francis Murphy." What am I now but his name, with an extra "s"?

"The women where my people come from in Ireland usually don't change their names," I explain.

"How come?"

"I don't know. I think because so many rural people had the same name, first and last, that people stuck their father's or mother's or grandparent's first names on theirs. To keep things straight. Johnny Mickey Pat, Mary Johnny Tom, like that. I don't think 'Mrs.' would work."

"They change their names these days?"

"Some do."

"So you say you live in a big Mafia steel town in Ohio and you're not changing your name because in the old days country people in Ireland had to keep their names straight?"

Put that way, it does sound odd.

"I gotta get me a notebook," Walker teases.

FRANCIS'S BIRTHDAY IS coming up in a few days. All I can find at the drugstore is a card with a blue teddy bear and some balloons. I put in a picture of me with the Reverend and me holding up a rabbit net.

Hi! Happy Birthday! I hope you have a wonderful day. What will you be doing? I wish you could be here with me for it. I'll call you that day, maybe around seven? Early, in case you decide to go out for a wild night. Love you to pieces ♥♥♥♥♥ *E.*

PS—Only a few more weeks, and we'll be meeting in Reno! I'm saving your present for then.

On the back of the photo, I write, *This shows a very early stage in what will eventually be a traditional Paiute rabbit net, not that the Paiutes use them any more—Reverend Parks and I are just making it to show people how it's done.*

After mailing the card, I wonder if I should have left the picture out. Francis might wonder why I'm teaching something I don't know anything about to people who don't need it, and who can probably do it better if they did. He might wonder why our honeymoon was interrupted for this and why he's spending his birthday alone. Now that it's too late –I've written it and sent it— I wonder a little, too.

CHAPTER EIGHTEEN

Ethnobabble

"*I 'kwye!*" LARRY MUṬTERS, sweeping Eddie's dice into the weeds in Jennie's yard. He's lost $5.00 to Curly.

"You owe me $4.00," Eddie demands, and Curly meekly hands him 80 per cent of his winnings.

"You know what that word means, don't you, the one Larry said?" little George asks Wilmalee Conroy, who's dressing a Barbie doll in a tutu and tiara. "It means something really bad."

"Huh."

"It *does*. It means...." He leans close to her and whispers.

"What does *that* mean?" She frowns.

"It don't mean that at all," Curly butts in. "It means one of those little willow hoops for lifting hot rocks out of a fire." He fires a rock at a yellow dog. Yelp. "Bingo."

"Oh, yeah," Eddie says. "Next time I stub my toe, I'm gonna yell, 'Little willow hoop for lifting hot rocks out of a fire.' Wow."

"Then what does it mean?" Larry demands. After all, Eddie has the inside track, being a Paiute.

"It means," Eddie says, never slow to seize his advantage, "the sound one coyote makes when he's calling another coyote. Or no, wait, no, it means a root like a parsnip that tastes like chocolate." He lies back against the tree and rips the tutu off Wilmalee's doll.

"That parsnip thing, that's *ja pá*," Larry says.

"Let her alone," Wilmalee shrieks, snatching the doll back and smoothing her stiff hair. "When I'm 12, I'm gonna have long hair like this." She stares back at Eddie. "You're gonna get a big surprise."

"Only one gonna get a big surprise when they're 12 is you," Eddie sneers.

"Okay, George might be right. I got a dollar says it means what George says," Curly challenges Larry. He glances at Eddie, perhaps wondering if he also deserves a percentage on ordinary bets too.

Wilmalee starts to cry.

Delaney ambles up and sits down to join us. "*I 'kwye.*" He scoops Wilmalee into his lap. "You don't need to cry."

"What does that mean?" Curly lobs a rock at Wilmalee's naked doll. "That word?"

"Yeah," Eddie blows on the dice.

Delaney winks at me. "'Bout time you took an interest in your own language," he says to them.

"What does it mean? *What?*"

Delaney raises his eyebrows. "You want to learn a little Paiute, you ask Mickey Kelly."

"What does it *mean?*" Eddie demands.

"You can't translate these things exactly." Delaney takes his time. "It means something like 'Shucks!'" He takes the dollar from Curly and gives it to Wilmalee, who hands it straight over to Eddie.

Over the weeks I've watched the boys' relationship with Delaney ("Elders, treatment of" and "Socialization, youth"). Delaney acts as a kind of benign sounding board for any new antics the boys want to try, shyly at first—at least in the case of Larry and Curly—and, if unchallenged, more boisterously. When they think he's half-asleep, they'll ask me questions about white girls, or they'll share a couple of bottles of beer under Jennie's tree, as long as the genteel Jennie is in her house and not on the steps. If one of them shouts, "Fuck!" in the heat of some quarrel or other, they all look at Jennie's door, alarmed, and turn quickly back to their cards or their pile of cat rocks.

"I've heard worse," Jennie says equably while we're talking in her kitchen. If Jennie thinks occasional swearing is okay, then I will too; I don't pursue the question of what she might hear that could be worse. As a result, I have few notes filed under "Obscenities and Imprecations."

After the kids scatter, I ask Delaney about Larry's situation. "Larry's mother's worried about him," I begin, although I don't like to say why.

"Yeah," he replies. "Reenie's older boy's in prison in Carson City. After that, she cracked down on Larry. Hard on her, though, working two jobs. But we keep an eye on him," he says with some satisfaction, as if he and Reenie are in cahoots. "When his brother gets out, Larry'll have somebody."

I knew this was unlikely to happen.

"Where's his father?"

"In the same prison, since before Larry was born."

"Does Larry go to see him?"

"Reenie's never told him anything about him. Fact is, he thinks his father is somebody else."

"Who?"

"Me."

"Why on earth does he think that?"

"I know what you're thinking," Delaney shakes his head. "Larry don't look much like me."

No, what I'm thinking is that Delaney is older than Mount Rushmore. But it's true, the two look like members of different species. Kingdoms. Phyla. "Whatever put that idea into his head?"

"I guess he don't really think it anymore. He just wants a father. I always talked to him, ever since he was little. Nobody else seemed to bother with him. He never said anything to me about it, but when he was a little boy, he used to tell Jennie all the time that I was his dad."

Delaney lowers his eyes, shy, pleased.

7 P.M. 7:15. 7:30. Every time I dial Francis's number, a different guy answers, and none know where he is. It's his birthday. I have to talk to him. I don't want to run to the casino for more change for fear Eddie might come along and take up residence in the phone booth. Here comes Jennie in her church hat, sailing sedately down the sidewalk. I'll ask her to hold the fort for me.

"Out on the town?" I call out to her.

"Out looking for you," she says, waving a piece of paper. "You got a telegram. Nancy at the post office asked me to give it to you. She had to go over to Schurz. I've been looking all over for you." Her tone is as solemn as if she already knows that the telegram can mean only bad news.

This is why I can't reach Francis.

"I don't want to see it," I say. "You open it."

"I already did. Nancy told me to open it, in case I had to tell you something bad."

"What does it say?"

"HAPPY BIRTHDAY TO ME. LOVE, FRANCIS"

We stare at each other, speechless for a moment.

"You forgot his birthday," she says finally. I've confused "solemn" with "disapproving."

"No, I sent him a nice card, and I got a present for him for when we meet in Reno and right now I was trying to...."

"Nancy says you haven't sent him a letter for a long time. 'The bloom is off,' she says."

Did I mail the card? I can't remember.

"What should I do?" I wail. "I can't get him on the phone."

"Nancy gave me a blank telegram form. Here." She puts it on top of the phone book shelf. "You need to write something pretty good."

"SORRY SORRY SORRY SORRY SORRY. DIDN'T FORGET. LOVE YOU."

Jennie says, "You go over to the post office first thing tomorrow morning and send that. Nancy says she'll be waiting for you."

The next day I do just as Jennie tells me, under Nancy's disapproving eye. But at least I've sent it. To escape Nancy, I go over and check my box. Thomasina and Charlene are hovering. There's always an air of disappointment when my mail isn't from my mother. Today, we hit the jackpot: two letters, along with a big box.

Dear Eileen,
The Vindicator *has gone out on strike, so you probably didn't know the Beatles movie is on here at the Palace. I was down there the other day because that nice girl, Karen, you know her, she's been named Miss Canned Soft Drinks, and she was handing out drinks. I'm glad you never won a beauty contest. I remember Miss Network Difficulty, that Doris. It's very hard on those girls—they get the notion life will be easy.*

That's not a notion I share, especially after my mother once told me I was "too plain to wear a hat." And Miss Network Difficulty has remained unspoiled, as far as I know. Her photo was chosen by a local television station to replace the usual snowy screen when the network signal breaks down.

My mother has packed candy in the box "for the children"—Bit-O-Honey bars, Chuckles, Flying Saucers, some multi-colored candy necklaces, three six-packs of Fizzies, some Charms, and a bag of wax lips. There's also a replacement *Simplicity* sweetheart-neck dress pattern #4196, size 24½, for Jennie. And a promise for next time of *Simplicity* suit pattern #5151, with optional fur cuffs.

For me, she's sent a picture of the dog, a grainy newspaper shot of the latest Mafia body dumped in the reservoir, and some more photos of the wedding reception.

Thomasina and Charlene have become used to my people being white and can even tell a few of them apart. But, strangely enough, they can't identify Francis and me.

"Is that Frankie?" Charlene asks, looking at a snapshot of me in a ponytail.

"No, here he is." I point to a pale figure with reddish hair.

"You two look way too much alike," she says, peering at his image.

"Paulette and Roger look alike. Doreen and Al look alike. So what?"

"White people think all Indians look alike. Paulette's completely different from Roger. And Al's a Shoshone, stupid. It's you two that look alike. So does that red-haired lady in the back row."

"That's my father."

The second letter is from the University of Nevada: "Begin planning the outline of your report and bring one sample chapter when we meet for the next seminar."

TIME TO BUCKLE down. "Ethnography" is my subject—a description of the way of life of the Paiutes, with a focus on my special topic. All through the night I write. Nothing works. The more I write, the less my words seem to have anything to do with real Paiutes.

I read some of the ethnographies in my tiny library—minus, of course, Driver, which is still missing. "The Tasmanians lived only for the passing moment," one reports, which probably explains why they were forced in hard times to "gnaw on kangaroo skins." A woman's activities revolve around "clambering for opossums, diving for shellfish, digging for roots, nursing her children, and quarreling with her husband."

This gives me no sense of the people. Other than the kangaroo skins, the clambering, and the diving, much of this is true at one time or another of my own family's activities and interactions, and I'm certain they must differ, at least in some respects, from the now-extinct Tasmanians, whose culture, according to one author, "was unquestionably the lowest of any people known to modern man." I wonder if an anthropologist studying Youngstown would pick up all the local detail and interpret it correctly.

For example, "the Tasmanians lived only for the passing moment." Does this mean that only the immediate was important and that the past and future had little meaning for them? Or that the future was in the lap of the gods, and planning was presumptuous? Or was it an ecological strategy to weed out the weakest during hard times? There are any number of other interpretations. We ask the questions and observe the situations that our theories and hypotheses suggest to us. Without these, our vista would be limitless, and the people in the societies we study would come across as feckless psychotics.

And I'm still constrained by the arcane corsetry of our traditional reporting format. The contrast between what we do and how we write about it is, to me, almost comical. Anthropology has a heroic, breathtaking scope. We cross disciplines between science and the humanities. We look for the universal and ask, "Why?" Is a practice rooted in biology? No? Well, does it meet some human societal need? We examine the particular and ask, "Why is something done in this place and not another?"

To get our answers, we look at current societies and past ones through cultural anthropology and archeology. We draw on linguistics and physical anthropology. Each of these subfields uses a wide range of methods, both qualitative and quantitative. In my own subfield, cultural anthropology, methods are designed to keep options open, responsive, and expanding as we work in unfamiliar societies. Sometimes, all we can ask is simply, "What should I be asking you?" What is grander than that?

Why, then, do we report our findings in such a prissy, constipated manner? If we need all this richness of scope to make our discoveries, why can't we draw on a richer range of narrative forms to convey it? Conventional academic reporting presents an interpretation, but other kinds of writing and other media—plays, films, novels, games, dances—convey additional or alternative layers of context and meaning. For instance, James Agee's *Let Us Now Praise Famous Men*, illustrated with Walker Evans's spare, powerful photographs, is part journalism, part anthropology, part poetic narrative, and part novel about three families of Alabama tenant farmers. Some of these families expressed pain and anger over how their innocent hospitality had been used, but others felt that it was a true account. Agee himself, however, said, "If I could do it, I'd do no writing at all here. It would be photographs; the rest would be fragments of cloth, bits of cotton, lumps of earth, records of speech, pieces of wood and iron, phials of odors, plates of food and of excrement."

Anthropology is a better foundation than others for conveying a sense of a society's way of life—that's what I believe and why I'm studying it. I don't agree with the British social anthropologist Edmund Leach, who said that most anthropologists would really rather be novelists. But I do think ours are not the only voices and that others have ways of presenting insights that we should be able to use, if we can.

Of course, the people we study should be able to include their own insights, too, and these should be circulated along with our studies. But that isn't going to happen now, or any time soon.

All this ranting is not producing any writing. I begin, "As has been noted by Lowie in his seminal work...."

A few hours later, and two pages along, I stretch and go out to get a couple of books from the car. Cyril's on the porch, leaning back on two legs of a chair, looking unworried for once.

When I open the car door, there's a bang so loud he scrambles up. His chair clatters to the floor.

"Don't do that," he gasps. "I thought I was back on Bataan."

Myself, I've flashed back to Youngstown and its Mafia wars.

Eddie slides out from under the car. "Whoops. I've got it up on a block on that side. Guess it slipped."

"A block?" Cyril shouts. "That was an orange crate. Rotted through."

"All I could find. I thought I'd give you some fancy lake pipes. Jazz up this bucket." He preens his new DA hairdo—DA, according to Thomasina, who cut it, meaning "A Duck's Ass. For a horse's ass," she added.

"I don't need side pipes," I retort, using their other name. I pile more terms on. "I had those kind of shorties on my car when you were still in grade school. The rocker panels have to be reverse-curved—you'd never be able to do that."

Eddie's expression is so comically stunned, I wish I had that camera I was supposed to be carrying with me at all times.

My father trained as a mechanic. Surely it's a universal rule that a mechanic's children have to stand and watch him tinker with mufflers, rocker panels, magnetos, differential flanges, and flywheels every Saturday, all day long, with only an occasional "Don't move" and "Don't touch nothin'" to break the tedium. I miss my father.

Eddie recovers. "What do you think of the Chevy V8 engine?"

"Flathead Ford V8's better," I say. At last, a round to me.

I FINALLY REACH FRANCIS.

"Are you furious with me?" I ask. "I really am sorry. I had the card ready and everything. I thought I mailed it. I'll have your present waiting when you get here."

"No, it's okay" he says. "I know you have a lot on your mind. I sent the telegram after I had a few drinks; I meant it as a sort of joke but..."

"It really scared me when Jennie handed it to me. A lady here," I explain because of course Francis doesn't know about Jennie. Or Delaney, or Thomasina, or...

"You know, I'll be glad when this fieldwork is over and we can be together for good," he says.

"Well, not for good, yet. I still have two years of graduate school. And my dissertation research."

Yeah, well," Francis sighs. "Let's talk when I get out there."

CHAPTER NINETEEN

Ruin...

I'VE LOST MY notes.

Only a few pages are gone. I can't focus long enough to reconstruct what's in them, and I've already sent the originals off to the university. When I was searching for the copies of my "Willie Jackson" notes for Wickham, I thought they were just misfiled. No.

I search my lockbox over and over. The last page before the missing ones is yet more about rabbit netting, but it ends with *I paid the bill and we left Rickett's at 8:45.* The next page begins in mid-sentence: *familiar, somehow, but it was too dark to be able to work it out.* What's gone is the ride home with Maybel that evening after our unpleasant supper at Rickett's. What else is on those missing pages?

Where had I last seen them?

In the post office, when I mailed the originals.

That must be where I left the copies. And the post office's Nancy "Razor Tongue" is the biggest gossip in Nevada. I will have to leave this time. If the notes are circulating in the community, I can't see any other outcome. First, people will be interested in the exciting items: X is having an affair with Y; A stole B's new transistor radio. Then, they'll become infuriated by the mundane: X thinks B's house is dirty; Y's dress is mail order, when people think it's from the city.

If the notes are out in public now, Cyril will be put in a difficult position, as host to someone who will be branded a spy. He's helped me with them some nights, straightening out genealogies and suggesting people to talk to. He may have figured out from my questions the kinds of things I'm writing about, although I doubt anyone can really grasp the level of seemingly trivial detail I've recorded.

For sure, he'll be one of the first to hear the news, especially since the lost notes mention Maybel. But he claims he's heard nothing about them.

"I'll have to go," I say, over coffee in his kitchen.

"You're not leaving here," he says. "You'll flunk your course if you do. If you want, I'll tell your teacher and your father"— my father!—"about it and say how it was an accident. Hell, I lost my teeth for three days once."

"It's not my teacher, it's the people here I'm worried about," I say. "They'll be upset I've written down so much about everything."

"Like what?"

"Like the fact it took 40 minutes and a complaint before Maybel and I got our supper order taken in Rickett's." He should know right now about the parts that refer to his household.

He set his cup down and sank a little in his chair. "I didn't know that."

"You know the kind of stuff I write. Not in the lost notes, but in other ones I still have—that everybody thinks Johnny Davis killed his wife, and Corbett's father was a white policeman, and Doreen says she sends Archie to church to get him out of her hair. I change the names, but people could figure them out if I lost them." I shouldn't be telling him this, it will only worry him, but I need to make him understand who and what he has in his house.

"Everybody here knows that stuff. Writing don't make it any worse or better." He's clearly uneasy now. "Hold on here for a couple hours while I go into town and see what's what," he suggests. "If they're floating around, somebody's bound to say something."

He sets off, refusing a lift in the police car, walking down the main road, a lone stocky figure in cowboy clothes, chin up, back straight again, resolute. Will I ever again watch a Hollywood cowboy striding into a new town without thinking he might be on the track of someone's anthropological field notes? Will I ever be an anthropologist? Do I want to be one?

This is the kind of mental self-flagellation Catholic-trained breast-beaters excel in. This carelessness—of people's confidences, of their innocence, of my professors' efforts, of Cyril's and Maybel's standing in the community—is nearly criminal. It's unprofessional. It's stupid. Why expend so much effort transcribing, checking facts, cross-filing, indexing, etc., only to leave my notes someplace? How will I explain to the people I've written about that I need to record this level of detail so I can understand their culture? I can say it doesn't matter because no one else will ever see them, but, in fact, everyone may already have seen them. Will anyone let me explain myself, or will they just want me to leave? And why let Cyril do my dirty work? Would he do that for a male anthropologist? I feel like Snow White, waiting for my hero to return.

"Didn't hear anything," Cyril reports that evening. "Nobody even mentioned you, except James Kelly wanted to know when your husband would be coming to get you. Could be Eddie heard something, not sure, because you can't never tell with Eddie." He pats my shoulder gently and goes to bed early.

I go to bed late, wondering for the second time this summer how I can apologize and say goodbye to people like Delaney and Jennie, Paulette, Walker, the Reverend, Larry, Thomasina, even Eddie. How can I make any kind of report out of what I already have? I still don't know what attracted people to the Reverend's church. Yesterday I was fretting over the niceties of writing my stuff up; now I'll have nothing to write.

As soon as I get up the next morning, I'm off to town to phone my mother. I swear not to tell her, but of course the minute I hear her voice, back there in Youngstown, I'm overcome with homesickness, and the story spills out.

"Why would people mind you writing down their names and addresses?" she asks.

"It's a lot more than names and addresses." I give her the details.

"Well, I can see why they'd be mad. If I went into Mrs. Johnson's house next door and wrote down that her curtains needed washing, she'd never speak to me again. Even though they do. Eileen, I don't want you exasperating those Indians. Let them alone."

That certainly puts anthropology in perspective. Exasperating the Indians.

To get my mind off my troubles, I go over to the church to help the Reverend. But I can't stop thinking about the notes.

Are they jammed down the back seat of the police car, lost in the lining of my suitcase, stuck to the bottom of my unused desert boots, sucked into the bedroom fan and blown around in unrecognizable shreds? All possible, but I've checked. Should I check again behind the cardboard lining of the glove compartment, which opens into God knows what? Or in the box the snakebite kit came in?

"What you making?" Delaney ambles over.

"Rabbit net," Reverend Parks replies.

"Huh," Delaney grimaces. "Who made it?"

"Me and the little lady here, mostly," the Reverend says. "In a week."

"I remember my father making a net, one afternoon." Delaney winks at me. "Musta been 50 yards wide. How big is that one?"

"Oh, near that. Maybe a little less." The Reverend bunches it up as Delaney starts to pace it out.

"Well, I don't know. In my time, with a rabbit hunt you got 50, 60 men with shotguns. You got about six yards a net here. They'd be shooting each other."

"Well, we ain't done yet. The little lady's got her heart set on this hunt. Don't take all the fun out of it for her."

"Women can't go on rabbit hunts," Delaney states.

"What?"

"Well, if it was a rabbit *drive*, like the old days, everybody walking in a V-shape, driving the rabbits, she might be able to beat the bushes and drive the rabbits, but she can't go on a hunt."

I take out my notebook to write down this instance of division of labor by sex. Probably a menstrual taboo. "Is it because..." I hesitate.

"Yep," Delaney agrees, not at all shy.

I write: "Menstrual taboos—see Rabbit hunting."

"See, a woman cannot use a shotgun. Physically impossible to fire a gun and hold both hands over her ears at the same time."

I write: "Humor—Paiute."

"'Course," he adds, "rabbit *drives* today are done in cars. I suppose she could be in that. I'd go with her, just to be sure."

Thomasina slouches by. The two men nod sharply toward the net. She grunts, squats down beside us, and starts working. Her fingers simply fly.

(Will Cyril let me take up the floorboards in my bedroom?)

"Those kids used to have an awful time at the orphanage," she says to Reverend Parks. "Paulette was telling us."

"What kids?"

"At the orphanage at Stewart. That's a sad story, what her and her brother and uncle went through. Even Morgan."

"Morgan wan't no orphan," Reverend Parks snaps. "And Stewart wan't no orphanage. You were an Indian, you wanted to go to school, that's the only place you could go in them days."

"Well, you better be sure you're putting that stuff about Indian kids at Stewart in your book," Thomasina tells me. "Paulette said they locked her in the attic one time."

We weave more *tules*. Sand and sweat grout the many paper cuts on my fingers, and it's getting hard to bend them. Thomasina is really fast and even adds little artistic twists.

"Larry's in jail," she suddenly announces, sticking a *tule* ornament in her hair. "For murder."

DELANEY HEADS FOR the jail so fast that he's there before me. Wickham's in the jail's little side office, leafing through a pinup calendar. He grins when he sees me, shaking his head as he looks from me to the calendar and back.

"*Toná"ta.*" Larry cuffs Delaney lightly on the shoulder.

"*Toná"ta?*" barks Delaney. "*You* say '*toná"ta*' to *me?*" He eases himself down on the bench in the visiting room, panting to get his breath back.

"I'm sorry, Delaney." Larry's eyes are red, swollen almost shut, as if he's been crying since his arrest last night.

I glance at Walker, who's waiting to go out on road detail. "It's what you say when you give someone a little punch as a joke," he explains. "Friendly-like."

"You don't give a witch a punch," Delaney scolds. "Not even 'sposed to *stare* at a witch. I was Dick Bennett, you'd be dead this minute. You of all people should know that, Larry. I had bigger hopes for you."

Larry, stricken, stutters, but Delaney goes on. "There's Archie Jim, me, Jennie, Paulette, the Reverend, and you. A few others. That's all of us left that knows the old ways. And Walker, acourse. And now lookit you. In jail for murder."

"I didn't...." Larry's crying again. Wickham leaves his office. We can all hear the squeaking toilet paper roller in the adjoining toilet.

"Don't matter," Delaney says. "You know we don't stand a chance with that guy, Wickham. He don't care about whether we did something or not—we're not humans to him."

Larry's stunned, perhaps not only at being held for Murder One but becoming a Paiute—perhaps even one of the elders—on the same day.

The roadwork truck pulls up in front of the jail, and the driver herds Walker and a couple of others on.

"Now, there's a good example," Delaney says. "Walker. What's *he* in here for?"

I'm about to say drunkenness, but maybe that's not common knowledge.

"Not drunkenness," he eyes me. "You don't spend 37½ days in jail for drunken driving, 'specially when you don't have a car. Or drink much. A little peyote's his thing. He's here because he's an informer."

It's my turn to be stunned. Where I come from, informers, if they're lucky, get a few days' warning to settle their affairs, and then they're assassinated.

"He's *your* informer," Delaney goes on. "Wickham arrested him when he passed through so's you can interview him. Yeah, he was drunk, but that's what, two-three days? Maybe there was something else, but I don't think so."

So, not an informer, an *informant*. And this is even worse than the infamous story told about the British social anthropologist A.R. Radcliffe-Brown. During his Andaman Islands research, so the lore goes, he strode into a police station and ordered the staff to "fetch me a Pygmy."

"Don't know that he minds. He's single now. And he takes some time out once in a while anyway."

The peyote news has surprised me, too. "I asked him if people around here used peyote, and he said only people from Bridgeport did."

"He's from Bridgeport."

"Why would Wickham arrest Walker for me?"

"To make a fool of both of you. Get things whipped up."

Wickham doesn't like Indians, or me, but arresting Walker—I'm sickened and ashamed.

"But he's careful," Delaney continues. "A police chief here got fired, some say for how he treated us. Wickham don't want nothing like that, so he pretends he's worried about us, dealing with our murders same as for the whites. He's having a good time with all this."

Larry's snuffling. "What about me? My ma's gonna kill me. She's on the night shift now and ain't heard yet. And I'm gonna miss the Reverend's rabbit hunt."

"Nah," Delaney assures him. "He won't have no rabbit hunt. The Revival's in August and there's no rabbits to hunt 'til the fall. He won't have a deer, neither, 'til the winter, unless it's road kill. I didn't like to say it to him."

"Why are we making the net, then?" I hold up my macerated, liver-colored fingers.

Delaney shrugs. Maybe high-intensity, purposeless net-making is considered a worthwhile activity in itself?

We turn our attention again to Larry, who's never had enough attention in his life and isn't getting it even now. I'm reflecting on the field research methods of a long-dead Brit, and Delaney is miffed about the inappropriateness of bantering with a witch.

"Why are you here at all?" Delaney asks. "I thought it was little kids they were looking for."

"They were. But I went over to Rickett's that day to see my ma on her 6:00 break. Willie Jackson was out back, drinking in the bushes, and those kids were with him. They had bats and gloves, just back from a baseball game."

"And?"

"I walked my ma over to the drugstore. They're expelling me from school for skipping all the time and I thought I'd tell her before anybody else did. She was ready to kill me. She had to work a double shift that day and said she was in no mood."

"So why'd Wickham get after you?"

"I was just hanging around. So I went on back to Rickett's to check what was going on. Willie still had one little kid there, and I knew he was talking to him the way he used to talk to me and Eddie and Curly. I chased the kid. The kid thought it was funny. Willie was okay then. I left with...." He looks at me sideways. Of course. I gave him a lift that night. That's the story in those lost notes.

"Maybe somebody said something about me to Wickham. My ma will throw me out after this. She's gone to see my Gram in Silver Springs for a couple of days but she'll send me to reform school when she hears this." Larry thinks his mother has the same legal and judicial powers as the State of Nevada. "I didn't touch Willie," he claims, looking only at Delaney, now. "I didn't touch him."

Delaney studies him for a long time. "Okay. I guess I know that, son."

Wickham comes out of the toilet, buckling his belt. "Two minutes," he grunts as he passes the visiting room door. I don't like the way Delaney stands immediately.

"I'll get Jennie and we'll go talk to your ma when she gets back. Could be she ain't even heard yet," he whispers and leaves.

The delicacy of all this impresses me: no mention by Larry that he skipped school to mess around with Paiute boys, and none by Delaney that he knows it's the Paiutes who infuriate Larry's mother. And I'm also impressed by his belief in Larry.

And I can't believe, after all the time I've spent with him, that is the first I've heard that Delaney is a witch.

❀

CHARLENE, THOMASINA, AND I sit in the car parked just down the street from the jail where we can watch but not be seen. We're hoping that Larry will soon be let out. It's a long wait in the 92-degree heat. I wonder what I can do for him. Find a lawyer? How would I pay for one? And except for what I've seen on television, watching *Perry Mason*, I'm not even sure what they do—people in Youngstown are as afraid of lawyers as they are of the police. I want to do something, but who am I? The Young White Woman, still wet behind the ears, who rushes in among the powerless Indians and fixes everything? All I had were my notes about Larry being with me that evening, and now I don't even have them.

I stick a tissue down the front of my tee shirt. My bra feels like a soggy wet poultice.

"Tell us about when you went to school in the old days," Thomasina suggests, fanning me with a comic book.

"It was awful," I pander to their lust for tales of brutality, deprivation, and suffering. "We had to get up at 6:00 in the morning...."

"Yeah, that way you beat the heat," she agrees, wriggling down into the seat.

"It was snowing," I correct her. Seems to me my entire primary-school career passed in the cold and dark of a short Ohio winter day.

"And we didn't have anything to eat because we had to go to Mass at 7:30, and you couldn't eat before that. You had to fast from midnight to go to Communion."

The girls shrug. Communion is clearly a mystery to them (as of course it's supposed to be).

I continue with the most enjoyably miserable parts of my day. "We had to walk nearly a mile through deep snow, with boots and heavy wool pants over our dresses and coats, and our gloves on strings, and scratchy wool hats pulled right down over our eyes, and scarves up over our noses so they wouldn't freeze."

"You're kidding," Charlene scoffs.

"And we had to carry all our books and two paper bags of food, one for our breakfast after Mass and one for our lunch."

"You had candy and stuff in the bags?" Charlene hid her share of the candy my mother sent and is still grudgingly sharing fluff-and-sugar encrusted Chuckles with Thomasina.

Actually, we had slices of cold fried-cornmeal mush. Unexplainable. "Sandwiches," I compromise. "After Mass, we'd go into the school, and—"

"Eat!"

"No, pray, and then Sister Concepta would collect money for the starving children in Europe"—little white babies, she called them—"and then...." Too tedious to go into the collection of milk money, the collection of mission money for the starving children of Africa ("little black babies"), the collection of old newspapers for the church roof fund, the collection of money for subscriptions we hawked for the *Catholic Exponent*. "And then we'd eat!" I conclude. "Right at our desks, eyes straight ahead, silently praying 'Sacred Heart of Jesus, I place my trust in thee' or 'St. Jude, patron of hopeless cases, help me.' Then we had to line up against the wall for catechism—questions about our religion."

"What kind of questions?" Thomasina picks at a broken nail.

"Well, for instance, what is the difference between actual grace and sanctifying grace? And if Sister Concepta caught one of us not paying attention, she'd whack our hands with a ruler."

Charlene sits on her hands.

"Then we had another prayer, and then we did arithmetic."

"I'm good at that. Give me any problem." Thomasina sits up.

I make one up. "A horse is tied to the corner of a barn on a rope 20 feet long. How much area can the horse cover?"

"What kind of horse?"

"Spotted saddle."

"Mare or stallion?"

"Gelding."

"I wouldn't tie up a gelding, myself."

"Okay, how about this. Mary Theresa sends 40 rosaries to the Missions in Africa and 17 come back because she didn't use enough stamps. What percentage come back?"

"Forty-two and a half," Thomasina says, even before I get the last word out.

I skip the next lesson, geography, because it's basically a tour of world shrines in the company of a little boy, Peter Martin, whose name changes to Pierre Martin, Pedro Martino, etc., as he moves around. Peter's interested in how many Catholics Peru has, and how many Catholics were crucified in China. He also has a fixation about the production of iron ore and principal economic products and the like.

"Then we had handwriting."

"I love handwriting," Thomasina says and writes, beautifully, in my notebook, *Eileen is a stupid pig.*

"Well, we wrote things like 'May is the month of our Blessed Lady,' or 'Jesus died for our sins.'"

"And then you went out to play," Charlene insists.

"No, no room outside to play. We had lunch then. We weren't allowed to talk then, either; we had to pray silently all through our meal. We said little prayers like 'Jesus, Mary, and Joseph, assist me in my last agony,' or 'Sweet Heart of Jesus, have mercy on us and on our erring brethren.'"

"And then you had...."

"More prayers. And then we had English. Correct this sentence: 'Patrick don't like Dominic's sister.'"

"Are Patrick and Dominic cousin-brothers?" Thomasina asks.

"Uh, yes. I guess so."

"Well it don't matter, then."

"And then history, the badness of Henry VIII, setting up his own religion and killing all those wives; and then spelling."

"What about science?" Thomasina asks.

"No science."

"I'd like that. I hate science," Charlene says.

"And then we had to put on all our wet winter clothes again and go over to church for a novena."

"What's a novena?"

"You pray certain prayers for so many days and you get some holy souls out of...or you cut down on the punishment for your sins...." Why did I ever begin this? "It takes about 45 minutes. We didn't have Novena every day, only on Mondays. On another day we might go to Confession. To confess our sins."

Charlene has slumped a little but perks right up now. "What kind of sins?"

"Disobeying our parents, telling lies, fighting with our brothers and sisters."

"Those ain't sins. That's just...*life*. So after that, you went home," she says.

"No, then I had to go back to the classroom to study for the city spelling bee. The nun would ask me to spell difficult words."

"Like?"

"Syzygy."

"They both giggle.

"We spent about an hour practicing spelling."

"Did you win?"

"I had to train first for a few years. But yes." My prizes were the key to the city, with a Mafia mayor's name engraved on it, and a typed postcard from our church pastor saying, *Congratulations on winning the speeling bee.* My father was congratulated by his mill supervisor, who said, "I had no idea you'd have a smart kid."

"And then you went home. I know, with your wool pants, and your I don't know what all. How old were you, anyhow?" Charlene asks.

"About ten."

"So you had dinner then?"

"No, my mother tested me on more spelling words."

And then dinner, lovely pork chops with green beans and mashed potatoes and plain green Jell-O, not with macaroni in it like the Protestants had.

"And then to bed. Before going to sleep, we said the 'Angel of God.'"

"The what?" Thomasina demands.

I recite it for them. "Angel of God, My Guardian dear/ To whom His love commits me here/ Ever this day be at my side/ To light and guard, to rule and guide."

Funny I can remember that and not the dates of the Jurassic, which formed the oldest mountains around here. Or the order of caste hierarchies in India, learned only last year.

Thomasina muses, "I like that. Angel of God.... I'm going to tell it to Larry."

WICKHAM STOMPS OUT of his office, sees us, and crooks his finger at me. Time for another interrogation session. I leave the girls in the car and saunter over.

"You know a lot more than you let on," he says.

He stuffs himself into an office chair behind a scarred plywood desk, while I perch on a low bench directly in front of it, where there's barely room for my knees and I have to face into the light glaring in the window. I tilt my head up and back to meet his eyes. He's sweating and smells of cold cooking fat and dirty hair. Poor Walker, trapped here for more than a month. Poor Larry.

"The kids say they were with you. They swear to it. You're always taking notes, you gotta have a record of all this."

"I remember a group of kids that I gave a lift to a game. I met them around 4:00 or so and took them to the baseball field. Then I picked up Maybel to take her out to supper."

"Maybel Watkins?"

"Yes, and I saw Willie Jackson later that night. I took Maybel over to Rickett's for supper, and he was drinking against a shed behind it when we left."

He laughs and shakes his head. Will he come right out and accuse me of lying? Not about Willie, but the supper. Maybel is dark; she and I were asked to leave a restaurant near Bridgeport once when we went to see her other sister. In his mind, Paiutes sweep out the kitchen at Rickett's, as Morgan did.

"Why would you take someone like Maybel to Rickett's?"

Because she's a U.S. citizen and, since a few weeks ago, she's legally entitled to go into any restaurant she wants to? Because I like her? Her stroke has left the right side of her face sagging like a torn pocket, but she always understands what I'm doing and vouches for me with hard-to-get people. But I don't dare say any of this to Wickham.

"To have supper, I told you."

"Okay, and you went in the back door because of her." This makes more sense to him.

"Yes. She's in a wheelchair from a stroke, and it's easier to get in that way." Also, the bar next to Rickett's doesn't care to have my police car parked in front at night; bad for business, the barman came out and said one evening after I'd eaten at the diner. But I know Wickham thinks we went in the back door because she's an Indian.

"And they served you."

"Yes." We'd got service only when I went up to the counter and reminded them we were there. Maybel was politely resolute and prepared to stick it out.

"So. Where was Willie Jackson when you came back out?"

"Near my car, still drinking."

"What time?"

"Quarter to nine."

"You sure of the time? You can be that exact?" He raises an eyebrow.

"We got there at 7:15 and left at 8:45," I insist.

"And you didn't come back."

"I told you, no. Wait a minute." I ponder. "Maybel left her glasses in the booth, and she can't read without them. We turned around after a few minutes and came back for them."

"And where was Willie?"

"Still in the bushes."

"So," he says, "this story of Larry's." He shifts in the chair to push his face closer. "He was out back with Willie, right?"

"Not any time when I was there."

"He's told me he was."

"Around 6:00, 6:30. Not when I was there later."

"Okay." Then, trying a new angle, "We got the call on Willie at 9:30." This is the first real piece of information I've got from him. "You were there right before 9:00. So Larry, he could have turned up there again right after you. Unless maybe he was with you?"

That "with you" sounds too off-hand. I have to be careful.

"I talked to Larry around 9:00 on his way out West Bridge Street. I saw him. Maybel saw him." That's the closest I can get without getting him sent to military school. "That's about what, a mile out of town?"

"That's a half-mile out of town, Miss Precise," he laughs. "So you got notes on this?

"No, I have to send them to the university."

"You got copies?"

"No," I admit. Those notes are the lost ones.

Wickham smirks as if he knows what's in the missing notes. "You and that kid ought to learn something out of this. He'll end up like that no-good brother."

"What have you got against Larry?" It mystifies me that someone so unassuming can attract such attention.

"Know his mother? That's all she talks about—how worried she is Larry will end up like the brother."

"But he won't. He's a good kid."

"You bet he won't—I seen to that. Got a friend, a guard there in Carson, got him to let the brother know when he got out not to show his face here again or I'd see the two of them in Carson for a good spell, him and Larry too." He snickers and adds, "This is what you get, sticking your nose in, hanging around them Indians. Trouble."

CHAPTER TWENTY

... and Reprieve

I HAUNT THE POST office, waiting for the university to send me photocopies of my lost notes. The department has confirmed what I already know: they didn't get any extra carbon copies from me. My fears are real. The carbons are somewhere in Yerington.

Thomasina and Charlene join me; they're still waiting for Paul Anka's reply.

Nancy hands me a bulky letter from my mother, with some photos and a newspaper cutting headlined "MAN FOUND DEAD OF BULLETS IN JAIL CELL."

Dad's still laid off. By the way, why are you writing me all these questions about the Mafia? They're not all bad—I remember when your cousin was laid off, that fellow Vince, I forget his last name, he turned up at the front door with money for the mortgage payment. The little man has to take his help where he finds it. Some say they're only interested in power and money, but most of them end up dead, so what good does it do them? They hurt themselves more than anybody else. By the way, do you ever hear from Francis?

Francis calls me twice a week now from Fort Monmouth, and about half the time I have a chance to talk to him. Sometimes Thomasina and Charlene run ahead, shouting "Frankie" and "Lover" into the phone before I get there, then rush off, screaming with delight. Francis talks about spit-shining his shoes, and I talk about the rabbit net and pine nut soup. How dull my life here must seem to him! I try to think of something that might be interesting to a white person.

"My young friend Larry is in jail," I tell him when he calls this evening.

"How old is he?" Francis asks.

"Fifteen. There are no males here between 17 and 35," I remind him, which reassures him.

"What's he in for?"

"Murder." I explain as best I can.

"Well, what are the formal charges? Where's the evidence? What's the court record say?" Francis sounds more authoritative, more in command since he got involved in that court-martial. "You gotta stop all that ironing and stuff, and get over to the courthouse or whatever they got out there."

CHASTENED, I HEAD for the courthouse first thing in the morning but stop yet again at the post office, hoping to find a package of notes from the university. They're here! I avoid the group who always gather when the mail comes in and hunker down in my police car, studying the photocopies.

The times I was in the diner are just what I told Wickham, including when Maybel and I came back for her glasses. The part about seeing Larry at West Bridge Street around 9:00 is there, too. And, unfortunately, so is that other detail—he was actually in the car with Maybel and me, because I gave him a lift from Rickett's, he and Thomasina. I race through the notes for the rest. The last line reads: *There was a sort of mumbling from the old man in the bushes now. Somebody else was in there standing over him. He was....*

Whoever has the notes must think I know who killed Willie. The next line is the first one on the page I haven't lost: *familiar, somehow, but it was too dark to be able to work out who.* On the page after that, after some other odds and ends, another paragraph I hadn't noticed before: *Whoever it was moved away, and the old man started singing.* Wickham doesn't know that, but if he does have the lost notes, at least he knows Larry wasn't around when Willie was still alive. He also knows that I avoided saying that Larry was in my car. Will that make him wonder about the truth of everything else I've told him?

The most likely person to have found the notes is a Paiute. Why would a Paiute pass anything on to Wickham?

I continue on to the stately courthouse. Larry's been in jail almost three days now, so I ask an elderly man in the lobby for the court records for the last few days. He eventually produces a book, then picks up a broom and starts sweeping. "Gonna leave those out," he says. 'Everybody lookin' for them yesterday and today—Indians, everbody." There's no reference to Larry, Lawrence, any boy his age, nothing.

"Has there been a hearing for a boy named Larry Kilmartin?" I ask the old man.

"Wouldn't know. I'm here on a sentence of my own. Obstruction of the sidewalk. Wickham. Can't stand us Mexicans. Pretended I was Irish, but he said he hated them even more."

"Are you in the court record?"

"Court record?" I leave him leafing through the book.

Back on Cyril's front steps I ponder the implications of all this, a change from my usual worries about my general lack of progress, my notes, my paranoia, and my marriage. Eddie turns up, a portrait of the busy, edgy man he's in the process of becoming. He's carrying a paper bag and a deck of cards. His shuffle is now faster than the eye can follow.

"I was talking to Cyril this morning," he says.

I wait.

"He's been nosing around for days, was nosing around again, so I says, 'Is this about the notes?' and he starts mumbling and worrying the way he does, so I told him calm down, I knew all about them, and to leave it to me."

"Of course," I say. Eddie's developing a knack for inspiring confidence in the easily duped, which I want to be at this moment.

"Here's the story," he says, flicking cards in the air and catching them. "Nancy found your notes and gave them to Paulette because there's something about Paulette's tablecloth in them. The one with the hole in it." He looks at me. "Paulette gave them to Charlene's mother because there's something about her pot plant in them, too."

He makes a temple of his fingertips and tsks. "Charlene's mother can't read, which she don't want Paulette to know, so she gave them to James Kelly, because they looked official. James Kelly thought maybe they were Morgan's Tribal Council minutes, which he's supposed to type up but never does. He thought you had way too much in them about Morgan and sent them over to Morgan to fix up."

That's right, I wrote up some further insights into that Tribal Council meeting. Thank God, at least now I know they're with Morgan. Then again, my observations of Morgan at the meeting aren't all that flattering.

"Morgan gave them to Officer Wickham."

"Why?" I groan.

"Morgan thought they were *lovely*. He wanted Wickham to see what an important guy he is. Wickham hates him." Eddie transforms himself first into the stubby Wickham, plunking each foot down as though he has a soggy diaper between his legs, and then into Morgan, equally stubby but clearly wearing a tutu. His performance is wickedly magical; does he ever imitate me? And, if so, what does he make me look like? Little Miss Muffet, probably.

He stops, and all the fun drops away. "What did you tell Wickham about Larry yesterday?" he demands. "About where he was?"

"I said I talked to him on West Bridge Street at 9:00. And that Maybel did, too."

"Nothing else?"

"No."

"Good girl," he laughs. "Smart."

"Why smart?" I snap, infuriated at his tone. "I *did* talk to him on West Bridge around 9:00."

"Only because he was in the car with you, had been all the way out from Rickett's. Thomasina, too."

I can't deny this. I'm so tired I think he must be tapped into some kind of cosmic information grid.

"How do you know that?" I demand.

"Gotcha!" He pulls Driver out of a paper bag and flips through it. "Remember I gave you this book back last week? When we were in the post office?" My lost notes fall out.

"My notes!"

"As usual you weren't paying any attention to me," he says. "You pulled some notes out and left them and the book behind."

"And Nancy...."

"Nancy nothing. I picked 'em up, yelled after you, but oh, no, you're already trotting up the street." He marches heavily on his heels. "Already busy poking into somebody else's business." So this is what I look like to Eddie—not Miss Muffet but a carthorse. Accurate maybe, but painful.

"But Wickham and Paulette and Morgan?"

"Nobody's seen them but me. C'mon, try to keep up. It's a good thing, though. Wickham saw those, he'd be really grilling you right now. They end only a few minutes before someone called Willie in dead. It could look like you knew who was in there with him. Oh, don't worry, *I* know you don't know."

How can he be so dismissive of my observational abilities, I who am supposed to be on top of all the local action? In fact, from what I've heard about Willie, I think alcohol poisoning is the most likely cause of his death.

"But, that ain't the problem. Wickham don't care what really happened."

"Why not?"

"Why *not?*" he spits. "You know how many Paiutes die one way or another and nobody pays any attention?"

"True." Certainly not the local paper.

Eddie plunks his cards down and ticks off his fingers in rapid succession. "Suppose it was another Paiute did it. Wickham can keep quiet, use your notes about Larry how he likes later on. Suppose it wasn't a Paiute. That'll make trouble. Or maybe Wickham thinks killing Willie was a good idea. A drunk no-good Paiute that messed with kids.

"Or *maybe*," he concludes, "Willie died a natural death. He had TB. He didn't have to be kicked to get the bruises he had, he was falling down drunk all last week."

"So what do you think happened?"

"Forget about it." He shakes his head at me. "What I want to know is why you write down all that shit? Don't bother," he flicks his wrist as I begin my stock explanation. "You coulda got Larry sent away, writing all this stuff. Changin' his name don't fool anybody."

"These notes will save Larry. Wickham believes I've got written evidence to back up Larry's story, and I do. Even if the notes don't say exactly what I told him."

"That don't matter. He's sure Larry didn't do it. Larry was hanging around inside the diner waiting on his mom. Plenty of people saw him in there and Willie was outside. He was still alive around 9:00—other people heard him, too, not just you. You're not the only person around here who sees things. Of course, you have it on paper, and Wickham being a cop, he's impressed by paper even if he don't see it."

"So why is he still holding Larry?"

"To give him a good scare, to show off to Larry's mother. Wants Reenie to see she needs a guy like him, that he can control Larry, keep him on the straight and narrow. He wants to move in with her. Of course, if he could show her official-like, on paper, that Larry was still hanging around with you and the Paiutes, that would be the best of all, he might be able to get rid of him. Reenie keeps going on about sending him to military school if he doesn't go straight, and Wickham is the man to do it for her. He's already told Larry's brother not to come back here."

"How do you know that?"

"Eddie *knows*," he mocks. "So Larry don't need notes like these proving he's innocent. No one on the reservation tells on him. He doesn't hang around with us in town. Why do you got to write about him at all?"

"Why didn't you give me my notes back before this?"

"Because they're *our* notes. Besides," he says, "I wanted to see what you'd do."

He stands, stretching, and looks lazily down at me, the way he looked at Wilmalee when he got bored taking her money off her.

"I were you," he says, "the one I'd watch out for is Paulette. I tell her about the tablecloth business, you're dead." He makes a gun out of his fist and fires at me. "By the way, Wickham let Larry out about an hour ago. When Reenie came back, went over there and tore Wickham up one side and down the other for picking on her boy. Delaney was with her. Said Wickham had no call to hold Larry, he'd found out Larry hadn't been charged in court, and Wickham could be had up for kidnapping."

Well, that shows me. Maybe, if I'd been smarter, I could have had Larry out of there yesterday. But I'm glad it was Delaney who rescued him.

Eddie catapults off the porch, tossing my notes back at me. When I look up, he's already gone. So is the copy of Driver.

So this is who Eddie reminds me of: he works out my worst fears, brings them to life for a while, and leaves a trail of muddle and mystification behind him. Coyote.

BUT EDDIE IS not who I think he is.

I'm mad at him for taking and keeping my notes, for not telling me instantly that Larry was released, and for an older complaint, egging Larry on to paint flames on my car. It's his responsibility to get them off my car. There's no way Reenie will let me near Larry, so I do the next best thing. I drive out to the Ranch to confront Eddie.

From my census, I know who's in Eddie's large extended family. Funny to think of Eddie actually *having* a family. His house is like the others on the Ranch, straggly fences, unpainted, odds and ends of rooms tacked on. A thin, mousy little woman answers the door. She's wearing a faded, shapeless dress and fur-edged slippers. Her sparse hair is scraped back in a knot. Must be his mother, Emmeline Conroy. Hard to believe such an ordinary woman produced a creature like Eddie.

"I'll tell him you're looking for him. He's not in any trouble, is he?" She eyes the car, the words "NEVADA STATE POLICE" not entirely concealed by the flames. "Are you sure it's Eddie you want?"

How innocent mothers are. How can anyone live with Eddie and not expect daily calls from thugs, social workers, angry fathers, and flim-flam men?

"Please tell him I'm looking for him," I say. There's nothing for it, but to go back to Cyril's and wait.

A little later, there's a knock on the door. A thin teenager, stooping to disguise his height, a mop of hair obscuring his eyes.

"My mother says you want me," he stutters.

"Who are *you*?"

"Eddie Conroy."

Not my Eddie.

Cyril joins us. "This here's Emmeline's boy. What do you need *him* for? Stand up straight for the lady," he snaps at the wide-eyed boy.

"I was looking for *my* Eddie—the one who's hanging around all the time."

"Ohh," says Cyril, "that's Eddie *Conroy*," as though the one in front of us isn't. He sends the boy home, with orders to pull back his shoulders and to say "Hey" from him to his mother.

"Where does my Eddie Conroy live, then?" I demand.

"No place, half the time," Cyril answers. "His grandmother moves around sometimes out in the country—the last of the old-timers—and Eddie stays out with her, gives her a hand. He can be very good to his grandmother." Cyril likes an upright moral order.

"What do you mean, wandering around the desert?" Eddie, the guy who dresses like a Las Vegas spiff? "How do they live?"

"The old lady knows a lot about the old ways, and Eddie, he's pretty inventive. And he brings her in often and they stay awhile with Thomasina's people—they're Conroys, too. Eddie keeps some stuff there."

So Eddie's a hunter and gatherer. Thomasina's an Irish citizen. Larry's an honorary Paiute elder. It's probably time for me to go home. Even if I don't really have one.

I meet Eddie later on, coming out of the phone booth. "I was looking for you," I say.

"I know."

Of course.

"Those flames," he says, "they come right off. Watercolor."

Wouldn't have worked in the rain-sodden east.

"A LETTER FROM SECOND Lieutenant Francis Murphy," Cyril salutes, handing me the envelope with a flourish. "Doreen dropped it out here. I remember the time I was on Bataan, dreaming of getting a letter from Maybel...well, I'll make myself scarce." He tiptoes off to the chicken coop.

I've been thinking a lot about Francis. Trouble is he's so...what? Tame? Careful? Of course, he's *very* safe. No leaping off porches, living off the land, languishing in jails. Nice.

Honey,

I'm glad they keep me so busy here, otherwise I'd have killed myself by now from missing you. Three more weeks! Will I make it? That court-martial kept me occupied, but now I don't have much distraction.

Can you send me some new pictures? How are you getting along with the Indians? Your letters—not nearly enough, by the way—sound like you're really on top of things. Who's that guy that keeps answering the phone? Eddie? How old is he? The girls seem very nice—do they really wear bikinis all the time on the reservation? I guess I was getting my ideas from those old-fashioned cowboy movies. It's nice talking to them, even when they can't track you down before my nickel runs out. Did that boy get out of jail? Terrible how they treat Indians out there.

I love you and miss you and just you wait till I get there.

Please call me.

CHAPTER TWENTY-ONE

The Killer

"HERE'S SOMETHIN' WILL interest you, Hotshot," Walker says when I stop by the jail on his second last day. "Somebody's joined the Reverend's church."

Finally! Someone fresh, who may actually be able to explain why the church appeals to the Paiutes. "Who?"

"Charlene."

No chance of an explanation there.

"Yeah, she came over with some Paiute ice cream her ma found at the bottom of the freezer. Boy, taste of that sure took me back. Anyhow, she says she'll be safer with the Reverend's Mission. Otherwise the Catholics might get her and she'd have to go to school in gloves and leggings and all. Said they were real cruel." He grins. Once again I pity the anthropologist who may follow after me here.

We sit awhile. A cowboy in full regalia passes the window. The gray dog with the bushy tail tracks him, ears up.

"You like Roy Rogers, Hotshot?" Walker asks.

"No, we never went to his movies." Watching Roy Rogers wasn't an option among the children in my family, or among my friends. Roy Rogers was a Protestant. Not that he *was* Protestant; we had no idea what religion he was. But Protestants liked him, or we thought they did. Or maybe we thought Roy Rogers was the best cowboy and Protestants, being Protestants, had first choice. So we had Gene Autry. Our parents didn't tell us this; we just knew.

"What about Hopalong Cassidy?"

"Not him, either." We never could place Hopalong. He wasn't Jewish, we didn't know many Jews. Maybe he was neutral. Or a boundary crosser? Maybe...no. Coyote has colonized my brain.

"What about movie stars?"

We liked Bing Crosby and Loretta Young, of course, because they were

Catholic, and the nuns loved them. The only divide was between movies—moral/immoral—and each year we had to stand up in church and pledge not to see immoral movies. I didn't pledge, probably, once again, to irritate my mother as she stood beside me.

Religion did apply to food, though. Protestants ate hot dogs; we ate hamburgers. They ate ketchup; we ate mustard. They ate vanilla ice cream, we ate chocolate. There were other differences too. They used first names for their parents, who wore dressing gowns when they got up. Protestants wore matching pastel blouses and skirts; drove Chevrolets rather than Fords; went to summer camps; named both their children and dogs Skippy and Biff. They ate dinner at 6:00; we had ours at 4:30.

"And Protestants don't believe in Mary, the mother of Jesus," I told Walker. My little sister explained this more fully once. "What they do," she'd told me, "is when they build a manger at Christmas, they put in the baby Jesus and everything, but they just put a photograph of Mary at the back, with an 'X' through it."

Walker nods his head. "This kind of division is the exact same as with us and the Navahos. The Navahos are afraid of ghosts and we aren't. We'd love to have our dead people back, the ones we've just lost. But if you want to give a Navaho the willies, just bring up the subject. Of course," he cautions, "we don't want them back as *dead* people. We only want them back alive."

"So are you afraid of ghosts?"

He pauses. "Nah. I'm not afraid of anything."

"W. Wilson not afraid of ghosts," I write in my notebook. We sit for awhile in companionable silence.

"Who's *your* favorite cowboy?" I finally ask.

"I dunno. Let's see, Tonto, maybe." He winks. In my few weeks here, I've moved on from thinking that Tonto can't be a cowboy because he's an Indian. I do wonder if he's a Protestant, though.

Since I know that Walker will be freed soon and no longer a captive for my research, I spring my most important question, hoping he'll give me an analytical response that can form the substance of my report. "Why do *you* think some of the people are going to the Reverend's church? Is it the religion? Is it him? Is he anything like the leaders of the past?"

"Nah. Way too short. And Jack Wilson was more of a businessman."

"What do you mean?"

"He had a good trade in souvenirs, cures and such. People used to write to him from distant places, looking for cures. But he and the Reverend, they're both smart. They know how to attract people."

"With miracles?"

"Jack Wilson, yeah. The Reverend, I don't know what it is. I'd say it's nagging."

Great: "Nagging as the Basis of a Religious Revitalization Movement"—I can't wait to see that in print. I press on. "The Assembly of God people go into states like trances sometimes. Did Jack Wilson use peyote in the Ghost Dance? Some of the other tribes did. Is that the link?"

"Nah, that came later, after Ben Lancaster brought it in from Coleville."

I go back to the Reverend's nagging. "You don't think much of the Reverend."

"Not true. He's trying to teach the kids something. Some of the old ways."

"Shouldn't it be Paiutes doing that?"

"Some are. And we will again. But look at it this way. We're the first whole generation to be cut off from our land, to be corralled like cattle. Jack Wilson understood that. He tried to give us something. But it wasn't enough for all that happened to us."

"What about the ice on the river? What was it, really? Is it true that those white Wilson brothers helped Jack Wilson fake it?"

"Who knows? Look, why would white boys in those days help an Indian? To help Wilson make fools of other Indians? Could be. Seems odd, though. Jack Wilson never made fun of people, at least that I know about. There's another way of looking at it."

"How?"

"Even if he tricked people into thinking he'd made ice, *why* did he do it? Maybe he needed to teach people something good, and he had to get their attention. He needed to get his message talked about and spread around. That's how people remember things. So it don't matter if it was real or not."

Another pause. Some odd little squawks outside. I glance out the window again. A few scraggy, dun-colored turkeys are scratching around outside in the dust.

"The King of Lovers," Walker muses. "You missed out. Don't look like much now, I know."

"Who? You?" I sputter, embarrassed.

"Not *me*," he grins again. "Those birds. Sage grouse. In the spring, when they mate, you never saw anything like it in your life. The males all get together and put on a real show, tail feathers up, those big ugly pouches on their chests puffing up, and making a sound like you've never heard. It's like a powwow, with all the females watching, all of them picking the best-looking guy or two. The rest are left in the cold."

How Walker must miss the outside world, locked up as long as he's been.

"BA-BONK, BA-BONK!" he squawks.

I stop writing.

"It's kind of hard to imitate. It's a little like a fish playing a horn, but not exactly. You got to come back next spring to hear it; you'd never forget it. Ask Hoot-ze about it. He can do it real good."

"Hoot-ze?"

"Delaney. That's one of his Indian names."

I'VE GOT HUNDREDS of pages of notes. I know enough kinship terms to cover the largest Paiute family reunion. I can make a rabbit net with the best of them. I haven't met and don't dare meet Mickey Kelly: my language skills haven't improved much, and they would only insult him. Generally, though, I'm feeling pretty smug; not three months into the project, and I'm nearly One of the People. I understand almost every issue, except exactly why the Paiutes had joined Reverend Parks in the Assembly of God—my main topic of research.

Delaney and I meet at Jennie's steps to sort out the last few things. Larry is back, as always, under Jennie's tree, this time drawing a *kah' nii* for Wilmalee in the sand with a stick. The *kah' nii* movement is catching on with the little kids in the frenzy leading up to the big Mission. Sometimes I see Larry huddled with Delaney, and he visits Walker every day, but he doesn't talk about his time in jail with me, and he shies away when I ask him.

"I worry about his future," Delaney whispers. "But he seems real interested in the same things as you are. Our customs. The language. Maybe he could do the kind of work you do."

Yes, I can see Larry having the patience to sit through endless sessions of Peoples and Cultures of the World, arguing with Professor Murdock about whether the Seneca had squirrel traps or not. But he'll never get that far; he'll never get the encouragement to spend nine or 10 more years in school.

"Tell me, how do I become an anthropologist?" Larry once asked me, and what could I say—that I wouldn't start from where he was? *Tell me, Brother,* Coyote asks Wolf, but their worlds are worlds apart.

"Maybe you don't think he'd be as good a anthropologist as you," Delaney continues.

"No, no, that's not it."

"Well, I'll tell you one thing for sure—he's never gonna be a Indian." He glances sideways at me. "Knowing about Indians ain't the same as being one."

We move on to my notes, and Delaney helps me clear up a summer's worth of unanswered questions in less than 10 minutes. "I don't know why you didn't ask before," he grumbles.

Charlene's *connordoreon* is a traditional instrument, but traditional to the local Italians; she was trying to say "accordion." The monster *Paizó?o* sometimes takes a woman's form; its one constant feature is slaughtering people with rocks. Despite his appearance, Mickey Kelly is not a Paiute at all; he's "black Irish" from Oregon. Johnny Mitchell had married Delaney and Jennie the day I arrived in Yerington; I interrupted their honeymoon moment by asking for kinship information, as anthropologists do.

"No need to write that part down," Delaney says. "We want to get used to it first. *I* want to get used to it first."

We sit there, thinking about getting used to our marriages.

"I forgot," I break our silence. "Walker told me to ask you about the sage grouse."

"Oh, yeah. BA LOOMP, BA LOOMP, BA LOOMP. That's the sound he makes. The sage grouse, he's a real ladies' man. But only one or two of the best gets the ladies. They all look alike; some must put in more effort. Same in life. You never know what the women will like."

I work my way around to the last point on my list. "I'm sorry I didn't know you were a witch."

"It's okay," he shrugs. "I s'pose nobody told you."

"I think they did," I lie. "I just wasn't paying enough attention."

"Don't worry. You're doing good. You'll get a good grade, I bet."

Another silence. We watch Jennie's yellow dogs tear a dirty rag.

"I know nobody told you," he says. "Not many left who know, Archie and Paulette and them. And Larry."

"How on earth does Larry know?"

"He knows, I don't know how. Odd kid. No bad in him, though."

"Does Reverend Parks know?"

"Heavens, no." Delaney's taken aback. "I wouldn't tell a reverend a thing like that. Here, you," he lunges at the dogs. "Let that rabbit net alone."

I help him retrieve the gray mess.

"I think it's because I'm not a doctor like Horseman or Jack Wilson was; I don't do cures. I'm only a witch. A good one, of course. I help people that have been bad-witched. I never tried bad witching, myself, don't really have the gift. Oh, yeah, I forgot, Walker would know, because he's the one of the last ones left that got bad-witched. An old lady over in Nixon did it. Those people in Nixon are crazy. I fixed him back up."

"Why did Walker get witched?"

"The old lady thought he was fooling around with his sister."

"Coyote did that."

"Well, maybe that's what put it in her head."

"I wish I'd known about you," I brood. Both his and my professionalism have been diminished by my obtuseness.

"Well, you don't worry. You can't know everything; you got enough on your mind. You ask Archie sometime, though; you say I said it was okay. He'll tell you I was pretty good."

Why hadn't Walker told me this story? Maybe because he didn't want to admit being witched by an old lady in Nixon.

"What happened to Willie Jackson?" I ask. If secrets are coming out, then I want to know all of them. I bet everyone knows but me.

"Well, I guess everybody knows but you. Fact is, he's the man who liked little kids, Indian and white, and not in a good way, if you know what I mean. The man Larry was talking about. 'Course Larry shouldn't have been talking about that stuff in front of you. Maybe Willie hurt Larry once, I don't know. The guy was okay till he got drunk, but people watched out when he was around. Thomasina even had her eye on him; she was nervous for her little sister, Wilmalee."

"And someone killed him?"

"Looks that way."

"Who?"

"Larry."

"He was with *me*."

"Funny how even though Larry's white, he can think like a Paiute and you can't. Don't have to be there at all to kill somebody."

Delaney smiles, as proud as if he were the father of a new Harvard graduate.

WALKER IS FINALLY being released from jail. There he is, leaning against the building's front wall and joking with Larry, who's also come to say goodbye.

They shake hands. "One jailbird to another," Walker laughs, and Larry, standing straight, beams. Wickham is nowhere in sight.

"So long, Hotshot," he bows to me. "How do you say goodbye in your language?"

I know he doesn't mean Ohioese. "*Go n-éirí an bóthar leat*—May your road be successful. That's not really goodbye, though."

"No," Walker agrees. He pats my shoulder gently. "*Toná"ta.*"

The gray dog, black-tipped tail stuck straight out, lurks in the brush.

"Waaa," Walker calls.

A few minutes later, all that's left of them both are the imprints of Walker's broken boot and a single line of paw prints. Walker's dog is a half-coyote.

CHAPTER TWENTY-TWO

The Mission

"INDIAN MISION REV∀IAL AUG 2–9!! ALL WECOME!" proclaims the banner over the Mission front door. A few cartoon faces decorate the edges. Charlene, the "I HATE TO DRA" girl, stares up at it. "I did all that," she marvels, more to herself than to me.

The main action at the moment, not quite a bustle, is outside the Mission behind the three-sided windbreak that circles the tiny *kah' nii*. The windbreak doesn't look 100 per cent traditional, even to someone who's never seen one before. It's built of sagebrush branches interlaced with ordinary fencing, reinforced by odd bits of old steps, drawer fronts, and scrap iron.

"Learnt that from the Shoshone," the Reverend says, rubbing his hands in satisfaction. "Did it entirely myself."

There are babies in cradleboards, men in string ties and good western boots. Thomasina is stuffed into my good batik top, one I've been looking for. The women are dressed in their best church clothes. Reverend Parks had suggested that the ladies wear native costume, which intrigued them until Jennie explained that this consisted of a buckskin apron. "And nothing else?" Paulette shrieked. So they turn up at the Revival wearing their good solid foundation garments under nice summer dresses, with cardigans for the night service.

The only white people here are the Reverend, Mrs. Parks, and me. I'm not sure what Larry has come as—a white person, Paiute elder, or senior witch. For his own sake, given Reenie's views, I hope he's not here simply as Larry.

Inside the windbreak is the kitchen staff—Morgan, cooking mounds of free food at two wood stoves and a barbecue, and Thomasina and Charlene washing up at a makeshift sink. The Reverend insisted they make a proper traditional fire by lighting it with braided sagebrush bark; he's gone into his trailer to light the bark from the burner of an ordinary gas stove.

Morgan's forays into various careers—shoemaker, janitor, hairdresser to

Negro ladies, thwarted WAVE—have clearly been wasted. He's a wonderful cook. Sitting around some crude picnic tables ("Did them entirely myself, too," the Reverend beams), people eat loaded plates of deer meat barbecue.

"God knows where it comes from," Delaney says.

"Where's the gopher and squirrels?" Larry asks.

"Ain't got any," Morgan replies.

"Or the porcupine? sage hens? grouse?" Larry's voice rises.

"Ain't got them, neither. Nor do we got mountain sheep, wild dogs, chukker, quail, duck, lizards, Mono Lake flies, pine nut worms, June bugs, *tapoós*, buckberries, chokeberries, bulrushes, elderberries, clover, rose buds, wild onion, or mountain rice. Smarty pants."

"What we *do* have," he continues, "is deer, currants, elderberries, sunflower seeds, and pine nut soup made the right way, in a *opýh* basket, using these here cedar tongs to lift the hot cooking stones out of the basket. And," he adds, "we got six platters of rabbit."

"Where did you get it?" I'm impressed. I know that the net, all 15 feet of it, hasn't been used. Too short and too soon, Delaney informed the Reverend.

"Eddie."

"Called in some debts," Larry says. "The rabbit dish is priced separately. He's getting a percentage of the takings."

"What's this?" Delaney asks, poking at a dish.

"Coleslaw."

"Huh. A little like squaw cabbage."

"Service starts at 7:30," the Reverend announces. This is the third of the daily services; the others at 10 a.m. and 2:00 p.m. were badly attended; in fact, Maybel and I were the only attendees at the afternoon service, and Maybel's a Catholic. Reverend Parks cured her diabetes about eight months ago, and now she's looking for help with her stroke. He invited us into his trailer rather than go into the empty church. I wondered, as he went down on one knee and put his hand on Maybel's head, how he and his wife managed to fit in the trailer's tiny space.

"Praise Jesus," he intoned at the end of his prayer, and Maybel replied, "Amen." But, as ever, I blessed myself with the sign of the Cross and then slapped my hand in irritation.

Now, people file in for the last service; about half—some young men and some middle-aged people of both sexes—are white. The Paiutes are of all ages, except, of course, between 17 and 35; one couple has made the 50-mile round trip every night from Smith Valley.

Guest ministers have arrived as well, not only from other parts of Nevada, but also from California and Oregon. They enter the church in solemn procession: Reverend Follis, a Modoc; Reverend Case, a Klamath; Reverend Hopkins, a Pomo; and two other white preachers, the Reverends Harley and Wilcox, plus an assortment of wives, other relatives, and a young white male quartet, the Apostles. Reverend Eaton, another white, pulls up to the Mission door at the last minute in a brand new Cadillac and wearing a large, loud tie.

No one person takes charge of the proceedings. Reverend Harley leads an occasional hymn, and Reverend Eaton conducts a contest to see which visiting youth group has the largest attendance. The Apostles sing, wonderfully, and at the end of one hymn invite people to come forward and testify.

Nine people do. Only one, the man from Smith Valley, is a Paiute, and he waits until last to make a quiet, unemotional statement of thanks for the food and the service. One white woman praises the quartet, and everyone supports her with their applause. She calls for a collection for them; the basket passes around quickly and fetches up two coins, a 50-cent piece and a quarter.

Mrs. Harley sweeps to the front. "My poor sister-in-law there, she's got possessed by the devil. She needs all your prayers."

The sister-in-law bridles, clearly displeased, and doesn't join in the prayers.

A teenaged white girl—Thomasina's *bête noire*, the too-cute Betty Ann O'Donnell—has been crying throughout the service. At last, she testifies, "I never heard singing like the Apostles, they're way better than Jimmy Gilmer and the Fireballs, and way better than the Hondells, too."

Thomasina and Charlene can hardly contain themselves, waiting for the next event in which people will answer the call to step forward and be saved. A throng surges to the front—about 10 children under 15 who, in my experience, have plenty of scope for repentance; some middle-aged Paiute women; a few white men and women, also middle-aged; and Betty Ann. The contrite don't include my two friends, who whisper that they're here only to see Betty Ann repent, that she's the best at it.

What a confusion. Other congregants step up to shout support for the weeping penitents, while the ministers wander among them, also shouting.

The rest kneel on the floor between the pews, praying, heads in hands. Betty Ann, merely hysterical at the beginning, begins to speak in tongues.

Mrs. Parks abandons the organ and summons me away from the tumult to explain the principle since she believes, I now learn, that I'm here in Yerington to find myself a new religion. "I saw you slapping your hand when you crossed yourself, and then I knew for sure. Speaking in tongues is a sign of the infilling of the Holy Spirit," she explains. "When we repent, we take on a new life and new tastes and we get an ability to speak a heavenly language. Listen to our Paiute brothers and sisters, for example. When they speak in tongues, it's neither Paiute nor English."

Betty Ann is white and isn't Paiute; she's repeating "Jesus" over and over, in plain English.

"It's the Holy Spirit in Betty Ann," claims Thomasina, when I return. "It's a lot of fun. A man paid me and Charlene a dollar to do it, once."

"Bet 50 cents she can't go on as long as we did," Charlene says.

"Bet a quarter the cute Apostle will come over and take her up in his arms. That's what she's aiming for."

But only women can offer support to women, so it's just the first bet that's still in the air when I leave. Betty Ann has been at it nearly an hour, with no sign of slowing down. I've caught enough of the spirit of the event to consider waiting to see if Thomasina and Charlene will be struck down by lightning.

It's interesting to compare the two groups of ministers, Indian and white. By a large margin, the Indian clerics have more formal education than the white ones, are better spoken, and more conservatively dressed. The Klamath Reverend Case has a master's degree and speaks a number of languages; Reverend Hopkins has a degree in theology. The whites, all ministers of local Indian churches, finished high school at most. The Indians are courteous, but Reverend Harley addresses Morgan as "Hey, you," and Reverend Eaton explains to me, over the barbecue, that "Some of the Indians is plain no good." He looks to me for support on this.

I can see now how this religion appeals to people who once turned to Jack Wilson and his fellow doctors, healers, and witches. It has little formal leadership; little pageantry or art; a lot of member participation; a simple hand-clapping and foot-stomping beat not too different from the traditional side-stepping circle dance; and curing by laying on of hands, which the Reverend is supposed to be pretty good at. Glossolalia, the speaking in tongues, can lead to the kind of trance-like state some people, still living, witnessed in Jack Wilson. The second coming of Christ, a fundamental point in Assembly of God religion, is marked, among others things, by a rider on a white horse descending from heaven. Morals can be controlled by public comment, such as the one Mrs. Harley directed at her sister-in-law—who, rumor says, is practicing birth control.

Such material is the bones of a nice paper. I can see it now: "Parallels between a Millennial Movement and Modern Evangelical Practice." Maybe it's not possible for a somber, hierarchical, baroquely ornate religion like Catholicism to appeal in such circumstances. Cyril and Maybel belong to the Catholic church, but few other Paiutes do; of course, the fact that St. Jude's is further in town may be the reason for its unpopularity. Morgan rejects all but the Methodists because the other churches have "too much kneeling," but that's not a theological argument—Morgan's knees are bad. And some churches barred Paiutes, as recently as 20 years ago. So much for my experimental controls.

And yet...where are the people? Despite the year's preparation, the heaped platters of free food, the great music, the ethnographically correct *kah' nii*, and the hard-won (and reasonably priced) rabbit, the numbers at the big Mission barely reach 30 at any one service, and half the attendees are local whites. Some services would have no attendees at all if the Reverend didn't mount the human equivalent of a rabbit drive with his bus.

In fact, this whole summer, I've been the rabbit driver. I've been studying something I've created myself.

Maybe it's too soon to know if people will officially join the Reverend's church; it's still relatively new here. Maybe his charismatic personality will draw people in. In the past, religious leaders were agreeable, low-octane characters who served simply as a focus for consensus. The visiting Indian ministers are rather like that. It's true some traditional figures, such as witches, were threatening and abusive, but the witches weren't really leaders. The three visiting white ministers at the Mission are robust practitioners of the fiery hell-and-damnation school; their performance is dramatic, all right. I remember Paulette saying the Mission is "all too emotional for her," and now I see a few others drawing away at the more demonstrative moments.

Most traditional leaders are remembered, perhaps fancifully, as fine specimens—tall, it's always said, and "smart." Although I'm very fond of him, if "smart" includes "shrewd," it doesn't describe Reverend Parks. He's also even shorter than I am. Another type of man may have entrenched the new religion more successfully. Despite this, many people on the reservation have a quiet fondness for Reverend Parks, although not enough to give him a hand building anything.

Sadly, leadership may become the issue in future because the real reason Reverend Case is here, it turns out, is to decide whether Reverend Parks should stay. The previous minister is anxious to return; he's already mounting an advance action, taking up a post nearby and consorting with a few of the disgruntled in Yerington. I, the atheist and neutral anthropological observer, take exception to this. Reverend Parks is a good minister, excelling, as I Corinthians 14:12 admonishes, in "gifts that build up the church," speaking admirably in the Paiute tongue, building *kah' niis*, making almost passable rabbit nets, and generally knocking himself out in the service of the Lord.

Of course, my central question is wrong. Traditionally, Paiutes didn't belong to any "church." They wandered as single families most of the time. Temporary leaders were called on only as needed. But all western American Indian traditional life has been ravaged, even earlier among the Paiutes than in some other places. Perhaps no one understood the lessons as well as Jack Wilson; his message tried to address and mediate the changed world for his own people and others. Sadly, as Walker had said, "It wasn't enough for all that happened to us." Today their lives continue to change, for the worse, mostly. Wilson's message, if he were around today, would probably be quite different, even if the basic Christian elements remained.

The Reverend Parks's message helps mediate the world for a new group, those younger, more acculturated, mixed-blood people who are more empowered and struggling hard to keep their place in the white world. In a few generations, they will be white.

Have I been snatching at academic straws? Maybe, like Delaney's verdict on the rabbit net, my experience here has been "too short and too soon" to learn and understand what I want to know.

CHAPTER TWENTY-THREE

The Parting

THE MISSION IS over. It feels like the day after my birthday, the day after Christmas, all those dead days when the world looks ordinary again. Some day when I'm old, perhaps I'll look at the one *tule* scar on my finger and remember this small event in a small town, one that meant so much. Or maybe it just meant a lot to the Reverend and me. And I might remember that I wasn't able to do what I'd come to do, find a neat correlation between the old and new religions.

But I do understand Coyote and the other tricksters. I always have. "Who's the trickster?" Walker asked. Who, indeed?

The trickster pretends to be something he isn't to get what he wants. He presents a new face to each person. He thinks he knows so much, and then he makes a fool of himself. Things backfire on him. He may be careful—if he keeps field notes, for example—and then the very thing he doesn't want to happen does anyway. He's a wise fool. In the words of Radin, he dupes others and is duped himself. He disrupts. He uncovers. He explains why things are the way they are today—why, for example, people are wary of strangers with notebooks. The trickster steals things from one world and gives them to another. He's not bad; he's amoral, not immoral. He's an inquisitive nuisance prowling around in in-between spaces.

Then again, he may not be a *he*—or a *she*—at all. He can be the *space* between boundaries—native and Christian, Indian and white, shyster and genius, duper and duped, savior and charlatan, god and man, educator and entertainer, animal and human, nomad and settled. These are not opposites, just as Walker said.

Perhaps he's something even more familiar. Walker said, "Wolf sets the world up, real careful, all perfect, rules and all, but who can live that way? Somebody's got to take the rough edges off the world. I think Coyote's working out how the little man can live. He breaks out of all the rules so he can get by, see what might happen, see if he can get something he wants, anything."

"We did whatever the white people let us do," Delaney had said.

"I know how things *can* be," Jennie told me.

"You could live if they'd let you," my mother had written.

Does the Paiute fondness for Coyote's most venal features, and the Youngstowner's partiality for people like Cadillac Charlie Cavallero provide a rough model for survival and perhaps even modest happiness in an alien world? For a while, the tricksters outsmart a system for which the group has no regard. The Paiutes, subject to capricious arrest and racist exclusion, were forced to send their children to distant Indian schools where they were gone for years. Nomads settled in 12- by 18-foot wooden boxes, they had to negotiate their lives through random interstices of local white culture. So too did the devalued Youngstown mill workers, who were abandoned by the national government and brutalized by absentee mill owners. As the mills failed and believing, in Springsteen's words, "Them big boys did what Hitler couldn't do," they developed their own anti-institutional strategies for survival.

Youngstown wasn't set up for the people who lived there; it was founded to move iron and steel. Every system, every institution was geared toward that. Immigrants—skilled workers in the early waves, unskilled at the turn of the century, political refugees from central Europe in mid-century—all understood this. After all, whatever they'd been in the "old country," the official systems hadn't worked for the likes of them there, either—whatever they got, they got through dodges, ingenious finagling, and rickety informal systems that mirrored the official ones. These were "shadow" systems, used by my mother and her sisters, struggling to create a co-operative support network against the treacherous insecurities of the mill; my dad and his coffee-break "machine calibrations"; local men "running the Bug" for extra money; hustles like Chicken Shit John's moonshine.

And who had the most organized shadow system? The Mafia, whom most people tolerated, even admired for their audacity, as long as they didn't interfere with the ordinary worker. They didn't; they had little to gain and a world to lose. The Mafia were more than a shadow; they were boundary crossers who *became* the police, the judges, the politicians. "THUGS RUN YOUNGSTOWN," the *Cleveland Plain Dealer* blared after one election. Then, under the cloak of probity, the Mafia ran things their way rather than the "official" way. Of course this meant Youngstown lost potential investment by outsiders, but mill owners were on record as having fought to keep all but their own related businesses out anyhow. When a family was saved from eviction by Mafia intervention, were they really worried about these larger issues? Older people remembered that the Mafia had once driven the Ku Klux Klan, which was targeting Catholics, out of town. And they remembered, too, that the church's Sunday sermons had little to say about work conditions and strikes, the stuff of their lives.

The Paiutes had their own shadow systems, ways of maintaining control. The lone phone in the Colony, installed so people could summon the town police if trouble broke out, was rarely used. Witches punished incest, cured illness, and righted grievances, although usually only their own. Even today, the Paiutes keep themselves to themselves—everyone knew almost from the beginning about Willie, except me.

The Paiutes moved, and still move, across worlds and boundaries as bizarre as any of those in Coyote's world. Not surprising that one of their own, Jack Wilson, brought temporary comfort to Indians all across America's western half.

Person or process, creature or space, alien or familiar—today most of us are too pale and cowed to toy with tricksterism. Life has ways of boxing us in. Only the most desperate or angry or mischievous or inventive people will risk playing with the world, mocking it, putting things in motion to see what comes of them. People like us. And like the Paiutes.

Maybe now, after this summer's experience, I'm ready to conjure up a trickster by assembling one from bits and pieces. Who will it resemble most? Jack Wilson? Eddie? Walker? The Reverend? Larry? Me.

MY TIME ON the reservation is over. People give me two going-away parties, gifts of handwoven baskets, a cradleboard, and a *pa'tú* stick for stirring pine nut soup. For my part, I give Driver to Eddie, or rather, I can't get it back from him.

In one corner of the second party, at Cyril's, Larry, Curly, and Eddie play squaw poker; they've abandoned the barbut ring.

"Come and join us, Hoot-ze," Eddie commands Delaney. Delaney's Indian name; I'd forgotten what Walker told me.

"What does that name mean in English?" I ask.

Delaney laughs. "You want to ask Jennie."

I find her in the kitchen, giving a stern talk to Thomasina. This time next week I'll have no way to keep up with Thomasina's new antics, or to see how the Reverend's filling his time now the Mission's over, or to follow Eddie's career.

"Delaney says to ask you what '*Hoot ze*' means."

Jennie giggles. "Sage grouse."

Cyril Watkins sneaks a crumpled packet into my bag; in it is the two and a half months' rent I paid him. I've spent a total of $373.33: $25 for renting the garage, $13.03 for gas and electric, $15 for food, $45 to a few "informants," $15 for gifts, and the rest for field equipment, much of which I've never used.

I leave the reservation late in the morning, driving north through the green Mason Valley, along the Wassuk Mountains, up toward the Desert Mountains and Silver Springs, through Wabuska, southwest over to Dayton, and on through Silver City and Virginia City to Reno. That's all it is: 90 miles, two hours, and a different world. It's the hottest day I've ever known, dangerous to be in the desert. The heat shimmers as midday approaches. Outside Silver Springs, I see a mirage, two figures dancing above the road. Very real, as mirages are.

It is real. Walker and his half-coyote. He's carrying some kind of large basket that's forcing him to stoop almost double as he trudges along the verge. I stop.

"Walker, hey. Where are you going?"

"Bridgeport," he grunts.

Going there will add another four hours to my journey, but that's nothing compared to the time he'd spent in that jail. Or I can take him to Reno and find him a bus from there.

"Get in."

"Thank you, ma'am, I'm fine. I'll make my own way up there, no problem." He covers the top of the basket with a rag.

"Walker?"

"Yeah?"

He doesn't know me. It's clear he doesn't know me.

"Are you okay?"

"I sure am. Just fine, thanks." He looks smaller, older, darker, nearly invisible in the shade of the rocks that just here line the highway.

He's probably never seen my police car before; all our meetings were inside the jail. You can't leave people in the desert at noon. I get out, light-headed just stepping into the sun.

No one's there.

Boulders and bushes litter the landscape. I search, keeping sight of the car. A heat headache blinds me, my pulse races. How has he survived out here? Dog prints—all four paws. Walker's half-coyote leaves only a single line of prints. But wait, it's not a set of four paws. It's two sets of single-line prints.

I can't see the car. Panic. There it is, directly behind me. In the shimmering haze, I've been turned around. I go back for a drink from my canteen.

Now what? The injured rabbit call Walker taught me that first day in the jail. "Waaaa," I call out. Then again, shorter. And again.

Far off, I hear a deep rich laugh echoing around the rocks. Then silence.

At the first gas station I come to, I tell the owner about the man and dog out in the hot desert. I call the one phone in the Colony, but whoever answers doesn't know me. I explain that I've just seen and lost Walker in the middle of nowhere. The man laughs. "Wherever Walker is, he'll look after himself, don't you worry," he shouts down the line.

The gas station owner, his weathered face embroidered with acne scars, says if he'd known it was Walker I was talking about, he'd have said the same thing himself. He reminds me I should be wearing a hat in this heat.

"By the way," he says, "you know coyotes put their hind foot on the same spot where their front foot is."

"Yeah."

"Maybe to fool us."

BACK IN RENO at the university, I write a comprehensive report and laudatory evaluation of the training program, larded with some waspish comments about all the useless equipment I'd been told to buy, especially the engineer's scale, which still baffles me. I mention the police car, although not as scathingly as I would have done in later years. My writing style is anthropologically perfect, written in a cool, "objective," passive voice, sprinkled with "the seminal work by ..." and "a view long espoused by...." Morgan becomes a social deviant, Delaney an elderly informant, Larry a child marginalized in two cultures, Reverend Parks simply a white preacher.

The few days' respite from the reservation has given me a little more emotional traction—not everyone is a trickster.

I write with a grandiloquent sweep. Local people always insisted they were all interrelated. I blithely describe this as a "vast indefinable system of ties," then document the kinship links between every single person and everybody else, and then all of the community back to three people—Horseman, Winnemucca Naci, and Chief Joaquin, just as Walker had said. Overlooking my own contradictory comments, I assure the reader the relationships are not complicated: "A cousin of one generation ascending from ego becomes an uncle or aunt; a great-aunt becomes a grandmother, etc. Thus, genealogical ties are maintained without extending the family relationships beyond the bounds of easy comprehension."

Underneath, the report is really an account of a drama, one directed by me, focused on me, and revealing my place, my history, my orientation, my perspective. It puts *me* in context. That's what this fieldwork has done.

"A longer program, I feel, would be more beneficial," I conclude majestically. Beneficial for whom? Walker has done about all the jail time he and his gray companion can tolerate, and some of the Reverend Parks's superiors are confused by the atheism of his most constant sidekick this summer. Morgan is unwisely beginning to reconsider nursing. Thomasina takes her depredations to new heights, falsely emboldened by her association with the police car. Larry's not on his way to military school, at least not yet, and no one's been charged with Willie Jackson's death. Wickham is gone, without Reenie, no one knows where.

Some of the people who helped me most were in a state of relieved collapse when I left, like parents who finally get a demanding baby to sleep.

One of the last things I did before I left was to read a passage from Driver to Delaney: "In the Great Basin, four bands allowed father's sister's daughter marriage and three permitted union with the mother's brother's daughter. There is no obvious explanation for this difference. Nine other bands permitted step-cross-cousin marriage. A person's step-cross-cousin is the stepson or stepdaughter of his father's sister or mother's brother."

"Yes, well," Delaney sighed. "You want to study that. They didn't teach us that up at Stewart. 'Course I wasn't there all that long. I'd say you could copy that down in your report and nobody'd know the difference. That way, you'd be sure to have it right."

Of course I can't do that, because I've learned a few other things this summer. Scholarly honor, for instance. Last week, Professor Murdock sent me a letter congratulating me on the work I've done on "our" book, but now we're finished, he said, he's abandoning the project, all 500 pages of meticulous analysis. He's seen that using kinship systems, his lifelong interest—his lifelong love, really—is not the most useful scheme for grouping American Indians into culture areas. He doesn't know what is, but we'll start again in the fall. He's sorry for the disappointment—and the year's work I've put in. He doesn't mention that he's paid me, or the decade of work he's put in himself.

And humility, for another. Most of those awkward anthropologists I'd scoffed at, well, they all survived their own first fieldwork, and more. Even now that some have concluded their nerve-wracking summer of carefully incubating me, they're off to do new fieldwork of their own. They haven't lost their notes. They haven't been accused of being involved in Murder One. And they haven't laughed at people who did both these things.

I'm worried, though; I've got so much from the Paiutes and given so little back. If a new researcher comes along later, the locals will just start all over again. It will be a long time, in another place, before I understand how to use anthropology to give people help doing what they want to do, rather than what I need them to do.

I SPENT $7.00 ON stamps, writing to my family and my husband. Now Francis is flying in to meet me, and we'll drive back together to Ohio. "About time we settle down," he says once again. I picture the banana boat sailing off without me.

Epilogue

ANTHROPOLOGY SURVIVED MY fieldwork. Or did it?

The history of anthropology since the 1960s would make a good bodice-ripper. We were very promiscuous with our intellectual neighbors, ungrateful upstarts who then pillaged our discipline and scolded us severely. We stopped talking to other anthropologists. Indeed, with the advent of postmodernism, some anthropologists no longer even *understood* each other.

I set out for Nevada having been cosseted in the bosom of anthropological silverbacks, Grand Old Men who had, at most, two or three gentlemanly tiffs going on at one time. The Four Fields—cultural anthropology, physical anthropology, archeology, and linguistics—were still bedfellows. Classificatory systems—races, language groupings, diagrams of human evolution, archeological eras—remained safely in place, awaiting our second-year exams. We still believed that "cultures" were unitary systems with neat boundaries. In Nevada, I drew maps of clearly bounded culture areas for my work on Professor Murdock's book.

But when I returned to the University of Pittsburgh in the autumn of 1964, anthropology had already fractured on ideological and ethical issues. The latest, centered on the infamous Project Camelot and involving one of my professors, was about to erupt. An earlier scandal was quietly fermenting in the records of the FBI, only to emerge decades later: in 1949, Professor Murdock had sent an unsolicited letter to FBI director Edgar Hoover, naming 12 anthropologists, all "personal friends," as Communists. Precision and carefully qualified accuracy were Murdock's scholarly forte, but not all were Communists. (Price 2004: 73–75)

Anthropology was also about to fracture along philosophical, theoretical, and practical divides.*

---

* For an analysis of the impact of Project Camelot (and of the post–World War II relationships between social science and government generally) on these developments, see Solovey 2001.

Little did I know I represented a dying trend, modernism, which was based on the natural sciences. Cultural acts and decisions were rational, and the task was to discover what explained these acts and decisions. Did they serve a function? Were they part of an overall theme or orientation? My questions—what's universal in cultural and social life? what's local? and why?—and my neophyte methods—i.e., searching for the universal through a minute study of everyday particulars—would soon be replaced by other ideas. Monographs such as Kathleen Gough's *Anthropology, Child of Imperialism* (1968) and Talal Asad's *Anthropology and the Colonial Encounter* (1973) gave fair notice of what was to come. Soon, "cousin-brothers" of anthropology (specialists in cultural studies, media studies, literary criticism, etc.) branded us as "colonialists," people who perpetuated stereotypes of "primitives." Clifford Geertz described anthropology as "a collection of quite differently conceived sciences rather accidentally thrown together" (2000: 90).

Some even thought, and still do, that we should drop our central concept, culture. Books and articles bear such titles as *Anthropology Beyond Culture* (Fox and King, 2002), reminding us that culture is now a "vexed" and variable concept. If, as we'd been taught, the concept of culture is the bonding agent for the overall field, its dismissal by some cultural anthropologists perplexes and alienates scholars in the other three fields. Today, more than ever, the answer to "What is anthropology?" depends on with whom you're talking: archeologists, interpretivists, postmodernists, critical realists, constructivists—even those valiant foot soldiers teaching in the classroom, whom Barrett dubbed "no-name anthropologists" (1999).

This state of affairs is not really new. Anthropologists have never agreed on what culture is. In my first year of graduate school, we were confronted by 250 definitions of culture, assembled by A.L. Kroeber and Clyde Kluckhohn (1963). We have moved from culture as E.B. Tylor's 1871 "complex whole," consisting of "capabilities and habits acquired by man as a member of society," to a rich variety of theoretical "schools." Some reject culture; others hold onto the idea of a "complex whole," but differ on what the whole consists of, what it does, how it changes, whether what one does falls into the scientific or humanistic paradigm, and therefore whether one describes, explains, or interprets meaning. Who should this "one" be who is doing the describing/explaining/interpretation? Can one generalize the findings or must one restrict oneself to the local group? And what is the anthropologist's role in relation to the group and the material studied?

Answers to these questions shape various interpretations of culture: culture as custom, as shared patterns and behavior, as responses to broad political and economic forces, as symbol and meaning, as a creation of the anthropologist's perspective. Even those who have abandoned the concept of culture itself have a view on the consequences of these conceptualizations. And, of course, proponents of each have strong views on the stances of others. Thus, we read about a Wickedness of Geertzians, an Upstart of Feminists, a Self-flagellation of Postmodernists (Salzman [2001] provides the most succinct account of what each thinks of the others).

Some anthropologists will argue that what might look like disarray is nothing very new and is, in fact, simply a reflection of our strength. Reck's rather tricksterish response is a good example:

> Anthropology's uniqueness and contributions reside, as always, in its simultaneously comfortable and uneasy location between things, between the sciences and the humanities, between history and literature, between ourselves and the other, between objectivity and subjectivity, between the concrete and the abstract, between the specific and the general. Living in the cracks between these worlds comes with the territory." (1996: 7)

One example: in the last two decades of the last century, postmodernism, drawing on French philosophy and English literary criticism (already fading in the cafés of Paris and the common rooms of backwater British universities), dominated anthropology. These included the interpretive anthropology, critical anthropology, and post-structuralism of Geertz, Clifford, Marcus, Jameson, etc. Adherents, aligning themselves with the humanities and literature, took a moral rather than a scientific stand, emphasizing the subjectivity of fieldwork and the belief that all truth is relative to one's perspective. Anthropologists asked, "To what extent are we as much the subjects of our ethnographies as the people whom we observe? Is ethnography really a form of autobiography?" Authors began to feature in their own work, the "I" as a factor in ethnography.

In my time among the Paiutes, I had several concerns. One was: "Whose voice?" That is, whose account of a people took precedence, and, if it was the anthropologist's, why? The second was how to convey multiple layers of meaning and perspective. Third, what were the Paiutes getting out of this? Postmodernism attempted to address the first two. It decentered the white, the western, the male, in an attempt to empower the voice of the Other; however, most postmodernist writing was an almost impenetrable, laborious monologue by that very white western male. "Whose ear?" would have been a better question—who were anthropologists writing *for*? And was there a next, more practical step after the market for excoriating self-exploration waned? Postfeminists, who pointed out that they'd been there first, said yes. The practical step was a political one: self-determined change by the oppressed, the Other.

Postmodernists also worried about representation. Could the written word ever adequately represent speech, and, if not, how could we do ethnography? My concern was that ultimately, language, even from multiple perspectives, represents only a small part of how humans comprehend.

Then globalization, among other factors, forced our hand. Shifting national and cultural boundaries, refugees and asylum-seekers, emancipatory ideologies and the process of "decolonizing" required urgent attention. Also, the development issues that applied anthropologists worked on were worsening. "Active citizenship" and practicality were called for. Now we've moved into "post-postmodernism," into various forms of "critical realism," "constructivism," etc., which draw from a variety of previous theoretical positions, recognizing that we need to be humbler about our abilities as observers and that multiple perspectives are critical—part of the co-construction of knowledge among us and the people we work with—but also stating that science does have some role in our research. This approach reflects my own work for the past two decades, and through it I found more insights into my questions. (Lewellen, 2000, provides an excellent, readable review of these recent trends in anthropology.)

So, today, it's "whatever works." Anthropology has always had several paradigms going on at the same time; most of us have managed, trickster-like, to hold totally incompatible paradigms in our heads and to skim off what's usable.

And now, the age-old question. What would I do if I knew what I know today and could be back where I was then—or even now—in Youngstown; or with the Paiutes? I do know a little more now: two years after my Paiute fieldwork, I went to Ireland to do my dissertation research on small industries; directed a National Science Foundation Field Training Program like the one I'd been on; joined the faculty of the University of Pittsburgh; went back to Ireland to help set up the first department of anthropology at St. Patrick's College, part of the National University of Ireland; and after 17 years there, became an applied anthropologist, working on participatory projects in Africa.

I now know that Youngstown has enough material to satisfy any anthropologist, as the following update will show.

SEPTEMBER 18, 1977, ends like most late-summer weekends in Youngstown. Steelworkers and others in the 400 related manufacturing businesses prepare for a new workweek.

On Monday morning, they learn there will be no new workweeks for 5,000 of their workmates, maybe no work for the rest of their lives. "Black Monday," the day Youngstown Sheet and Tube announces its closing, is only the first in a series of black days. Other mills close, and by 1982 more than 40,000 people in the area, almost 20 per cent of the work force, are out of work.

Who will help? Various strategies are proposed, and a civic-church coalition tries to buy back the mills. All efforts fail. Most U.S. presidential candidates, from that period to today, have visited Youngstown at election time and offered help. Not much has been delivered.

Enter the sheriff, the one person who is still remembered by the townspeople—indeed, he's remembered by millions, thanks to his career choices. The badly-toupeed James Traficant, sheriff of the Youngstown area from 1980 to 1984, refuses to serve eviction orders on the foreclosed homes of unemployed mill workers and spends three days in jail as a result. In 1983, he is charged with and acquitted of accepting Mafia bribes, despite confessing and acting as his own lawyer (even referring to himself as "my client," making direct examination awkward). He wins a Democratic congressional seat as champion of the little man in 1984 and in eight subsequent elections, often with more than 70 per cent of the vote—even when, in later years, he often votes with the Republicans in the House. His own local Democratic chairman once tries (and fails) to have him declared legally insane; as a result, Traficant often proclaims that he is the only legally sane person in Congress.

After serving nine terms in the House of Representatives, Traficant is convicted in 2002 of racketeering, taking bribes from the Mafia, obstruction of justice, tax evasion, and such assorted mischief as using on-the-clock public employees as farm hands on his horse ranch. Expelled from Congress by a 420–1 vote, Traficant (a.k.a. Federal Prisoner 31213–060) is released on September 2, 2009, to a heartfelt welcome-home dinner attended by 1,200 supporters at Mr. Anthony's Banquet Hall. He plans to run for office again.

What did Traficant do right? Both as sheriff and congressman, he was strongly pro-labor, supporting a raise in the minimum wage and protection of Social Security and voting against free trade and illegal immigration. Most important, he was, as most local workers were, deeply anti-institutional, convinced that the federal government and large corporations had left Youngstown adrift. The only institution that didn't fail Youngstown was education, which is still held in high regard. Traficant has two Masters' degrees and can deploy high-flown language in downhome ways. "I will grab a sword like Maximus Meridius Demidius, and as a gladiator I will stab people in the crotch" (see http://www.freetraficant.com). His nationally mocked polyester suits were exactly what many older men wore. In local parlance, these clothes were the "full Cleveland"—usually a plaid jacket; solid, coordinating-colored pants; white tie and white shoes— that my own father was buried in. Traficant was, to borrow a campaign slogan from the ex-con mayor of Washington, DC, "Not perfect, but perfect for Youngstown."

Although these events may be difficult for outsiders to follow, many older people believed one thing: Traficant was on their side. And the forces they hate were out to get him. They've held that view throughout his imprisonment and afterward. To those 1,200 who attend the "Welcome Home" dinner, he's still "Our Jimbo"; as one attendee says, "[he's] the only one who ever did anything for us."

I call my brother, who still lives in Youngstown, to ask his opinion of Traficant's behavior.

"Well, he hurts himself more than anyone else," he says.

"I don't know about that."

"So who does he hurt? Huh? The *government*?" His voice rises, incredulous; it's clear he thinks I've been away too long.

But things are changing and have been for some time. It's been said that FBI agents working in Youngstown in the 1990s had the greatest job security in the country (Linkon and Russo, 2002) because the Mafia controlled everyone from the sheriff to a county prosecutor to the coroner. But in the late 1990s, an FBI sting netted 70 public officials, mob boss Lenny Strollo, and, of course, Jimbo.

Suburbanites and a younger emerging professional class have less reason to tag along with the legacy of the Mafia, and some resent Youngstown's national image as a failed, corrupt city. To these people, Traficant and the others are a symbol of Youngstown's disgrace.

Today, a glance at the snapshots of Jim Traficant's welcome-home dinner as posted on the Internet may help to explain not only the nature of his support base but also the direction attitudes may eventually take. His is an aging demographic—men and women with softly creased faces and bodies stiff after a life in the mills; yet, they still have enough mental flexibility to come out for a night and rally around a known criminal. The median income in Youngstown today is $22,000, the lowest of any medium-sized city in the U.S. That's not the way it was when the mills were firing balls of gas into the night skies, they say. But it's the baffled young people, raging now on the Internet about what Traficant and the Mafia have done to Youngstown's image, who will decide the future.

So, WHERE WOULD I start studying Youngstown today as an anthropological project?

One fruitful area, class, has been seriously neglected by anthropologists.* We seem to have taken our cue from the American public, most of whom ignore the topic and, if pressed, see themselves as "middle class." So we have approached the subject obliquely, frequently partnering it with race, ethnicity, and gender.

I might first explore the concept of "working class" itself. I'd draw on my experiences with the working classes, in both the historic "capitalist" period (my father's generation) and the more recent "late capitalist" period (in which my niece, a "part-time" minimum wage employee, on her only day off, takes three buses to attend a mandatory 7:00 a.m. "team-building exercise," where she learns she's been written up for forgetting to say "Hello My Name Is Ellen, Welcome to Shoe Heaven, We Have a Special

---

* We have a long way to catch up with other disciplines; in 2009, out of approximately 250 presentations at the multidisciplinary Working Class Studies Association Meeting in neighboring Pittsburgh, only three people were identified as being affiliated with anthropology or anthropology/sociology departments.

on Leopard-Print Flats Today, How May I Help You?" to each customer). They suggest that the social, cultural, economic, and political constituents of working-class life are variable enough to make seeking common signifiers an important exercise.* However, British research shows that another element may be important. A recent study there shows that the percentage of people claiming to be working class (the majority of people) has changed little in almost 50 years and has taken on the characteristics of "caste," including people in professional and managerial positions who feel that the class one is born into is the class one really "belongs" to (Heath and Curtice 2009). Would occupation, which Sherry Ortner argues for in her study of her 1958 high school class (2003), be a sufficient signifier of class in my study?

The reader won't be surprised that I might cast my work instead in terms of class resistance and the "ambiguities of resistance" (Ortner 2006: 62). "Resistance studies" draw on literature, cultural studies, history, and anthropology to look at how people both resist and in some ways are complicit in their domination, such as, in Youngstown, characterized the relationship between the workers and the powers that controlled steel production. Scott's "everyday forms of resistance" (1985) resonates: steelworkers sabotage the workplace but not enough to jeopardize the production process and their own self-interests, while saying little when their work-related inventions are privately patented by individual managers as their own. Also relevant are Linkon and Russo, who offer the most extended commentary on the mills and the Mafia in Youngstown. They conclude that "...distrust of institutions and a belief that individuals and groups that challenged and even violated traditional rules were the community's best hope, reflecting a 'politics of resentment'" (2002: 218). Bruno's *Steelworker Alley* (1999) explores this resentment and the often satisfyingly ingenious ways that many steelworkers developed to get around poor wages and oppressive conditions.

Working-class people's tolerance and sneaking admiration of the Mafia, and later of people such as Jim Traficant, was a double mockery. The Mafia made a travesty of the official institutions when they held official positions and nose-thumbed them when they didn't. But how did a people who obeyed the laws (except for those related to minor gambling), put money in

---

* For example, in 1977, the year in which Youngstown's "Black Monday" occurred, Willis's classic study described British working-class boys as contemptuous of education, but education was one of the few institutions Youngstowners never rejected.

the church collection each Sunday, and prided themselves on their sparkling lines of laundry reconcile their moral and social rectitude with their regular votes for Mafia candidates? Because of their admiration for the audaciously cunning stunt? Or did they share a Paiute-like amusement with Trickster? Or something more?

So, my proposed study, I would also look at Youngstown's version of "shadow systems": the legal, judicial, and economic arrangements created by dominated people all over the world when, by neglect, poor fit, or design, the official systems ignore their needs.

Most anthropological comment on Youngstown, the Mafia, and Traficant exists only in the form of media interviews by the late Mark Shutes of Youngstown State University, who was actively involved in community regeneration efforts. The idea that Youngstowners were victims of gangsters was "crap." "Their values are our values," he said, citing the disillusionment of local people at achieving their ends through orthodox channels (cited in Grann 2000). As one local commentator said of the newly released Traficant, "He actually represented us. Yes, he is loud, crude, vulgar, stubborn, opinionated, straight shooting, and everything else those folks in Washington didn't like—and so are we" (Levinthal 2009).

But even if I knew in 1964 what I know now, I couldn't study Youngstown then—not in my own place, not on American life—not if I wanted to get my degree.

WHAT ABOUT THE Paiutes, the Numu now, the people I actually set out to study in 1964?

I ride back into Yerington, Nevada at noon, November 16, 2009, down the deserted main street, past the faded stage-set wooden storefronts. A couple of tough men in Stetsons and boots squint at me, giving nothing away. One spits at a loping yellow dog. I'm in yet another deceptive vehicle, a new Lincoln Navigator, the only one left at the Reno rental agency. I pick up a copy of "The Only Newspaper in the World That Gives a Damn About Yerington" and go to the Tribal Council Meeting, in its impressive new building on the Ranch. Here are faces I knew on people who hadn't been born when I left or who had been the teenagers Delaney fretted so much about, almost all of them grandchildren of the models for my characters.

"Did you ever meet my grandmother?" "My parents were..."; "My uncle was..."; all I can manage to say is how proud I am to have known them.

In a bizarre twist, the Numu have leased part of their land to a boys' reform school, although more humane than the kind Larry might have been sent to. On the plus side, their houses have been rebuilt, and new ones added; they have a complex of modern buildings, food security, and a good care system for the elders. They get Social Security. A monument to Wovoka marks the entrance to the Colony, and people in Yerington celebrate an annual Wovoka Day.

On the minus side, one in four of the Numu has diabetes, the closed mine is a source of serious water and air pollution, people are "still getting used to reservation life," and some whites still dismiss them as Indians. Many still eat at the back of the local restaurant.

Few people speak Paiute. At the Elder Center I have lunch with some of them, people who were there in my time, a few of them graduates of Stewart School, children of nomads. Our lunch includes the Reverend's favorites, pine nut soup and buckberry sauce. The Reverend is gone, replaced a year after I left by people not quite as ethnographically sympathetic to his interests. "Where's the church now?" I ask, looking around. "You're sitting in it," they answer. I can almost see Clarence in his cradleboard and Roberta firing wads of paper at fellow Missionettes.

I'm told that no one goes to any church now, although there are churches nearby. Reverend Parks's theory that people came to his church "for the eats" may not have been so far off; pastoral charity may have been the real attraction, and people are more secure and better cared-for now. In the old days, people had a word for "prayer" but not for "religion." Today, they pray to the spirits. A few use the traditional, recently built sweatlodge.

And Delaney, Jennie, Archie, Paulette, Morgan? All gone, too. I think I see Eddie slipping around the corner of Main Street and Center, and that girl on the curb looks awfully familiar, but...

But no. They never existed. Even most of the people who helped to embody them, who contributed parts of themselves and their stories to their characters, are gone. Coyote's still here, though—I see the tracks. Should I study whether they still need Coyote today?

The female elders say Coyote is "bad"; men say there's nothing worse you can call a person. But the stories still flow—outrageous, subversive, satisfying. One old lady joins in enthusiastically. Is she less prudish than the others? More traditional? An enticing new hypothesis hovers. But no, she's just helpful. "What got you so interested in small animal research, dear?" she asks me. But it's clear that Coyote is still alive: this is not the end.

So what work would I do with the Numu today? They are quite able to study themselves, and have been—little Earl, for example, he of the rubber tomahawk, is now not only Karl Fredericks, a chief of police, but also an astute ethnographer, and has worked with the anthropologist Michael Hittman and Numu historian Marlin Thompson to recover much of the twentieth-century Numu story. So perhaps I would do something practical.

Pasquinelli argues that others have furtively appropriated our anthropological concepts and methods "with a depressing dearth of thanks" (1996: 60). In recent decades, I've associated myself with the biggest pillager of all: participatory research and action, a relative of critical realism, and one of the many cousin-sisters of anthropology. And I follow the counsel of anthropologist Beatrice Medicine, a Lakota: "...as anthropologists, we should do more participatory research," using Native People as co-directors of research projects. "Thus, they can learn research techniques and initiate and implement their own 'needs assessments' and application strategies to improve the quality of life in their own communities" (2001: 330–31).

With this in mind, I would have to consider that one of the major problems facing American Indians is high school student drop-out rates, absenteeism, and low achievement test scores. Participatory research and action approaches are among the most successful at doing what Medicine suggests; people can learn how to do it themselves and pass it on to other groups and communities. I could share that process.

ONE THING, FINALLY, that I've learned from all these years of working in fields that have borrowed so much from anthropology: in the end, no other discipline does what we do, as well as we do it. Lewellen (2002) sums up my thoughts perfectly: "Anthropology needs to get its nerve back." And today's students are the people to do it.

And I do know why you've been reading this far—what you really want to know. Yes, I got a good grade on my report. And Francis and I, children of our culture, stayed together another two years. But we'd crossed too many boundaries, and finally we said goodbye at yet another of my airport gates, this one marked "EI 104 Dublin." We'd each found our own banana boat.

Discussion Points and Exercises

1. "The past is a foreign country: they do things differently there," is the opening sentence of L.P. Hartley's 1953 novel, *The Go-Between*. You can look at a "foreign country" in your own family, or among friends and neighbors, by looking at the past. Arrange to interview a couple who were married in the early 1960s (don't use a questionnaire). Try to learn what it was like to be a young couple then, about to get married and start married life.

2. Before you begin, imagine that after the sessions (there may be more than one), you'll want to become a time-traveler, and go back to the 1960s yourself. You will need to know enough to fit in, undetected. Think about what you'll need to ask. Some possible questions are: What did each person expect from marriage? What did each hope for? What roles were each expected to play? What was each responsible for?

   Would you like to have been part of a marriage in the 1960s? Why or why not?

3. After your interview, reflect on the session. What concerns did you have before you went to meet the people you interviewed? How does the 1960s marriage you looked at differ from marriage in your community today?

4. Wovoka, during an illness, had a vision that led to the creation of the Ghost Dance. Some societies and religions encourage visions; others, such as the Catholic Church, usually do not. Why do you think visions are acceptable in some religions/situations and not others?

5. "I decided to police my field notes and be one hundred percent objective, saving myself a lot of time."

   This sentence presents the difference between the "scientific" paradigm of the first half of the twentieth century and the more "humanistic" model of the second half, which is based on the belief that all ethnography is "subjective." Could I have achieved my aim?

6. In 1996, the American Anthropological Association concluded that anthropology was "severely handicapped" in understanding cultures by failing to attract students from ethnic minorities and underrepresented groups. Do you think experienced anthropologists can study their own people in ways that others cannot?

7. James C. Scott (1985, 1990) says that dominated peoples understand how power is used against them and develop "everyday forms of resistance," as the Youngstown mill workers did. Can you think of other examples of "everyday forms of resistance"?

8. In a survey of minority anthropologists in 1973, the American Anthropological Association found that some felt they could not recognize their own people in the studies done on them. Would you recognize a classic anthropological study of your own community? What would you think the study would capture? What would be missing?

9. Some famous tricksters are listed on page 71. Do you know of any others, from films, books, or your own ethnic traditions?

10. In anthropology, postmodernists argue that a researcher's previous experience, personality, group identity, gender, and age shape his or her treatment, perceptions, and interpretations. Do you think some of the material in this book would be told differently if I had been a male student or a middle-aged person? Do you think your own interview with a 1960s' couple was affected by such factors?

11. In western marriage today, how do a couple decide they're "made for each other?" Was it the same for the 1960s' couple you studied? Was it the same for the traditional Paiutes?

12. Anthropologists Russell Thornton (1998), a Cherokee, and Beatrice Medicine (2001), a Lakotan have explored the problematic history of anthropological relations with American Indians. Do you think it would it be reasonable for an anthropologist to expect as much support today as I got in the 1964 Tribal Council meeting?

13. Alice Beck Kehoe, in her Introduction to this book, says Americans don't like to think about the concept of class. Do you agree?

For the Paiutes, which factors—class, race, or religion—do you think most influenced their daily lives, and how?

14. In your first or second year of university, you might study anthropology, sociology, psychology, and biology. They all look at the human being. How do they differ from one another?

15. Until about this point in history, some anthropologists liked to think they were studying "traditional cultures." Is it very likely that these cultures were traditional? What do these field notes suggest to you?

16. What are Coyote's main characteristics? Walker says that stories tell you "more about the teller than the tale." What do you think he means?

17. In the early 1970s, about one-third of the people earning PhDs in anthropology were women. At the turn of the millennium, more than half were. Do you think this has led to, or will lead to, differences in the emphases/insights/interpretations in texts?

18. The title of Lewis Hyde's book, *Trickster Makes This World* (1998) describes one of Trickster's major roles. How does Walker think Coyote, Trickster, "makes" the world? Which world?

19. If you become an anthropologist today, you will probably do applied work rather than teach. What kinds of work might you get? If you've concluded that the ethnographer's gender, experience, age, etc., affect what is learned, how do you get practical, reliable information that can be used to help people?

20. *My Name is Red*, Orhan Pamuk's 2002 murder mystery, is set in sixteenth-century Istanbul. Trouble begins when the Islamic world is shocked to discover that western art uses perspective, rather than representing flat scenes, and that people in portraits are recognizable, rather than being identifiable only by badges. In my story, I get a surprise when I teach cartooning to Paiute girls. How do you think culture affects the way people draw and interpret drawing?

21. Beatrice Medicine (2001) says that many American Indians complain that anthropologists' studies are not available to them to help in projects that might improve their quality of life. If you study and write about a group, how will you deal with this issue?

22. Traditionally the nomadic Paiutes wandered in small, often nuclear family groups. Why? What influenced the composition of a group?

23. Look at your answer to the last question. What influenced the composition and residence patterns of family life in Youngstown?

24. People usually think their traditional stories and literature sound better and are more meaningful in the original language (for example, Walker tells me some of his stories in Paiute). Is this because they may be less familiar with a second language, or do you think there are other factors?

25. I worried about introducing barbut, the Turkish dice game, to the Paiutes, although not enough to stop. Is it possible, even for someone far more careful that I was, *not* to introduce new ideas and practices?

26. Clifford Geertz suggested that anthropologists do "thick description," that is, a very detailed study of context and meaning within a culture (1973: 5–6, 9–10). How can we convey meaning and insights about a group in ways other than those traditionally used in anthropology,?

27. What factors influence your ethnicity? Do other people think of you as belonging to a particular group? Why? Can you think of anything that would change your ethnicity or "disqualify" you from belonging?

28. "Post-colonial" studies began in anthropology about the time I was doing my fieldwork. Anthropologists themselves have been criticized for being "colonizers" by perpetuating views of some people as primitive or simpler. Fardon (1990) has called anthropology "colonialism's twin." What is your view?

29. Alice Beck Kehoe, in her book *America Before the European Invasions* (2002), shows how complex and sophisticated pre-invasion American Indian societies were. What do you think a book or books on the history of North America would be like if various American Indian groups wrote it? What would be some possible chapter headings? What might the maps look like?

30. Harsh "Indian schools" existed from 1878 to the 1930s. What do you think the student's life was like after leaving? For more information on Indian schools, look at http://www.kporterfield.com/aicttw/articles/boardingschool.html#section1. Do you think the children in Indian schools were taught about Jack Wilson and the white horse?

31. Walker says, "So you say you live in a big Mafia steel town in Ohio and you're not changing your name because in the old days people in Ireland had to keep their names straight?" We think our customs make sense, whereas those of others often sound odd. But consider that breasts and beards are both secondary sexual characteristics: in western societies, why does one have to be covered in public and not the other? Would you be interested in joining a movement to demand that men wear "beard bags"?

32. You may have noticed that Delaney often tells young people it's about time they learned something about their culture. However, there were very few young people between the ages of 17 and 35 in the community. What impact do you think this had on the passing on of Paiute culture in the following years?

33. In my notes, I ponder how to present a richer description of culture—for instance, drawing on "many voices," allowing as many perspectives as possible to emerge, from various disciplines and people—insiders, outsiders, old, young, men and women, people of different status. Can you think of any other voices? Would your study of a 1960s' marriage be poorer if you had interviewed only the husband?

34. Think back to earlier today when you were in a place where other people could see you. Your actions were "public," but how would you feel if you found out that someone had written down everything you did? If you questioned the person about this, what would you say?

Would the respondents of your study of a 1960s marriage be happy if you wrote down everything they said and showed it to your classmates?

35. At one point Delaney says about Wickham: "We're not human to him." However, some weeks before, Delaney had told me that a police chief had been fired and that some people, both Paiute and white, believed it was because he had treated Indians badly. What else have you learned about Paiute–white relations in this book?

36. My schooling differed from Morgan's and Paulette's Indian school days, and both differed from yours. What assumptions did each type of schooling make about what children needed and the best way to pass it on? Are these cultural assumptions? How?

37. Does anyone other than the researcher have rights to see notes made in an anthropological study?

38. Now that you know about my experiences, think about an ethnography you've read. Does the author discuss the problems, obstacles, and mistakes that affect every anthropological study? Should the study include these?

39. "Eddie's a hunter and gatherer. Thomasina's an Irish citizen. Larry's an honorary Paiute elder." Some people describe surveys and questionnaires as "objective" and "scientific." Would I have ever learned this information by doing a survey?

40. Ethnicity is self-defined and based on shared symbols, myths, and memories. What were we Irish-American children in Youngstown doing when we divided the world the way we did, i.e., Catholic/Protestant, Roy Rogers/Gene Autry, etc.?

41. I used the English word, "witch," to describe Delaney's role, but it really is not quite accurate. He was probably a curer or doctor specializing in healing the bewitched. What do you think the functions of witches and doctors were? Do you think they have survived in Paiute society to this day? If yes, why?

42. Walker says that Jack Wilson's message was right for the circumstances of his time but not enough for all that has happened since. Do you think Jack Wilson, if he returned, would do something similar to Reverend Parks?

43. We in the west tend to think of tricksters and tricksterism as "bad." Has your own view of Coyote and tricksters changed after reading this book?

44. "The report was really an account of a drama ... revealing my place, my history, my orientation, my perspective." In recent years, some anthropologists argued that this was true of all ethnography. What do you think?

References and Further Readings

Agee, James, and Walker Evans. 1941. *Let us now praise famous men: three tenant families.* Boston: Houghton Mifflin.

American Anthropological Association. 1973. The American Anthropological Association's *Report of the Committee on Minorities and Anthropology.* See http://www.aaanet.org/committees/minority/minexp.htm.

Arensberg, C.M. 1937. *The Irish countryman: an anthropological study.* New York: The Macmillan Company.

————, and Solon T. Kimball. 1940. *Family and community in Ireland.* Cambridge, MA: Harvard University Press.

Asad, Talal, ed. 1973. *Anthropology and the colonial encounter.* New York: Humanities Press.

Barrett, Stanley R. 1999. "Forecasting theory: problems and exemplars in the twenty-first century." In E.L. Cerroni-Long, ed., *Anthropological theory in North America.* Westport, CT: Bergin and Garvey.

Bowen, Elenore Smith (Laura Bohannon). 1956. *Return to laughter.* London: Gollanz.

Bruno, Robert 1999. *Steelworker alley: how class works in Youngstown.* Ithaca and London: Cornell University Press.

Chambers, Robert. 1983. *Rural development: putting the last first.* New York: Longman.

————. 1997. *Whose reality counts? putting the first last.* London: Intermediate Technology Development.

Driver, Harold E. 1962. *Indians of North America.* Chicago and London: University of Chicago Press.

Fardon, Richard, ed. 1990. *Localizing strategies: regional traditions of ethnographic writing.* Edinburgh: Scottish Academic Press.

Fox, Richard G. and Barbara J. King, eds. 2002. *Anthropology beyond culture.* New York: Berg Publishers.

Geertz, Clifford. 2000. *Available light: anthropological reflections on philosophical topics.* Princeton: Princeton University Press.

Goodenough, W. 1963. *Cooperation in change.* New York: Russell Sage Foundation.

Gough, Kathleen. 1968. "Anthropology: child of imperialism." *Monthly Review* 19,11: 12–27.

Grann, David. 2000. "Crimetown, USA: The city that fell in love with the mob." *The New Republic* (10 July). https://www.tnr.com/article/politics/crimetown-usa?page=0,3.

Hartley, Leslie Poles. 1953. *The go-between.* London: Hamish Hamilton.

Heath, Anthony, and John Curtice. 2009. *Identity in the 21st Century: new trends in challenging times.* London: Palgrave.

Heizer, Robert. 1944. "The use of the enema by the aboriginal American Indians." *Ciba Symposia* (5 February): 1686–93.

Hittman, Michael. 1984. *The Yerington Paiute Tribe: a Numu history.* Yerington, NV: Yerington Paiute Tribe, 1990.

———. 1996. *Corbett Mack: the life of a Northern Paiute.* Lincoln, NE: University of Nebraska Press.

———. 1998. *Wovoka and the Ghost Dance: a source book for the Yerington Paiute Tribe.* Lincoln, NE: University of Nebraska Press.

Hoebel, E. Adamson. 1958. *Man in the primitive world: an introduction to anthropology.* New York : McGraw-Hill.

Holand, Hjalmar R. 1957. *My first eighty years.* New York: Twayne.

Hostetler, John. 1993. *Amish Society.* 4th ed. Baltimore, MD: The Johns Hopkins University Press.

Hyde, Lewis. 1998. *Trickster makes this world: mischief, myth, and art.* New York: Farrar, Straus and Giroux.

Johnson, Edward C. 1986. "Issues: the Indian perspective." In Warren L. d'Azevedo, ed., *The handbook of North American Indians: Great Basin*, Vol. XI. Washington, DC: Smithsonian Institution.

———, Melvin D. Thom, and Stannard Frank. 1975. *Walker River Paiutes: a tribal history.* Schurz River, NV: Walker River Paiute Tribe.

Kehoe, Alice Beck. 1981. *North American Indians: a comprehensive account.* Upper Saddle River, NJ: Prentice Hall Professional Technical Reference.

———. 2000. *Shamans and religion: an anthropological exploration in critical thinking.* Longrove, IL: Waveland Press.

———. 2002. *America before the European invasions.* New York: Longman.

———. 2006. *The Ghost Dance: ethnohistory and revitalization.* Longrove, IL: Waveland Press.

Kluckhohn, Clyde. 1949. *Mirror for man: the relationship of anthropology to modern life.* New York and Toronto: Whittlesey House.

Kobler, John. 1963. "Crime Town, USA." *Saturday Evening Post* (9 March): 71–76.

Kroeber, A.L., and C. Kluckhohn. 1963. *Culture: a critical review of concepts and definitions.* New York: Random House.

Lash, Scott, and John Urry. 1987. *The end of organized capitalism.* Cambridge, UK: Polity Press.

Lee, Richard B. 1969. "Eating Christmas in the Kalahari." *Natural History* (14–22 December): 60–63.

————, and Irven DeVore. 1968. "What hunters do for a living, or, how to make out on scarce resources." In R.B. Lee and I. DeVore, eds., *Man the Hunter.* Chicago, IL: Aldine.

Levinthal, Dave. 2009. "Where might James Traficant, itching for a political comeback, get capital?" *Capital Eye Blog*, September 7. Reply to blog by MaVoter, September 13, 2009.

Lewellen, Ted C. 2002. *The anthropology of globalization: cultural anthropology enters the 21st century.* Westport, CT: Bergin and Garvey.

Linkon, Sherry Lee, and John Russo. 2002. *Steeltown USA: work and memory in Youngstown.* Lawrence, KS: University Press of Kansas.

Medicine, Beatrice. 2001. *Learning to be an anthropologist and remaining "native": selected writings.* Edited with Sue-Ellen Jacobs. Urbana and Chicago, IL: University of Illinois Press.

Mooney, James. 1896. "The Ghost-dance religion and the Sioux outbreak of 1890." *14th Annual Report of the Bureau of American Ethnology*, Part 2.

Moore, John H. 1996. "Cheyenne work in the history of U.S. capitalism." In Alice Littlefield and Martha C. Knack, eds., *Native Americans and wage labor.* Norman, OK: University of Oklahoma Press.

Murdock, George Peter. 1934. *Our primitive contemporaries.* New York: The MacMillan Company.

————. 1949. *Social structure.* New York: The MacMillan Company.

Ortner, Sherry B. 2003. *New Jersey dreaming: capital, culture, and the class of '58.* Durham, NC: Duke University Press.

————. 2006. *Anthropology and social theory: culture, power, and the acting subject.* Durham, NC: Duke University Press.

Pamuk, Orhan. 2002. *My name is red.* London: Faber and Faber.

Pasquinelli, Carla. 1996. "The concept of culture between modernity and postmodernity." In Vaclav Hubinger, ed., *Grasping the changing world: anthropological concepts in the post-modern era.* London and New York: Routledge.

Petrillo, Larissa, with Melda Trejo and Lupe Trejo. 2007. *Being Lakota: identity and tradition on Pine Ridge Reservation.* Lincoln, NB: University of Nebraska Press.

Poldevaart, Arie. 1987. *Paiute-English English-Paiute dictionary*. Yerington, Nevada: Yerington Paiute Tribe.

Price, David H. 2004. *Threatening Anthropology: McCarthyism and the FBI's Surveillance of Activist Anthropologists*. Durham, NC: Duke University Press.

Reck, Gregory. 1996. "What we can learn from the past." *Anthropology Newsletter* 36 (4): 7.

Redfield, R. 1930. *Tepoztlán—A Mexican village*. Chicago, IL: University of Chicago Press.

Rideout, Henry M. 1912. *William Jones: Indian, cowboy, American scholar and anthropologist in the field*. New York: Frederick A. Stokes Co.

Salzman, Phillip Carl. 2001. *Understanding culture: an introduction to anthropological theory*. Long Grove, IL: Waveland Press.

Schneider, David M. 1984. *A critique of the study of kinship*. Ann Arbor, MI: University of Michigan Press.

Scott, James C. 1985. *Weapons of the weak: everyday forms of resistance*. New Haven, CT: Yale University Press.

———. 1990. *Domination and the art of resistance: hidden transcripts*. New Haven, CT: Yale University Press.

Solovey, Mark. 2001. "Project Camelot and the 1960s epistemological revolution: rethinking the politics-patronage-social science nexus." *Social Studies of Science* 31 (2): 171–206.

Stevens, Phillips, Jr. 2006. "Witchcraft." In H. James Birx, ed., *The encyclopedia of anthropology*, Vol. 5. Thousand Oaks, CA: Sage.

Thornton, Russell, ed. 1998. *Studying Native America: problems and prospects*. Madison, WI: University of Wisconsin Press.

Vidich, Arthur J. and Joseph Bensman. 1958. *Small town in mass society; class, power, and religion in a rural community*. Princeton, NJ: Princeton University Press.

Watkins, Mel. 1998. *Dancing with strangers: a memoir*. New York: Simon and Schuster.

Williams, Melvin D. 2002. *The ethnography of an anthropology department: an academic village*. Lewiston, NY: Edwin Mellen Press.

Willis, Paul. 1977. *Learning to labor: how working-class kids get working-class jobs*. New York: Colombia University Press.

"Wovoka's message: the promise of the Ghost Dance." 2001. *New Perspectives on the West: Archives of the West 1887–1914*. http:/www.pbs.org/weta/thewest/resources/archives/eight/gdmessg.htm.